Tried For Heresy
A 21st-century Journey of Faith

Andrew Furlong

BOOKS

Winchester, UK
New York, USA

Copyright © 2003 O Books
46A West Street, Alresford, Hants SO24 9AU, U.K.
Tel: +44 (0) 1962 736880 Fax: +44 (0) 1962 736881
E-mail: office@johnhunt-publishing.com
www.0-books.net

U.S. office:
240 West 35th Street, Suite 500
New York, NY10001
E-mail: obooks@aol.com

Text: © 2003 Andrew Furlong

Typography: Graham Whiteman Design, Halifax, Canada
Cover: Nautilus Design, Basingstoke, UK

ISBN 1 903816 52 1

A CIP catalogue record for this book is available from the British
Library.

Printed in the UK by Ashford Colour Press Ltd, Gosport, Hants.

Tried For Heresy

A 21st-century Journey of Faith

Contents

Acknowledgments

I thank the editors of *The Irish Times*, *The Church Times*, and *The Church of Ireland Gazette* for permission to quote from their newspapers. I am grateful to Mark Jarman who consented to my incorporating his poem 'Psalm: First Forgive the Silence'. My consultants who advised me during the time leading up to my trial agreed to my including their responses to my ideas and I appreciate their kindness in doing so and the aid they rendered to me. They were Professor Andrew Mayes, David FitzPatrick, Professor Maurice Wiles, and Rt Revd John Austin Baker. There are a number of people who read through the text, in whole or in part, when it was in preparation. They include Professor Andrew Mayes, Dr David A. Hart, David FitzPatrick, Most Revd Dr Richard Clarke, Revd Patrick Semple, and Archdeacon Patrick Lawrence. I am indebted to them for helpful suggestions. Members of the staff and students at the Irish School of Ecumenics shared in a seminar with me about this book, and I warmly acknowledge their useful contributions. I am delighted that a photograph taken by Barry Hollowell has been chosen for use on the front cover with his permission. My publishers in the USA and in the UK gave me considerable assistance and I thank them most sincerely.

Introduction

These pages are more than the story of a lonely struggle to survive and rise above the literalism of much Christian belief in the liberating search for a credible faith and spirituality. For they are also the chilling account of how a Church sought to divest itself of one of its clergy because of his interpretation of the faith. I am that questing person, and I am that member of the clergy, whom many, both in my own Church, and in other Churches throughout the world, turned against. I had seen myself as someone deeply dedicated to his tasks and his relationships with people as their priest. I had lived for 30 years with the thought that what happened might never come to pass. But that it did shocked others who saw the Church as broad enough to accommodate the ideas of a minister like me, whose life-long quest for a credible faith has taken me along a path, which others have also traveled on. I describe this path, as I write about my journey of faith – a faith that offers me no certainties. I believe in God, but I do not believe that God is knowable to us during this earthly stage of our human journey. So I look on all my religious reflection and theology, no matter how profound it may be, as inevitably speculative in nature. It is not surprising that it is different in certain respects from the reflection and interpretation of others who also seek to connect to the diverse riches of the Christian tradition, as they explore for meaning in the twenty-first century.

You may not be aware of the details of my story, although, in fact, it has traveled around the world. It concerns a heresy trial, something that is regarded by most people in the world today as a thing of the past. However, on 8 April 2002 I came before a Church heresy trial for several reasons, but primarily for denying the divinity of Jesus. A heresy trial was certainly a very unusual event for the Church of Ireland, a small autonomous Province within the worldwide Anglican Communion, to which I belong. Only Church historians could remember when the last one had taken place. I had worked as a clergyman for nearly 30 years, and at the time was the Dean of Clonmacnoise, which meant having responsibility for a small cathedral and its parish, about 35 miles from Dublin. This trial (see Chapter 9) was preceded by an initial period of three months beginning on 5 December 2001 when my bishop, Richard Clarke, imposed on me a three-month period of leave of absence, during which time I did not have his authority to work as a priest. It was intended by him to be a time for me to reflect on his concerns about my beliefs.

   I had known my bishop since student days, at Trinity College, Dublin, in the late sixties. We had often socialized in the past. I knew his wife, Linda, and had entertained Richard and Linda in my home. We had been curates in adjoining parishes in both Belfast and Dublin in the seventies and early eighties. While he would not have always been up to date with the developments in my thinking, he was not unaware that I held liberal views on Christianity. He knew that I was not of a fundamentalist outlook. During almost five years in which I worked in the diocese of Meath and Kildare, where he was the Bishop, I had given him copies of articles I had written (see Chapter 2), and had had several conversations with him about belief. He once contrasted his situation in relation to belief to mine by saying that while he had difficulties believing in God, he could more easily believe in the Incarnation, while I seemed to have less difficulty believing in God, but did not believe in the Incarnation.

I was stunned when he told me that he was giving me three months' leave of absence, for I was busy in my parish preparing for Christmas. His own views would not have been identical with mine, but he looked on himself as a liberal and a radical in the world of theology and morality. I was now being given a brief period in which to consider my position; to his mind some of my views were outside the goalposts of Christianity. He wrote to me saying that "This situation will be reviewed no later than 4 March 2002, at which time, if matters have not been resolved to my satisfaction and approval, decisions concerning your future ministry within the Church of Ireland will be addressed." I felt threatened and insecure.

I realized many people disagreed strongly with my views; I had my enemies. As I left the bishop's house, having just been informed of this enforced leave of absence from my work, a remark he made to me, as we parted, triggered a memory of one of Shakespeare's plays. I found I had Julius Caesar's anguished words, unspoken, on my tongue: "Et tu Brute." I felt as if I had been assaulted, I felt let down, isolated, and alienated. It was as if I had been stabbed by a friend.

After the three-month period had elapsed, I was asked, in March 2002, to meet with Richard Clarke again. A few days later, I received his letter inviting me to resign, failing which he would have no other recourse, he claimed, but to take the matter to the Court of the General Synod of the Church of Ireland. I declined his invitation to resign. Among its membership the Church of Ireland has some laity, academics, and clergy with similar views to mine, though not everybody wants to put his or her head above the parapet. These clergy are concerned, like I have been, about the consequences of being too explicit and transparent about a liberal interpretation of the faith. My neck was seen now by many as resting on the block; the guillotine had not been used for longer than most people could remember; the blade had become rusty and would need to be sent away to be sharpened. I did not myself believe that I deserved such a fate; others clearly did. I was angry and anxious, desperately uncertain about the future, but determined to fight. After an adjourned hearing of the Court of the General Synod of the Church of Ireland, I very reluctantly changed my mind and decided, for various reasons, to resign (see Chapter 10). I did so on 7 May 2002, just three days before the Court was due to sit again. Many people felt relieved; it felt to me as if I had signed my own death sentence. In my working life, I had not known anything else but to seek to serve as a priest. It looked as if I would need to seek a new identity, but what might that be? I remain a priest, but with no authority from a bishop to work as one, I have no license authorizing me. It feels like being in limbo; people ask me – are you still a priest? I have to answer – well, yes and no! It doesn't sound right. It doesn't feel right either.

I consider that religious faith finds its most appropriate home, and only authentic home, in a pluralist setting characterized by metaphor and symbolism, diversity and debate, tolerance and respect, innovative thinking and provisionality, and critiquing and acknowledgement of mistaken or outdated interpretations. In my view, the Christian vision is of a world embraced by one great mysterious love. I look on people, who claim for themselves a Christian identity, as both struggling to, and as also resisting, living out their response to that ultimately faithful mystery which I call 'God'. My vision of the Church, at its best, is not of a people at enmity with each other because of the different ways in which they express their beliefs, though sometimes indeed that is the reality found on the ground in many religious contexts. Rather it is a vision of a people struggling together in a common task.

That work has several inter-related strands. These strands include to connect to and to critique our Christian heritage, to understand the changing and diverse social realities in which it is found, to seek to diagnose the neuroses and spiritual and moral evil of our day and to point to the symptoms. Furthermore, having done so, it is to seek both courageously and prophetically, through debate and action, to participate and share with others in the healing and development of our lives and the life of the world. Within my vision of the Church this work is undertaken, to use an all-fashioned phrase, for the glory of God. An alternative expression might be to say that we seek to honor the mystery behind and within life and to honor each other, by taking the gift of life with the utmost seriousness and accepting the responsibility of doing so. Religious pluralism is both natural and perplexing; it may be partly accounted for by differing cultures and social realities in which the Churches exist and have existed, by the world-view of the period of history to which its members belong, and by their differences in personality. It may also be explained by the differing levels of theological understanding and by the varieties of life experiences, but no explanation is ever completely satisfactory. As I mention in the Epilogue, W. Paul Jones seeks for an explanation for theological diversity by looking at how a religion such as Christianity functions in a person's life; he lists five possible worlds in one of which a believer will feel most at home. Each world is viable in its own right; in effect religion both does and means different things for different people.

This book explains my beliefs as I hold them now. It is an attempt to tell the story of what happened from my perspective and of why it happened. I ask the question, whether my case should have been handled differently. Wasn't there a role for a conflict mediator? I write of the effect of what happened on the members of the parish where I had been working, and on my bishop and myself. I share the responses of some of my consultants, and of those who wrote to me, or to the media. I include an interview I gave *The Church Times* as well as some editorials from *The Church of Ireland Gazette* and *The Irish Times*. I try and look at what the case means for the Church today, and for the possibilities for Christian belief in the twenty-first century. I consider what lessons need to be learnt and write about how I now see the future.

This book also contains articles, on some of which the charges of heresy were based. You will notice some overlap between some of my papers; some were earlier drafts of others. I am not a university academic and these articles have not been prepared to a sufficient standard for an academic journal. Perhaps you would be better to look on them as discussion papers, which express where I have been on the journey of my religious quest so far. I am not saying that I am right in what I think or believe. Nobody can know that for certain. The religious quest is a lifelong one, characterized by tentativeness, modesty, and openness to new ideas and understandings, allowing for the fact that other people will see things differently from oneself. Montaigne said that we do not value people's conjectures so highly that we burn people at the stake for them! I agree, and with Barth who said that theology is rational wrestling with mystery. There is no scope for certainty or proof, and especially not if you start with the assumption that God is not knowable to us in this life. An attitude of openness and a willingness to change one's mind are essential.

I believe that the Universe in which we are making our home has an origin outside itself, to which we give the name 'God'. This is not something that I can prove. I believe that all religions are human creations. They have not come down to us, here on planet Earth, from the skies. They are our attempts to try to make some sense of our lives, to find a purpose and a meaning. It is true that the way people understood their religions, in the past, made it seem as if religions had come down from above. It was believed that a god might have said something like this to his people, "You are my chosen nation and the people whom I love." Now it is more credible to say, "A people believed about themselves that they were the chosen people and the favored nation of their god." There is a sense in which theology is being turned on its head. In my view it starts from below, from our experience; it does not start from above, from a god's self-revelation or self-communication. Once upon a time, people believed that there were the 'talking gods' who regularly communicated with humankind; now do we not need to accept that what we have is the 'silence of the gods' (unless in our stories we make them talk)? Both Judaism and Christianity make claims of a God acting in human history, which, to my mind, is very much open to question today.

I think that Jesus of Nazareth, without whom there would have been no Christian religion, was a human being like the rest of us, though a very extraordinary and inspiring one. I do not think that we will ever have a great deal of genuine knowledge about him. His life will remain shrouded in mystery. What we can glean from his teaching about his alternative vision of life remains challenging. However, I recognize that within the Church there are powerful stories to do with this historical person who lived in a very different age to ours. These stories are far from being simply historical reconstructions of his life. They are faith stories, which, to my mind, are metaphorical ways of expressing beliefs about God and God's relationship with us and our world. These faith stories speak of him as being a divine savior as well as a human being. To me, they are metaphorical stories and I do not understand them in a literal sense. However, I ask myself what are these stories claiming about God? What do they tell us about ourselves? I ask myself too, in what way are these stories linked to the story of the human being, called Jesus of Nazareth?

The story of the Son who is sent by his Father to leave heaven, who lives out a human life and then who dies for the salvation of the world is not, I consider, a true story in a literal sense. Nor is the story about his being raised from death and his returning to his heavenly Father an account to be taken literally. In my view, nothing like that ever really happened. It needs to be understood today how it was that such stories came to be constructed about Jesus, this remarkable and enigmatic person who belonged to the ancient community of Israel. We know much more today, than we did a hundred years ago, about his Jewish background and culture, and his world-view. What was it in the cultural and religious life of the time that permitted his followers to use such ideas, of being divine and of being a Savior, in these faith stories about Jesus?

I look on the 'Jesus story' as an ancient way of pointing to a faith claim that as human beings we are of sacred worth. We are loveable and forgivable in the sight of an infinitely compassionate, merciful, and loving God, who is mysteriously involved in the life of the world in a way that transcends our understanding. Furthermore, I take this religious story to be suggesting to us a belief that the most important thing we can do is to model this story in our lives, by seeking to be both caring and compassionate, just and merciful, and generous and self-sacrificial. To my mind, the best understanding we can have of God is that she/he is the embodiment of these values. The human Jesus has been taken up and incorporated into the Christ symbol. This is a symbol, which points us to the self-sacrificing heights of being human and to the depths within the suffering and victorious love of God. A symbol can be highly important, for it can take us beyond the realm of words and points us to realities no words can describe.

In the future, I do not think that this metaphorical story of Jesus as a divine Savior will make much sense to people; it may be gradually abandoned, others think differently. I accept that many believers still take the story to be in some way literally true, but I think more and more people are coming to question this approach, which to my mind is unsustainable in today's world.

How far faith is metaphorical and symbolical, and how far, if at all, it is historical and factual is a much-debated issue among Christians. The Sea of Faith Network has a special page on its website, http://www.sofn.org.uk/diversity.html, dedicated to exploring diversity of belief that states:

> This page has been compiled in order to assist with a study being undertaken by SoF UK on the allowability of doctrinal diversity in the Christian tradition. The study focuses on the current situation, rather than on the history of doctrinal conflict and diversity, although of course some understanding of the history is necessary.

There is much interesting information on this site, including reports of surveys done among lay people and clergy to see what percentage still believe, for example, in a literal understanding of the virgin birth or the resurrection of Jesus. I think that what many people are looking for are alternative ways in which to try to speak, using fresh metaphors and symbols, of a faith claim about both the meaning of being human and about the mystery of God and God's ultimate commitment and faithfulness to us. Anyone, who knows about the story of how Christianity has changed and adapted from one age to another since its beginning, will be aware of it as a cumulative and an evolving tradition. Indeed, I believe that all religious traditions evolve. I consider that it is important to search for a religious understanding today that helps us to have a greater sense of our responsibility as citizens of this precious planet that we inhabit. It should give us a stronger sense of our worth and dignity as individual human beings and members of the human race. A good religion helps provide an identity for its adherents. This should be, to my mind, an identity that transcends race, genders, color, class, creeds, and that dreadfully insidious type of nationalism that has led people to commit awful acts of violence against other people, sometimes leading to the horrendous atrocities of genocide. I consider that religions that began, as the major ones did, in a pre-scientific and pre-critical world, today need radical modernization and transformation. I hope this book will give you some idea of why I think this to be so.

I do not know if the major ancient faith traditions will survive the twenty-first century; perhaps they have had their day and the questing human spirit will find some other ways for us to express and explore our religious life and to live out its challenge. However, in the meantime, all the great world religions have something important to contribute to human society. They can challenge us to strive toward the heights of our humanity and to seek to avoid the depths of our depravity. They provide us with an ethical code that binds us to the rest of humanity. The values of this code, to my mind, challenge us all to reach out in solidarity to those in the greatest need, and to make great sacrifices on behalf of them. Our world needs changing, it is a very unequal and battered place. Life is so very hard, difficult, and unfair for hundreds of millions of people. Should not religions be at least 80 per cent about how we live out our lives? Then, perhaps, they can be 10 per cent discussion and debate about beliefs, and the remainder will have to do with religious practices in relation to self-development and worship (if that is seen as part of the religion's meaning).

My understanding of the Christian religion, which at present is still a minority understanding, means that I look on Christianity as being on a level platform with the other religions of humankind. I accept that the majority of Christians believe that there is a uniqueness about Christianity. It is centered on their interpretation of Jesus Christ as the Revelation and Incarnation of God and as the Savior of the world. This interpretation, to their minds, makes it a 'higher or better or truer' religion than others. What the minority and the majority viewpoints within the Christian 'family' have in common is both a belief in a God of all-embracing inclusive love, to whom people are of equal worth, and a recognition that many of the religions share a similar ethical code. I believe that my interpretation of Christianity can contribute more to peace between the religions than the traditional interpretation.

I also think that my interpretation of Christianity can help transform it from being a sexist, gender-biased, patriarchal religion to one in which both feminine and masculine metaphors can be used for the divine. Although others disagree with me, I think it has the potential to be re-shaped to become one in which women and men can be affirmed in the diversity of their humanity and in which they can have full and equal opportunities for leadership – and hopefully a different sort of leadership. Let the exploration of gender and the search for gender equality advance. Too many have suffered too long on account of powerful self-interest and, with respect, because of misguided theories about what we are meant to be and how we are meant to live in the diversity of our humanities.

There are many books available today in which the authors put forward ideas similar to the ones that you will find in this book. I have included a list of such authors and their books that I have found helpful, whether or not I agreed with all their ideas. I have tried not to be too technical, and I hope that most people will not have undue trouble in making out my meaning. I was advised to write, if I could, a book that such people could read and understand. "Keep it simple," I was told. You will be able to decide for yourself whether I have done so. I resonate with words that T. S. Eliot used of himself, in communicating with Paul Elmer More: "I am not a systematic thinker, if indeed I am a thinker at all. I depend on intuition and perceptions, and although I may have some skill in the barren game of controversy [I] have little capacity for sustained, exact and closely knit arguments and reasoning." You will not find that this book answers all the questions that will come into your mind, nor will it have answers to all the objections that you may make to my ideas. Perhaps, though, some of the other authors I have listed will help in this regard.

While part of the motivation in writing this book has been to tell 'my story', my main concern is to add whatever little support I can to an understanding of religion as a human creation within an evolving tradition. Theology is to a considerable extent autobiography; it cannot function without human experience. It comes out of the muck and mess of our lives, as well as out of our most sublime moments. Inevitably, therefore, all religious traditions will contain diversity, because there is both commonality and plurality between people and their experiences. I also wanted to affirm the journey and quest of other people who think in similar ways to me, some of whom have wondered whether they are alone in their thinking. I believe part of our identity as human beings is that we do not truly know who we are; we remain a mystery to ourselves, with all our contradictions, despite our increasing knowledge. For me, believing in God is profoundly important and 'reaching out to God' in trust and praise, in anger and love, in bewilderment and confusion, and in penitence and gratitude, remains a spiritual activity that I practice on a daily basis. Others see no point in it; I accept that. I value a time each day for quietness, silence, and stillness. Sometimes my deeper insights into my own life, both good and bad, into my relationships with others, into life in general, and into my vision of what God may be like come to me in such times.

You may have been surprised at the title of this book. Why is it called *Tried for Heresy: A 21st-century Journey of Faith* when in fact the full trial before the Church Court did not take place, and no verdict was therefore handed down? My response is that while this is true, on the other hand it is also true that not just in Ireland, but in many parts of the world, I was tried for heresy by countless people in their own minds. In taking me to court,

Richard Clarke was seen as charging me with heresy, and many agreed with his attitude to my beliefs. Others had a different vision of the Church and the place of believing in all its diversity within it. I support that sort of pluralistic vision. Ultimately, what we believe will relate to our own unique life stories and the insights we have gained into the deep mystery of life. You are going to be reading more than enough of what I think and believe in the pages that follow, so let's take first some worldwide responses to my story from other people, which reflect considerable diversity of thinking and some strong emotions. How would my case have gone if they had been my judges?

Worldwide Responses

As a result of the publicity surrounding me, I have had many people communicating with me. Some have done so by telephone, some by letter, some by e-mail, some by speaking directly to me face to face. Other people responded to my situation by writing to the press or by speaking to the media. In what follows below, I have put together just a sample of these responses. I have not put people's names, but I have included the country, where known, that they live in. You may be interested to read the variety of views that is gathered here. I have not drawn on the many well written articles by journalists, although in the Appendix there are some editorials and an interview from newspapers.

I just heard the news of your license being suspended. Scandalized to hear it. I have directed so many people from all over the world to your parish website since discovering it. It's the best I have seen. Keep your vision clear. It's worth so much to our contemporary world. *New Zealand*

Small world: I was listening to our public radio station yesterday and the BBC news was on. Guess what? Your trial was featured in a news brief. I must say, heresy trials just don't fit the Anglican ethos … there is something else going on here and this is just the tip of the iceberg. USA

I am a recently retired Anglican priest. I have experience of the Church at its best – open, caring, brave, honest – but more typically, and increasingly, as cynical, uncaring, dishonest, escapist, and oppressive. I am heartened by your seeming determination to expose its hypocrisy by fighting on. Most of my clergy acquaintances, many senior in their dioceses, hold views similar to yours (and mine) but manage to keep them well concealed, so as not to rock the boat and risk their status and their security. It is, in my opinion, vital that this reality is exposed as soon as possible, and before all men and women of integrity are forced to leave. *England*

Thank you for articulating so well in 'Pain and Integrity: reform from within' thoughts that I have struggled to formulate on my own for many years. I am grateful to see these ideas expressed (in public no less!) in such a sincere, brave, thoughtful, and positive manner by a studied member of the clergy. I found your article on the web after reading of your situation today on the CNN website. Good luck to you (you are certainly going to need it!). Please keep up the good work and draw strength from the many positive notes you are bound to continue to receive. USA

Courage? Bravery? These people need to open up a dictionary! You, Mr Furlong, are far from a brave and courageous man. Spending 30 years in a lie is not a good example of courage. Misusing your ordained position and violating your pledge is not bravery. USA

Greetings from Japan! The other day I read a newspaper article about your upcoming trial for heresy, and was alarmed enough by the story to have spent this Sunday morning reading the excellent articles on your website. What you have to say there resonates very strongly with my own experience over the past few years. Although baptized and confirmed an Anglican, I have never felt part of the Christian Church, as I have never been able to believe so much of the doctrine, which (as you rightly point out) dates from a period in time utterly different from our own. I therefore find myself unable to attend any place of Christian worship, since I cannot abide feeling like a hypocrite. (The Meetings of the Society of Friends are an occasional exception: at least they are silent most of the time.) Nevertheless, I have very much enjoyed reading the works of many radical theologians over the last few years, people like John Dominic Crossan, John Shelby Spong, Burton Mack, Marcus Borg, and Don Cupitt, to name but a few. *Japan*

My main question to you is how could you over the last four years stand up in front of your congregation, who looked to you to lead our worship weekly, and live a lie? *Ireland*

I sincerely hope that the situation in which you find yourself will be happily resolved and that you will be able to resume your full ministry very soon. The Church of Ireland will be the loser if the outcome is less than favorable to you. *Ireland*

Dean Furlong may be a much loved member of his Church community, but unless, as its priest, he can seek to teach, proclaim, and, more importantly, live the Gospel, he will fail it badly: he will be unable to feed it with anything other than human rhetoric ... The Dean is free to believe what he does ... but it should not be within the Church's ministry. *England*

Dean Furlong has used the facilities of the Church of Ireland website to make his radical anti-Church views public, while simultaneously drawing his stipend from the same Church whose doctrines he rubbishes ... I opine that this action has turned mere hypocrisy into treachery; so, to be true to his employers (and himself), I feel that Dean Furlong should do the honorable thing, and resign. *Ireland*

I am compelled to write to you to express my absolute horror at your refusal to resign your position as Rector of Trim and Athboy Parishes. Have you no idea of the amount of damage you have done to the vast majority of the parishioners by your selfish pursuit of your idea of what you think we all should believe? *Ireland*

The response by the Church authorities was to have been expected, I suppose. But I hope that, despite that, you'll accept my best wishes for the stand you are making. In particular I respect greatly your capacity to have stayed in, despite what I imagine must have been extreme tensions. What you are saying needs desperately to be said. *England*

These days, it's very common to read about priests who won't admit they have serious problems. It's refreshing to read about one with a problem of a very different sort, and one who is brave enough to talk about it. *USA*

All that I would now ask, hope, and pray, is that, if there are any other like-minded bishops, priests, or deacons in our own Church of Ireland, or in any of the other Christian Churches, that they no longer hide, like you did, but come out into the light. We that are for Jesus Christ will stay together, let all else depart from our Church. There is absolutely no room for compromise on this issue. As I have said elsewhere, the divinity of Christ is non-negotiable. *Ireland*

A much-respected twentieth-century Anglican Archbishop of Armagh remarked to me that as members of the Church of Ireland we are so ignorant that we do not even realize how ignorant we are. *Ireland*

If we do not form our organizing myth from the stories and teachings of Jesus, we have nothing that binds us together as a community. If I were your bishop, I would be inclined to grant you permission to say what you like about Jesus as long as you don't leave Jesus out of your teaching and preaching. If you don't like the Jesus that you have received, make up a Jesus that better suits you. That is what Christians have always done right up to the present, with Tom Wright inventing one Jesus and Marcus Borg another. *USA*

It is a pleasure to read such a refreshing view of Christianity in our times. Keep up the good work, my thoughts are with you. *Thailand*

Who has defined Christianity's limits? If the creeds did that or the council of Chalcedon, it is strange that it took four centuries to come to those conclusions. Those limits are human limits imposed primarily for political purposes. Your bishop needs to be informed. What can we do to be supportive? If the Church punishes its internal reformers it is doomed. USA

It is the Bishop of Meath and Kildare, Dr Richard Clarke, who should resign, not Dean Furlong. Clearly the Dean loves and cares deeply for his parishioners, and is an immensely experienced priest ... Let the Church of Ireland kick Dean Furlong out of office. It will be yet one more hammer-blow to the crumbling edifice of the dying Church of Ireland and Church of England ... The Bishop of Meath and Kildare seems incapable of dealing intelligently with intelligent staff. *England*

The action your Bishop has taken against you is deeply troubling. Some of the people in the hierarchy truly seem to have a death wish: "Let's do our best to kill off any signs of imagination, relevance, and new life." *USA*

I am part of a minority ... who are sad at the recent resignation of Andrew Furlong. I really appreciated his intellectually credible slant on God and faith ... perhaps our best hope is that another breed of bishops will emerge who will not blindly follow the status quo. *Ireland*

I sit in front of my computer near tears. For decades I have had (I believed alone) the same beliefs that you have conveyed in your articles. The tears I hold back are those of joy, awakening. Someone shares my views. I am not alone. *Canada*

I just wanted to tell you how much I have enjoyed reading your articles on the web. I love your forthrightness and perception. I am delighted that they are available on the net. *England*

I first came across John Shelby Spong's books about a year ago; his approach was a revelation. Although the scholarship he cites is not new, it was new to me. I have since found other useful reading, including Maurice Wiles' *Reason to Believe*, which you mentioned in an *Irish Times*' letter, and the website of The Center for Progressive Christianity, mentioned by another *Irish Times* correspondent. It is very refreshing to move on from the theology of Victorian hymns. Perhaps Christmas was an appropriate season for starting the debate. *N. Ireland*

The whole central theme of Christian theology causes revulsion to Jewish belief. I hope that you will survive this theological, indeed physical, ordeal. I would like to think that your integrity would find another platform in religious life. It has to be rabbinic. What a challenge that would be, but how fulfilling. *Ireland*

My brother or sister, the belief that the Supreme Being is a Trinity is false and completely inconsistent with the words of Jesus as presented in the Bible. God is one, not three. He is a perfect unity. If you are interested in the truth about God and your relationship to Him, we invite you to investigate the religion of Islam. *Country not known*

Thank you for the excellent and lucid presentation of your spiritual perceptions, which, as I understand the term, represent 'new paradigm' Christianity. I share most of the concepts which you have so fluently set forth, and would have little to add. It is my hope that my beloved Episcopal Church USA opens its mind and heart just enough to let in some fresh air and sunshine. *USA*

Bring him to trial on a charge of heresy. Blank out his websites. Sack him from his job and try and starve him into submission. What a Christian way to treat a sincere and honest man. Don't let them break your spirit. *Ireland*

The sad situation in which the Dean of Clonmacnoise finds himself demonstrates, yet again, that the peculiarly Christian desire for doctrinal uniformity can only make for division and enmity. *Ireland*

Part One:

CHARGED BY MY BISHOP:
MY HERESY TRIAL AND RESIGNATION

Chapter 1

Beginning the journey in life and ministry

For as long as I can remember I have been interested in religion. The word 'God' and the mystery it signifies have had a special hold over me. The vision of a world at harmony with itself and with its Creator has had a good feel to it. The sense of a God of infinite compassion, understanding all there is to be understood, and looking on us as people of sacred worth and eternal value has been of precious importance to me as a profound belief to hold onto and to cherish.

When I was a baby I was baptized in the Church of Ireland. In the school, Brook House, Dublin, that I attended from the age of eight to fourteen, there was a stable yard. During my time in the school, part of it, an upstairs hay barn, was converted into a school chapel. It had been used as a playroom with a table tennis table and a large clockwork train set on the floor. Particularly at the weekends, if it was raining outside, the boarders would go and play there. Church pews from some redundant church and other pieces of church furniture were acquired. There were two lovely small stained glass windows. This upper room was probably about seven meters wide by eighteen meters long, and was able to seat the 10 teachers and 90 or so boys. I enjoyed chapel services, as I did in my secondary school chapel, at St Columba's College, Dublin, which was a larger building designed by the Victorian architect, William Butterfield. I had not been a rebel when it came to going with my family to the local Church of Ireland parish church in Dalkey, County Dublin on Sunday mornings; I largely enjoyed it. I would have thought of myself as a devout boy who took his religion seriously, although one who was constantly failing to live up to its demands in ordinary living, as I have always done.

Speaking of failure, although that is not by any means my whole story, and looking back now over the years of my life, I recognize that, regrettably, I have failed many people, harmed or hurt them. I have caused people to feel angry with me, let down by me, disappointed in me, disgusted with me and alienated from me. Where it has been possible, I have expressed my apology and where appropriate sought forgiveness. In some cases, I have tried to make up for the wrong that I have done, and subsequently I may have tried to change myself in some way for the better. That has not been easy. Thankfully, I have often been the recipient of mercy and forgiveness, compassion and understanding, acceptance, tolerance, and love as well as the sincere criticism that brought home to me more clearly the nature of my flaws and the need to address them. I am deeply indebted to such people and very grateful. If we are to seek mercy and forgiveness because we need them then, to my mind, we must also be prepared to offer them to others in their need. But back to my account of growing up, which I had been describing.

In 1965 I went from school to Trinity College, Dublin to study Mathematics but, finding it incredibly hard, changed to Philosophy. I would sometimes attend lunchtime seminars organized on religion by the University chaplains. It began to become clear to me, that in relation to religion, things were not so straightforward as I had imagined them to be. It was a shock at the time. I was being introduced to biblical scholarship, a subject, like many others, that began to make significant progress over two hundred years ago. Up until the time I entered University, I had not noticed, nor do I remember being taught (although perhaps I had been), that there were two differing accounts of Creation in the opening chapters of the Book of Genesis. There were two dissimilar accounts of the story of the Flood as well. There were two stories of Goliath being killed, by two different people. I was learning that most modern scholars did not take all the Bible stories literally. There was no scientific evidence for a worldwide flood, the story of Jonah and the whale was fiction, and the Creation stories were not scientific history.

The New Testament authors had a different idea about writing history than ours: for example, some scholars think that Jesus was not born in Bethlehem, that was simply a way, used by the Gospel writers, of asserting his alleged Messianic credentials. For there had been a strand in Judaic thinking that linked Bethlehem, the city of King David's childhood home, with the idea of a Messiah who, like David, would be a leader par excellence. It all seemed very confusing at first, but also intriguing. I was learning that a story could be true in other ways. It could, for example, contain moral or spiritual beliefs that were held to be true. I was learning of the use of metaphor in speaking about God. I was becoming more aware of the importance of seeing religion as essentially symbolic. God is like a fire, like the wind, like a king, like a judge, like a shepherd, like a rock, and so on. We draw on our human world to speak of the ineffable and the divine, that strictly speaking transcends our understanding.

Shortly before I started my final year in the University of Dublin (of which Trinity College is still the sole constituent college), I was often pondering about what my working life might be after I had finished my degree course. Although I was also thinking of accountancy as a possible profession, I found myself becoming more attracted to what I felt to be the challenge of the ordained ministry of the Church. To work among people, especially in times of their suffering and crises, appealed strongly to the compassionate and loving side of my nature, to the spiritual side of my being. Please note, though, that I affirm that one's spirituality can be expressed in a host of differing forms of employment. Although I knew such work would be demanding, I also sensed that it could be very rewarding. That such work would be done against the background of a vision of faith in a God of all-embracing inclusive love, was also important to me. After much thought, prayerful reflection, and conversations with others, I attended a selection conference of the Church of Ireland in 1968 and it was agreed that I could go to Cambridge, if given a place there, to study in preparation for ordination. I was delighted when offers of places in both Jesus College, Cambridge University and at Theological College at Westcott House, Cambridge arrived.

I completed my degree in Philosophy in Trinity College, Dublin in June 1969. My father had been my professor and had spent virtually all his working life at Trinity College. After four years myself at Trinity, I was conscious of needing my own space. I was also looking for a larger Theology faculty than was on offer in Trinity College, if I had stayed on there. So I set off, full of excitement and anticipation, in October 1969, for Cambridge University to read for a degree in Theology and, in addition, from 1970-72, to do the rest of my ordination training at Westcott House. I knew that I was privileged to be going to a great and distinguished University, and to a theological college with a fine reputation. I felt really proud. In Trinity, I had been awarded my University of Dublin Pink in recognition of the honor of playing for my country in the Irish (under-23) hockey team. I was also intent on winning, if I could, my Cambridge Blue for playing hockey, the sport that I have enjoyed the most. If I were to come away from Cambridge, three years later, having developed a deep and strong relationship with a good and lovely woman, that would be another major bonus! I succeeded in achieving my sporting ambition, but failed to realize the much deeper desire of finding love and companionship.

Little though, as I arrived in Cambridge, did I realize the struggles of conscience and the profound changes in my understanding of Christianity that would lie ahead in the next three years. I would cease to believe, in a literal sense, in Jesus as the Savior of the world. I would no longer see him as both human and divine, in the sense required if it were to be claimed that God had entered our environment and become a human being. Should I have proceeded on the route to ordination? At the time it seemed to me, in the context of what I was taught, that this more metaphorical and symbolical understanding of Christianity was the way forward for the Church. It kept the commitment to love and caring, while presenting it in a way that was fully in tune with modern knowledge. My spirituality changed in Cambridge, from being Christocentric to being theocentric. I had moved from a devotional life very focused on Jesus to a meditative life, in which a sense of the mystery and unknowability of God were combined with an awareness of my 'vision' of God as love: love without limits and love without end.

The academic staff of the Cambridge University Divinity faculty was made up of theologians of varying outlooks – some were quite conservative, like

Charlie Moule, others such as John Robinson and Geoffrey Lampe were liberals. John Neill, who was one of my judges for the trial, and since then has become Archbishop of Dublin, was in Cambridge a few years before me. When the senior leadership of the Church of Ireland agreed to us both studying there, they were aware we would encounter a variety of theological thinking, as would have been true to a lesser extent at Trinity College, Dublin. John Neill seemed more drawn to the conservative and evangelical viewpoints, while I was more attracted to the liberal perspectives. Did it show that, at the time, the senior leadership of our Church at home was prepared to accept for ordination people with a range of differing theological views, regardless of whether they had been trained in Dublin or in places such as Cambridge? I think it did, for the Church of Ireland has always struggled not to be a narrow, theologically monochrome Church, although the majority viewpoint has been conservative. Though this does not mean that there cannot be radical thinkers, in the true sense of the word, among conservatives, traditionalists, and fundamentalists. I believe diversity and pluralism are inescapable features of life and should be welcomed, even though in practice it may be very hard for unlike-minded people to get on together in the same organization.

My period of transition from being a layman within the Church to being one of its ordained members was soon to conclude, although, as I often reminded myself, I would still basically be the same person. It is not uncommon for people coming towards the end of their ordination training to have some doubts about becoming ordained. My main doubt, some weeks before my ordination as a deacon in December 1972, related to my concern about the amount of poverty in the world, and the rate of over-consumption in the West. I had been wondering to myself whether I should look for work that would be more closely related to this massive issue, and give up the idea of being ordained. I shared my doubts with Canon John Brown, who at that time was working as the principal of the Church of Ireland's Theological College in Dublin, where I had been required to study for one term after leaving Cambridge. He suggested I go and think about it a bit more, which I did. I then decided to continue to plan towards ordination.

While I am a little uncertain now of the exact nature of my reasoning at that time, in relation to being or not being ordained, I think I may have been influenced by some thoughts I had had a few months earlier. For, during the summer of 1972, having left Cambridge in June, I worked and traveled in the USA for two and a half months, before returning to Dublin for my final term of training. During my time in the USA I was conscious of Ireland as a tiny little island on the other side of the Atlantic Ocean, on the western fringe of Europe. It was hardly the center of the world, if the world can be said to have a center! And the world was certainly a much bigger place than Ireland! I recall deciding then, as I considered the prospect of a working life of 40 years or more that would soon begin, that I would seek to spend a part of it somewhere else in the world. It may be that as I pondered on whether to take the final step towards ordination, I thought of the idea of having a chapter of my working life in the Third World. I do remember that in the early seventies a number of reports had come out, such as the Club of Rome's *The Limits of Growth* about both poverty in the world and the exponential rate at which the earth's finite resources were being used up. I felt very concerned about these matters. It seemed to me to be a great priority, and an urgent one, to encourage people in the 'developed world' to think about their lifestyles and to change them; otherwise we might all soon be doomed.

I think there was some eccentric idea in my mind at this time that I should parade around Dublin, dressed in rags, with a placard proclaiming a message of doom if we did not take more responsible care of our precarious planet and share more with those in desperate need. I think I must have decided that that sort of witness would not have made any enduring difference, and being an eccentric in that way did not appeal to me. Anyway, one way or another, I overcame this nagging doubt about the rightness of being ordained; and that particular doubt did not trouble me in the same way again. It was my sense of the Church needing to change its theological understanding that was to be the thorn in my side in the years to come and my own perception of being part of a minority outlook swamped by the convictions of the majority.

On 21 December 1972 (St Thomas' Day, as it was then), I was made a deacon in the little church at Glencraig, a few miles from Belfast. I was conscious, of course, that I would now be 'in uniform'. I realized that for many people this uniform symbolized trust, confidence, spirituality, and care. At first, though, I did not particularly like wearing clerical clothes. This was partly due to shyness about what I felt was a display, in public, of my inner being, and particularly my tenderness, but also because it seemed to make me feel different from other people, which in part it was intended to do. However, eventually, I got used to my uniform and came to value, in my pastoral work, what it symbolized. I recall feeling very green and inexperienced. My first post was in a Belfast suburb at St Mark's, Dundela, where William Butterfield had designed the church, as in the case of my secondary school chapel. It was the parish in which, many years previously, C. S. Lewis had lived as a child; one of his grandfathers had been rector there too. I did not share my worries about my theology with George Quin, the Bishop of Down and Dromore, who had ordained me, or with my first rector, Edwin Parke. I had just completed a year at St Mark's when Edwin Parke died and Robin Eames (now the Archbishop of Armagh) came to take his place.

While I do not remember speaking directly to my new rector about my theological convictions, I do recall that he would have listened to my sermons in which some of my theology relating to Incarnation was expressed. For instance, I remember drawing on a book by H. A. Williams called *Poverty, Chastity and Obedience* and what he wrote in it about Incarnation. It was a truth, he believed, not just about Jesus, but about every human being. The two verses from St John's Gospel, "I and the Father are one" and "the Father is greater than I" were true not just of Jesus, but of us all. I recall preaching about H. A. Williams' views and saying that they made sense to me as credible beliefs, for clearly God is greater than any of us and at a profound level we are intimately connected, to my mind, with the divine. I was conscious that most people would argue that Incarnation refers to a unique event – the life of Jesus – and think that metaphors such as transcendence and immanence are more appropriate to use in relation to other human beings and their relationship with the divine.

Robin Eames stayed for a little over a year, as he was appointed to be Bishop of Derry and Raphoe, and was succeeded by Jimmy Moore (later Bishop of Connor) with whom I did speak quite openly about my concerns about my theology, and whether I should stay on in the ordained ministry. Liberal theology was under attack and its proponents at this time were sometimes told that they were not true Christians, and they should leave the Church. I used to try to spend some time reading theology each morning and I continued to wrestle with the implications of liberal theology for the way Christianity was interpreted by the majority of people. In St Mark's I would listen to the more traditional sermons preached with sincere conviction by my three rectors and fellow curates, and I felt an outsider. Particularly at Christmas and Easter, the liturgy focused on Jesus and the hymns spoke so literally about him being human and divine, God come to live a human life on earth. It continued to make me feel so uncomfortable. I arranged to go over to Oxford and visit both my former principal, Peter Walker, from my time at Westcott House, who was then a suffragan bishop in the Oxford diocese, and my former supervisor from Jesus College, Cambridge who was then an Oxford professor – the late Peter Baelz. Both encouraged me to stay on, and assured me that there were many others of a similar viewpoint, who also struggled with these issues of theology and conscience as I was doing.

Some months later, I left Belfast and went to join Samuel Poyntz, who was Rector of St Ann's and St Stephen's with St Mark's in Dublin and also Archdeacon. I recall discussing with him *The Myth of God Incarnate*, edited by John Hick and published in 1977. I shared with him my basic agreement with the liberal theology expressed in the book. After Samuel Poyntz left the parish to become the Bishop of Cork, Cloyne and Ross, the late Billy Wynne joined me – my fifth rector during my time as a curate. I look on all five as having enriched my life in different ways, as did other clerical colleagues, and the people I sought to serve. During the time he was rector, I had written and had had published a six-week series, in 1978, in the weekly *Church of Ireland Gazette*. It was, primarily, about the significance of Jesus. I called it

Christianity's self-scrutiny: a conversation between friends. It consisted of
dialogues between a conservative believer and a liberal one (Appendix I).

Shortly afterwards, Billy Wynne invited two clergy, Victor Griffin (then
Dean of St Patrick's Cathedral, Dublin) and Noel Willoughby (then the
Archdeacon of Dublin) and Frank Luce, a lay reader, to the Rectory one
Saturday morning, so that we could discuss my beliefs together. It was a
cordial meeting over a cup of coffee. It was clear that we all agreed in our
faith claim about a God of all-embracing, inclusive love. Whether or not it
was credible to believe in some literal or historical sense that God had
become a human being was where we most differed. The liberal voice in the
Gazette dialogues had been mine, which a number of letter writers to the
Gazette following the publication of the dialogues had picked up, although I
had not stated this to be the case. At no time did any of the people with
whom I had shared my theology, either in Belfast or in Dublin, suggest it was
not appropriate for me to stay in the ordained ministry. I am sure that they
were surprised that I held such views, for the Church of Ireland was largely
quite conservative. I went to speak to Harry McAdoo, who was my
archbishop in Dublin, about my continuing concerns about staying on. He
simply encouraged me to go on reading and to go on thinking.

About this time, at a meeting of the annual Dublin and Glendalough
Diocesan Synod, Harry McAdoo had given a presidential address in which he
spoke about our identity as Anglicans, and he referred to the "faith once
delivered to the saints" and "the Christ who is the same yesterday, today and
forever". During this synod I very nervously made a speech in which I
mentioned the archbishop's remarks. I went on to say that this faith was
under considerable investigation in the theologians' 'laboratories', that a
debate was engaging many minds about the significance of Jesus and over
ways to interpret him today. I imagine I had a collection of essays such as
The Myth of God Incarnate in mind. I did not, however, speak about my own
specific beliefs during my speech. I just wanted to give my listeners the
opportunity to read between the lines. I hoped that they would see that, to
my mind, at least, it was being a little simplistic to speak about the "faith
once delivered to the saints". For there was deep debate about how to
interpret that faith, and a controversy was raging over whether the metaphor
of 'incarnation' was just a metaphor (speaking of a reconciling God) or
whether it pointed to something which people believed could be historically
true as well. In 1979, the late Professor Geoffrey Lampe, the Regius Professor
of Divinity in Cambridge University, was in Trinity College, Dublin to give a
lecture. I spoke to him afterwards and at his request I sent him *Christianity's
self-scrutiny: a conversation between friends*. He replied that it would be
helpful if these dialogues could be made available for readers in England too.
I did not, in fact, follow up this suggestion. He also said in his letter to me: "I
have read them with great interest. They seem to me to be a most valuable

exercise in communication and just what is so badly needed to plug the gaps between the study, the pulpit, and the pew."

In my Dublin parish, I spent four out of my six years there, specializing in hospital chaplaincy ministry. It was often very tough, but I liked the sense of being part of a multi-disciplinary team. I felt very close to many of the people who, as patients, or as members of their families, I was coming alongside, as well as to members of staff. My work involved me in meeting all sorts of people. I listened to many stories, and to people's hopes and fears. I regarded it as a great privilege to be there for people in their struggles to cope with their uncertainties and suffering. I admired the courage of many people as they sought to come to terms with new situations in their lives that were exceedingly difficult to accept and adjust to. Sometimes a person would share with me the pain of profound questions about the meaning of suffering that neither of us could answer. My only response was to stay with such a person, as they faced such times of questioning. I tried not to increase the pain with a superficial reply or a hasty exit. I had entered that person's world, to some extent at least. I brought into it, as best I could, my love, my faith, my unknowing, and my friendship.

Taking both my Belfast and my Dublin parishes together, I had now been a curate for a little over 10 years. This was a much longer time than most of my contemporaries, but then this was largely because of the opportunity, for which I was deeply grateful, provided to me to work as a hospital chaplain. However, I was beginning to be approached by parishes in Ireland that needed a new rector. Was that what I wanted to do? I remembered the idea I had had of working somewhere else in the world and, to cut a long story short, I approached a missionary society about work in the Third World. When I was interviewed, in London, about possible work as a missionary for the United Society for the Propagation of the Gospel (USPG) I was open about my theological position. It did not prevent them recommending me to the then Bishop of Harare, Peter Hatendi, for work there. The Anglican Church in Zimbabwe was supplemented by quite a number of clergy from several countries. I went first to USPG's training college in Birmingham, UK where there was a wonderful international mix of people. I began to learn the Shona language, to study about Zimbabwe, and to think more about the world's inequalities and injustices, especially in relation to the Third World and what could be done about it all. A new chapter in my own development had begun.

It is natural to want to share your deepest beliefs, and your interpretation of them, with other people, and while I was not speaking completely openly from the pulpit about them, I was often on the lookout for someone with whom I could speak freely and transparently. I found a few such people both when I was in Zimbabwe and subsequently when I lived and worked for a few years in Leeds, as a hospital chaplain. Working in Zimbabwe, which I did for 11 years, helped to deepen my concern for issues of poverty and justice in our unequal world and for other human rights issues too; it made me think about the concept of development in its broadest contexts. Being in Zimbabwe, from 1983-94, was a wonderful experience. Naturally, I did not enjoy everything, such as racial prejudice when I encountered it or the constant shortages of goods that were needed for the many building projects in my parish that I was sharing in. I was fascinated by the new cultures I was learning about, stimulated by the change living in a new country brought into my life. I felt I was now in a society where the individualism of being human was balanced by the sense of the corporate dimension to human life. I was making new friends, regardless of color or race. I became very involved in the work of the parishes I served in, both urban and rural. I was still conscious of my 'hidden isolation' and sense of alienation brought about by my theological views; but so much else was going well that I could continue to live with this aspect of my life.

If people are going to marry, I believe that it is much the wisest thing to spend a considerable time first getting to know one another. I went against this wisdom by proposing to a lovely person (after about 30 days in total in her company over a two-year period) who I became attracted to on first meeting her, in England, on a visit home in 1989. I was in my forties and wondering if I would ever get married; had I been looking for an angel that did not exist? Living on two separate continents, we hardly knew each other when we became married. After arriving with me in Zimbabwe, following our marriage in England, she was soon held in high and affectionate esteem by many in both parish and community. Unfortunately, she and I shared two stressful years in Zimbabwe before we left. Our relationship was not going well. My experience of marriage was shattering and humiliating for me in many ways, though I do not blame my former wife in any way.

To my mind, God does not protect us from making mistakes, even very serious and deeply painful ones. I wish such a good person well, and I hope she finds the love and joy I failed to bring into her life. Shortly after our return to England I left her; our lives would now go on in their separate ways; our marriage was in the final process of ending. It was not an easy time for us, nor for our families and friends. I was conscious that she was very sad about the ending of our marriage. She had been the one who had continued to say we should stick at it and persist in working to improve our relationship. I, rightly or wrongly, had been the one who had felt strongly that, regretfully, we would be wasting our time by doing so. I had considered that it would be better for both of us to move on in our different directions. I found fulfilling work during this time as a hospital chaplain in Leeds but after three years I was on my way back again to live and work in my own home country of Ireland. A chastened, and I hope wiser, man, though still a person battling to cope with his loneliness.

While still working in Leeds, I had traveled over several times to Ireland and had visited 11 vacant parishes within the Church of Ireland. I had finally decided to apply for work in the Trim and Athboy Group of Parishes in the United Diocese of Meath and Kildare, where the bishop was Richard Clarke. As it happened, the same day as I had had my interview in Trim, I had gone that evening to another vacant parish for an informal meeting with their nominators. The previous rector had been Paddy Semple, someone with whom I would soon re-connect and with whom I would have good theological conversations. I remember one of the people asking me whether I would encourage the people of their parish to question and to think, if I were to come as their next rector. It was what Paddy Semple had done, and they had liked and benefited from it. I was very pleased to have been asked such a question and replied that indeed I would. I see the religious life as being, for some people at least, a part of the search to become more fully human and so, to my mind, it is a lifelong quest.

That parish was not going to begin its official interviews for some months, so when I was offered the post in Trim, I was happy to accept it. It seemed as if it would suit my purposes. I did not want to live in a big city with all its congestion and traffic; life in Zimbabwe had made me used to the wide, open spaces and the sense of belonging one finds in a smaller town. This group of parishes would offer me a sufficient amount of pastoral work, there was minimal administration to do, and I would have most mornings free for reading and study. It also meant I would have Richard Clarke, whom I perceived to be one of the Church of Ireland's more liberal thinkers, to work with as my bishop. It was also close to Dublin, where I had family and friends. I wanted, now that I was coming home again after 14 years, to re-connect with them, as well as to make new friends in a changed Ireland. I was instituted into my new parish on 20 March 1997. I had become the Rector of the Trim and Athboy Group of Parishes and the Dean of Clonmacnoise. I was not expecting a turbulent time ahead of me.

Chapter 2

Becoming more open and transparent about belief

I was conscious that I was putting my roots down again in Ireland and becoming well settled in my parish. In the last few years of the nineties, plans were being made to celebrate the millennium. The twentieth century was drawing to a close and there was considerable discussion about how the millennium would be celebrated. The Churches around the world were planning to mark the birth of that remarkable person held to be the founder of their faith. Although historically I doubt it is true that Jesus of Nazareth had it at all in mind to found a faith in his name, he simply thought of himself and his disciples as being Jews. Something in me began to stir: a new century was about to dawn. Perhaps the time had come, in a more pluralistic Ireland, to be more transparent, though I was still very apprehensive about doing so. What was it then that encouraged me to lift the veil? I remember feeling that the country had moved on considerably from the time when I had left 14 years previously, in 1983. People were generally more outspoken, many were more articulate, and many had more self-confidence about expressing what they thought or believed about a wide range of issues. It was particularly apparent within the media that this was so, or at least that is how it seemed to me.

While people were discussing how they would celebrate the millennium, I had an invitation in 1999 to read a paper to the Diocesan Clergy Society and I decided that I would take the risk of speaking transparently about my radical beliefs to them. Perhaps some of them might recall my 1978 six dialogues in *The Church of Ireland Gazette* and remember being told that the liberal voice in those dialogues was mine or perhaps they had worked that out for themselves. My paper was called 'Treasure in Earthen Vessels: reflections of a reformer' (Appendix B). To nearly all of the small group, perhaps about a dozen people, who listened to it, my paper came, to my surprise, as a great shock. After I had read my paper I was asked whether bishops were privy to my views. I replied that I had had some discussions with Richard Clarke about my beliefs; he was not unaware, I felt, of their general tenor, and that I also had had conversations with Harry McAdoo, a former Archbishop of Dublin, when last I worked in Ireland.

Normally in the minutes of these Diocesan Clergy meetings there would be a brief summary of the paper read and of comments about it. In my case a decision was taken not to have any summary of the paper or any reference to comments made, and who they had been made by. It was agreed that the paper would receive further consideration at the next meeting, and the paper due to be read was deferred. Once again, no minutes were kept in relation to the discussion, which was largely critical of my ideas. There were some clergy who questioned my right to stay on as the dean, while others doubted whether I ought even to continue as a member of the Church. Some time later a number of the senior clergy were to say to Richard Clarke that if there was a Eucharist at the cathedral in Trim, perhaps for some diocesan event, and if I were the celebrant, they would not feel able, in conscience, to communicate. Though it created a rift between me and most of my fellow clergy, we remained on friendly terms. No campaign was started by them to have me removed from the diocese.

In 2000 I received permission from Richard Clarke to take a six-week mini-sabbatical, so that I could do some more intensive reading, studying, and writing. In the autumn of that year a series of seminars was being organized on the future of Anglicanism. Over the period, a number of papers were to be read by authors from around the world, and discussed by those present. They were going to be held at St Deiniol's Library, in Hawarden, Wales. I was delighted when the Warden, Peter Francis, agreed that I should be one of the people to read a paper on this theme. Picking up the theme in my title, I called my paper 'The implications of radical and liberal theology for the future of Anglicanism'. I subsequently re-wrote this paper for another visit to St Deiniol's, the following year, and re-named it 'Pain and Integrity: reform from within' (Appendix A).

During the six weeks I was there for my sabbatical in the autumn of 2000 there were a number of weekend seminars and courses that I also attended. At one of them Richard Clarke was reading a paper to do with matters relating to the Lambeth Conference held in 1998 and a report called the Virginia report about increasing the authority of the Archbishop of Canterbury, about which he was critical. I enjoyed his paper, which was well received, and while at St Deiniol's I gave him a copy of the paper that I had prepared for the series on the future of Anglicanism. It was good to be able to be open and transparent about one's deepest convictions, and to meet other people, with similar convictions, who felt the same difficulties of belonging to and ministering within the Church. Bishop John Shelby Spong also came to give some lectures, and he kindly agreed to read my paper. At the bottom of the final page, he wrote, "Thanks, Andy. This is a revealing and provocative piece of work. It places your questions and comments in our conference into a whole new context. You write well and you clearly have courage – rare gifts in the Church today. Why don't you expand this into a book and start a dialogue – it will be threatening to many – but you can't make an omelet without cracking some eggs. I have enjoyed meeting you, so has Chris. Stay in touch,

Jack." This is to some extent that book, although other events were to take place in 2001-2 that this book is clearly concerned with too.

The Church of Ireland has a journal called *Search* that is published three times a year. I decided to send my paper, read at St Deiniol's Library for the 'Future of Anglicanism' series, to the editor, Very Revd Stephen White. I was not completely surprised when, on 22 January 2001, he replied that he had read it, and had asked two others on the editorial committee to read it too, and that the committee had decided not to accept it. He wrote

> In essence this was, I think, for two reasons:
> The article argues for new models of worship, etc for those who do not have a Trinitarian understanding of faith, but it does not significantly address the prior question of why such an understanding is felt to be inadequate – in other words it argues for change without looking at the theological grounds for such change.
>
> It leaves to one side the very important practical issues that such a shift in understanding would bring – how, for example might one preach and speak about faith in a parish, or how might one relate to others in pastoral situations such as bereavement: how in such circumstances could one (if at all) speak of hope, the presence of God's love, etc?

I may be wrong, but I do not think it was the sort of article that *Search* wanted to get a reputation for publishing, if it were to hold its traditional religious readership. As far as the reasons given for rejecting the article are concerned, I had thought that my article had provided reasons why I did not find it credible to believe in a literal understanding of the Incarnation, and therefore, by implication, I considered the doctrine of the Trinity was not needed for my views. Second, I would have thought that if Jesus could speak about faith and hope in God, then I could too. Like me, to my mind, he very definitely did not subscribe to a belief in a Trinitarian conception of his God. After all, he was a Jew. As *Search* was the only journal within the Church of Ireland, I would have been glad if they had accepted it. It would have been one more way of seeking to broaden a Church, some of whose members, at least, wanted fresh winds and new thinking to be allowed in. It was not as if today's reader is simple fodder for indoctrination, and many people benefit from thought-provoking articles, even if they agree with little the author has written.

However, this rejection of my article increased my sense of frustration. I was not an academic theologian with a range of journals to send articles to. I was looking for a forum within the Church for debate and discussion. The Church is the community that receives the stories of our faith, interprets them for our day, and passes them on to the next generation. There has always been debate about how to do this. There have constantly been diverse interpretations of the stories of our faith. My frustration was caused by feeling that there was no real desire for debate or for open acceptance of pluralism over the issues that I, and others, were concerned about. I felt the debate was much needed, as Christianity had come out of a pre-scientific and pre-critical world, and to my mind needed modernizing and radical re-interpretation.

In addition to having sent my St Deiniol's paper to the editor of *Search* in November 2000 I also sent it to Patsy McGarry, the religious correspondent of *The Irish Times*, to see whether he would be interested in it, or in a condensed version of it. He replied, in January 2001, that he would be happy to receive an article of not more that 800 words for the 'Rite and Reason' column. However, he said that it might be a considerable length of time before it would be published, as he had a backlog of articles already. As my St Deiniol's paper was much longer than 800 words, I straightaway started to write a much shorter version that I called 'A Faith Fundamentally Flawed? Working towards a radical and revolutionary transformation of Christianity'. When I refer to this article again, because of the length of the title, I will just use the first part of its title. Later the same month (January 2001) I decided to show it to three members of the parish. My main purpose in doing so was for them to look through it, in order to see if it was written in a way that was sufficiently non-technical for the intelligent layperson. I had said to each of them that they would not necessarily agree with what I had written, but that I was primarily interested in whether they could understand it and follow the argument.

In February 2001 I took my annual leave, this time to a beleaguered Zimbabwe, to visit friends and former members of the parishes I had served. I wanted to express my solidarity with them over the many hardships that they were having to endure. There was massive unemployment and poverty. Countless thousands were suffering from AIDS. As a result of this there was widespread bereavement. The country was poisoned by political corruption. Harsh and often violent oppression by the government of its opponents was diminishing democracy. There was deep and pervasive uncertainty over the future of agriculture and the entitlement to land. A continuing brain drain of talented people was impoverishing the country. I know so many talented and dedicated people in Zimbabwe, and it made me very sad to see the vast majority of citizens in this part of the world having such a hard time, compounded too by mistaken and ill thought out policies of the World Bank and the IMF.

On my return, one of the parishioners who had read my article said to me that she could understand it all right, but that my views would not be hers. A second person said he had had a quick look through it and saw nothing to worry about in it. The third person, with whom I had often had theological discussions and who shared many ideas in common with me about the faith, thought it was a good article and that it would stir up debate. Two of the three members of the parish who looked through this article became some of the most outspoken critics of my position after Richard Clarke had withdrawn his authority for me to work as a priest later – in December that same year. However, to my mind the strange thing is that neither of them, at this time, in March 2001, had questioned my right to be their rector or its appropriateness. They had not, to my knowledge, brought any concerns about me to our bishop, nor had they started a campaign against me in the parish. I could not detect any change in their attitude to me.

It seemed that I could genuinely hope to be more transparent with my views on the need for Christianity to be modernized. Ireland had moved on, people were more used to pluralism, to diversity of opinion, and had the tolerance, breadth of mind, and self-confidence to cope with this. Was it not incumbent, particularly on a person with a theological training like me, to continue to seek to serve the cause of truth, to seek for appropriate ways to interpret the faith for the twenty-first century? With hindsight, I think that Richard Clarke and I ought to have given much more thought together, if I was going to go public, on how to prepare members of the parish for such an event. Part of their pain, undoubtedly, related to being so unprepared for the bombshell I dropped in their midst by becoming more transparent about my beliefs.

I eventually sent my article, 'A Faith fundamentally flawed?', to Patsy McGarry on 21 March 2001. I have not included this article as an Appendix, because most of it is included in 'Pain and Integrity'. It can, however, be found on my website. I was emboldened by the prospect of having one article that was due to be published in a number of weeks time, as I then expected, though in fact *The Irish Times* never did publish it. I was still nervous about the reaction to it, but I decided to send Patsy two more articles for his 'back burner' for the 'Rite and Reason' column. On 29 March 2001, I sent him 'Revelation: does it happen?' and 'New Worship, New Symbols', also to be found on my website.

Next, I sent both Paddy Semple and Richard Clarke 'A Faith Fundamentally Flawed?'. I shared my worries with Paddy Semple: "I am wondering and somewhat fearful as to what reaction there will be here in the parish, although some people who know my views are supportive." What would Richard Clarke have to say about it?

Richard Clarke did not like the article that I had sent him on 10 April 2001. I e-mailed him as follows:

> Richard, as you will know *The Irish Times* runs an opinion column for issues relating to ethics, religion, and spirituality called 'Rite and Reason', which normally appears on Tuesdays. Patsy McGarry hopes to use the article below at some stage and I thought you might like to have sight of it; it may or may not arouse some debate, although everything

in it has been said many times before by others, as you will well know. I hope your book is selling well. *Regards,* Andrew

I did not have long to wait for a reply from Richard Clarke that showed his annoyance and disappointment:

Dear Andrew

Thank you for doing me the courtesy of sending me your proposed 'Rite and Reason' piece for *The Irish Times*. I hope that what I want to say will not seem hurtful but it must nevertheless be said. I would ask you to withdraw the article and rewrite it. This should not present a problem with timing, as Patsy McGarry has asked me to have copy with him by tomorrow for next Tuesday's 'Rite and Reason' column, so it seems reasonable to assume that mine will be the one to appear next week. My reasons for asking you to withdraw the article and rewrite it are as follows.

Although, as you know well, I have never sought to stifle good theological debate (including radical debate), and I hope that I may even have contributed to it in my own way, you should realize that your article in its present form has absolutely nothing constructive to say. 'A Faith Fundamentally Flawed' is not the first part of a lecture being given to people who are well versed in theology, to be followed by some positive and creative suggestions. All that people will read is what is on the printed page. I think you would agree that a Cupitt or a Spong (although I am certainly not in doctrinal agreement with them) always advances constructive philosophical/ theological propositions. You have not. Secondly, your use of adjectives in relation to orthodox Christian belief – for example 'deluded', 'bizarre', 'crazy' – may seem to you to be provocative. They read as gratuitous insult. They are not the terms that one would expect to find in any objective appraisal of an issue, and I am at a loss to know why you would think of using them in the context of a general article in a daily newspaper.

I am sorry to write in this way. I have never asked you to pretend to be something you are not, and I am not doing so now. Nevertheless, I am certain that you have totally misjudged the context in which you are seeking to advance theological discussion. As the article reads, you appear not so much to be asking questions, as to be answering them to your own satisfaction in the questions themselves. The article should be withdrawn and rewritten.

I hope that what I have said is of help to you. I have no wish to hurt you but I value you far too much to wish to be placed in a position where I would not be able to give you support.

Obviously if you wish to come and talk about this, I would be more than happy to see you, but I would have to say that I will not change my views of this particular article.
With best wishes
Richard

My reply to this letter was sent on 12 April 2001:

Dear Richard, thank you for your response and reactions to my article. I wonder what you have been asked to write about yourself; I look forward to reading it. As you know, the articles are restricted to 800 words. In 'A Faith Fundamentally Flawed?' I did not find it possible in such a short article to include 'Part 2' – the constructive ideas. However, I still think that one can serve the truth by inviting people to ponder over the reasons for questioning aspects of the faith or objections to it. In fact, I have written other articles and submitted them to Patsy McGarry, one of which is a follow-up to 'A Faith fundamentally flawed?', that I hope he will also have printed in due course. In case people might feel affronted, I have removed adjectives such as 'deluded', 'bizarre', and 'crazy' from my article, and will resubmit it to Patsy with those changes.

You wrote in *And is it True?* about "an integrity that I hope encompasses both a ruthless honesty and also a wholeness of being that seeks to leave no place for compartmentalization within the self." Perhaps you will agree that there is a difficult path to be sought out between "a ruthless honesty", when describing one's own viewpoints, and yet at the same time expressing respect for other people and their differing viewpoints, and not making them feel that they may have been insulted by what one has written oneself about one's own position. Below you will find the amended 'A Faith Fundamentally Flawed?' and a second article, 'New Worship, New Symbols'. I appreciate the fact that you support open debate and the possibility of radical viewpoints being expressed. Please do respond again if you wish to do so. *Good wishes,*
Andrew

Richard Clarke did not reply to this e-mail. He had criticized me for not having anything constructive to say in the article 'A Faith Fundamentally Flawed?'. However, perhaps the second article, 'New Worship, New Symbols', indicated that I could be positive, even though in a most radical way. I was reminded of the 12 theses publicized by Bishop Spong at the Lambeth Conference in 1998. He had written below the theses the following: "These theses posted for debate are inevitably stated in a negative manner. That is deliberate. Before one can hear what Christianity is one must make room for that hearing by clearing out misconceptions of what Christianity is not."

Here are some of the radical views I put forward in 'New Worship, New Symbols' that, I assume, Richard would have read in April 2001:

> In the article 'A Faith fundamentally flawed?' … it was argued that Jesus was neither a supernatural being, nor divine nor the Savior of the world [I was meaning in a literal sense] … The time has come to leave Jesus to his place in history; and to move on. As Kahlil Gibran observed: "For life goes not backward, nor tarries with yesterday." Christian worship has presumed that Jesus is divine. If he is no longer to be thought to be divine, then the whole pattern of such worship needs to be changed; a revolution is required. No more Eucharist or Mass (or priesthood); no more prayers, hymns, or devotions addressed to Jesus; Christmas, Good Friday, and Easter lose their significance. An enormous challenge lies ahead for those who do not want to give up on the Christian tradition, but who recognize the need to radically reform it. This twenty-first century may well see a great burst of creativity, as new forms of worship are developed to reflect the new understanding.
>
> Poets and dramatists, novelists and painters, potters and sculptors, musicians and song-writers, film-makers and liturgists can share in this new spiritual searching for appropriate ways to respond to the mystery in life together with the 'ordinary person', young and not so young, people "unafraid to reason and unashamed to adore" (*The Collage of God*, Mark Oakley). Great art, and theology too, begin in the unconscious; sometimes artists and theologians have to wait until, in Bergman's words "the gods throw down their fire". A new 'vision' is awaited of God to emerge and enthuse, to "deepen the mystery though not to resolve it," (*The Collage of God*, Mark Oakley)… The days of the "faith once delivered to the saints" have gone. Each generation is free to construct their own faith in response to their world. As Kahlil Gibran wrote of children: "You may give them your love but not your thoughts, for they have their own thoughts. You may house their bodies but not their souls, for their souls dwell in the house of tomorrow, which you cannot visit, not even in your dreams."

Although Richard Clarke had written in his letter to me that "I value you far too much to wish to be placed in a position where I would not be able to give you support", yet the interesting feature of his letter is that he did not offer any criticism of the main conviction that my article, 'A Faith Fundamentally Flawed?', contained; he only expressed discontent with some adjectives I had used and the fact that it concentrated on what I did not believe. The key statement in 'A Faith Fundamentally Flawed?' was "Some may find this a provocative, disturbing and controversial article; it gives reasons for questioning some of the fundamental doctrines of Christianity. It implies that a revolution is needed in belief and argues that Jesus was neither a supernatural being, nor divine, nor the Savior of the world.' A similar statement of my thinking had been expressed in my dialogues written in 1978 (see Appendix I): "I consider that Jesus neither died for the sins of the world, nor is he the mediator between God and man" (Part 5). Perhaps Richard, as a person interested in liberal theology, and because they were written by a friend, had read those dialogues when they were originally published in *The Church of Ireland Gazette*, which was during the time when we were both curates of neighboring parishes in Dublin, never once thinking that we would work in a another diocese some day as bishop and dean.

Is it not amazing that, in April 2001, having read my article 'A Faith Fundamentally Flawed?' there should have been no comment on my theology in his letter to me asking me to rewrite my article? Particularly, since in referring to Cupitt and Spong, he had written, "I am certainly not in doctrinal agreement with them." I find it surprising that in April 2001 he offered no criticism of my stated and written belief that "Jesus was neither a supernatural being, nor divine, nor the Savior of the world" given the attitude he took to the same theology just eight months later. What had persuaded him to change his mind? Indeed, the striking statement in his letter is this one: "as you know well, I have never sought to stifle good theological debate (including radical debate)."

Chapter 3

The parish website – a controversial reception

In May and June 2001, each Tuesday I would open *The Irish Times* hoping that one of the articles I had sent to its religious correspondent, Patsy McGarry, would be published that day. But in fact none of them were. Each week I felt disappointed, but in other ways I felt relieved. I anticipated a storm, and wondered how to weather it. I have now learnt from Patsy that he spoke about my articles to a number of people within the Church of Ireland, but not to my bishop. He did this because he recognized that they could have serious consequences for me, and would be very distressing to many of my parishioners and to others. The people whom he consulted with had both my and my parishioners' well-being in mind. The advice they gave him was that they thought it would be better not to publish my articles, for the time being at least. Patsy agreed with this advice, and decided to await developments.

As it turned out, those developments would concern my articles, which were uploaded onto our new parish website. So let me tell you the story of the parish's website. Some months previously, the two Select Vestries in the Trim and Athboy Group of Parishes (similar to Parish Councils) had decided that it would be a good idea to have a parish website, as many churches are doing today. It was agreed that I would work together with one of the members of the parish on this project. He and I enlisted the help of a web designer who lived locally. I began to think about it in the spring of 2001 and by July 2001 it was launched.

I got advice from a range of different people. One person urged me to try to find a way of encouraging people to return to the site on a regular basis. As we developed our thinking we agreed to have an introductory page with some basic information about our parish and some photographs. I did not want the website to have an over-emphasis on pictures of buildings; I wanted the main visual images to be of people. In other words, the visual message of the website was that Church had more to do with people than with buildings. This introductory page would attempt to give something of the ethos of the parish as I envisaged it. It would provide a welcome to those who might be looking for a spiritual home in our area of County Meath. Both Trim and Athboy, and other smaller towns nearby, are growing rapidly, with many new houses being built. A younger generation moving into the area, where house prices are cheaper than nearer to Dublin, which is approximately 50 km away, might well use their computer to explore the area they had come to live in; the website would enable them to discover us. This is what I wrote for part of the introductory page:

> WELCOME: We are always glad to welcome visitors to our services, as well as new members; and people who are exploring, or seeking a spiritual home, are welcome to come and see if either of our churches and our congregations provide them with the sense that here is a place in which they could come to feel at home, ask their questions, go on growing in their spiritual journey; and through belonging to a caring, compassionate, supportive community find courage, vision, commitment, and love to seek to go on trying to change both themselves and their world. As a group of people here, we see ourselves as called to try to make a difference in the world, for good and for God. People in this group of parishes find themselves in different places on the theological map of believing: some are evangelical, some are conservative and traditional, some are radical and liberal, some are still processing the faith they received in childhood and working on it in order to achieve a more credible and mature faith. There is a sense that different people have journeyed in different ways, as well as a spirit of respect and tolerance for others' beliefs. There are conflicting viewpoints but there is the shared unity found in seeking to serve the truth of God within the one vision of Love as the ultimate reality in life, its source, its central and deepest mystery, its hardest, harshest, and most crushing paradox, and its eternal hope.

The introductory page had photographs of the Cathedral in Trim and St James' Church in Athboy. There were also some photographs of groups of parishioners, of the bishop and canons, the churchwardens, the organists, the teachers from the church school and some pupils, the diocesan choir, and a picture of myself and the Deanery. There was a photograph too of an African mother and her baby to indicate our concern for the wider world with its injustices and unequal sharing of power. By the time the site was ready to be launched, I had had the picture of the Ring come into my mind and this then became the opening page (see Chapter 23). Also on this opening page were links to our guest book for people's comments and a chat room facility. We had a link to a website that gives parents advice about their children's use of the Internet.

Then we had our 'news' page, which was updated each month. I managed to have a monthly theme and related the stories and photographs to the theme. It was very visual; my idea had been to have something that would be full of life, bright and colorful like *Hello* magazine. Although naturally not all the news would be upbeat, some would be very sad. The news was primarily from the parish. Now that it was on the Internet, it meant, for example, that a couple, who had been married in one of the churches of the parish, could tell friends around the world to look up our website to see their wedding photographs.

Next came our 'history' page: we had a considerable amount of interesting material, including an article written some years ago about Trim's famous Dean, Richard Butler. Then came the pages that we hoped would draw forth a response from people around the world. One was an 'Images' page and the other a 'Wisdom' page. This is how the 'Images' page was introduced:

> We live in a visual world where images, graphics, pictures and symbols are common and often powerful. The world goes on changing and always has and will do. Our symbols and images change too. We would like to build up a database of images, graphics, pictures, and symbols which are contemporary, but which also reflect the different cultures of our world. Every month we will choose some words, and invite you to submit an image, graphic, picture, or symbol, which expresses for you the meaning of the word or demonstrates something of its power or the vision or values linked with it. You may submit images, etc. for more than one word, if you wish. We would like you to submit, too, if you would, about 50 words explaining how the word and symbol are related to each other.

Some of the words for which we invited contemporary images were: freedom, wonder, awe, evil, victimized, destiny, hurt by the Church, terror. Our plan had been, with both the Images and the Wisdom pages, to upload some of the contributions we might receive each month if appropriate. There were some responses, and the picture of the chained gate with the horizon beyond it, used for the front cover of this book, was one of them. It was submitted by an American friend of mine, Barry Hollowell, who had trained with me for ordination in Westcott House, Cambridge. He is now a bishop of the Anglican Church in Canada. His image was in response to the word 'Evil', and his explanation read:

> So often we think of evil as dark, dank, muck and mire, yet all too often evil is experienced amidst the light and beauty of ordinary days – experienced as chain and barrier which shuts out, even though one can see through and beyond – it restricts access and blocks through the chain links of unchallenged assumptions, unquestioned history, and presumptive prejudice, fused all too often by fear.

However, it became clear that we would have to learn how to market this page, and the 'Wisdom' page, more effectively. It could be very interesting to see what visual images would come into the minds of people from the five different continents, with their many cultures and religions, if they were to think, for example, about words such as dignity, awe, vulnerability, glory, or abuse. I would be fascinated to see their images or symbols.

The 'Wisdom' page had this opening invitation:

> The world is full of people who have much wisdom to offer, which can help all of us in our own seeking to live well. Every month, we will invite you to submit a wise saying or some good advice on various topics. We hope to be able to upload some of these onto our site each month so that eventually we will have built up, with your help, a database of good advice and wisdom that will cover many areas of human living that people may share in common.
>
> However, we expect there to be some conflict in the wisdom that is received, because people in differing cultures and countries, and with differing world-views, will have various ways of looking at things. Such diversity of wisdom, gathered together, will be a way in which, in a global village, we may become more sensitive and understanding towards each other. And that helps in making for a more harmonious world, with less misunderstanding, for future generations to live in. Remember that, by sharing what may be your hard won wisdom, you may be able to help other people in the living out of their lives, through their times of confusion, or bewilderment, or searching, or growing, or hurting, or relating, or loving. A group of people or an organization, for example a Senior Citizen's group or a therapy group or a youth group, might wish to plan a Wisdom event or series of such events.

Some of the issues for which we invited people's wisdom were these: the future of women, accepting yourself, grieving, delegating responsibility, learning from a differently abled (disabled) person, leadership, responding to violence, euthanasia, reforming the Church.

The remaining page was the Dean's page, which contained some background information about me and some photographs including ones of me and of my parents, sisters and brother, and wider family circle, as well as of clergy who had been my colleagues over the years. It also contained the controversial articles that would cause the storm, the ensuing stressful months, and my eventual resignation. The member of the parish working with me on the website had expressed his opinion, at the beginning, that it might be better to have my own personal website with all this material, and simply have a link from the parish website to mine. I disagreed with him and had my way. Either way, I was going public with my ideas about how I saw Christianity needing to be transformed. I had introduced the articles as follows:

Some of what is written here is highly thought provoking. If anyone is offended by anything that they may read in these articles, then I ask for their forgiveness and am sorry to have so offended them. Remember that I am writing from my own perspective and viewpoint, which is not necessarily yours too. No one can force you to change your ideas, understanding, or beliefs, but perhaps by pondering on what I have written, you may find that the vision at the heart of your faith has been enlarged. We all are responsible for seeking to serve the Truth. It is a puzzling fact about the human family that within a range of different religions people may study their Scriptures and tradition and come up in every generation with such diverse and conflicting interpretations; nobody seems to understand the reasons why. Are the reasons psychological, sociological, moral, cultural, or something else? I would be interested in what you think yourself, will you let me know?

In the weeks that followed, the parish site was receiving hits from all around the world and the responses that I was receiving about the site in its entirety were encouraging. I was pleased. There was no immediate storm. For it was liberal parishes and radical thinkers who were passing the word to each other, I suspect, about the website. However, when my bishop's intervention into my life became worldwide news in December 2001, then my articles began to receive attention from the conservative and evangelical wings of the Church. Later that same month the parish website was closed down. I responded by having my own site put up and in my guest book on this site there are both severely critical as well as supportive messages in relation to my views and beliefs.

Chapter 4

Confronted with episcopal authority

As I have just mentioned I had been pleased with the way the parish website had been developing. Every month there was an increase in the number of hits that it received. And as I noted, initially, there was a good flow of positive feedback coming from all over the world, which was very encouraging. However, ominous clouds began to appear in the autumn of 2001, when the site was just a few months old. Some people had started to object to my articles and their liberal contents. In November, an Irish Catholic newspaper carried a report about them. I was "Outsponging Spong" it was alleged by David Quinn (*The Irish Catholic*, 29 November 2001). He had never before come across such liberal views as mine. Quite separately from the attention being paid to my so-called liberal beliefs, there was a worrying discovery about our website. It was reported that it was possible to access pornographic material.

My presence was demanded at the Bishop's house. On 5 December 2001, I arrived mid-morning to meet with Richard Clarke. He showed me into his study. Generally speaking I found I got on quite well with Richard. We shared a friendship going back over 30 years. If I had to compare and contrast myself with Richard, I would say that we undoubtedly have different personalities and temperaments. He is good at certain areas of the Church's work that I am not so good at, and in which I have little interest. I think particularly of the bureaucratic life of the Church. We both have our flaws and weaknesses like anyone else. I suspect that religion functions in differing ways in our lives. On this particular day, my friendly enquiries about his wife and family were dealt with in a manner that suggested he had other more important things on his mind. The previous week, he had e-mailed me that he had been alerted to the fact that it was possible to reach pornographic networks through the chat room on our parish's website. He had ordered me to close down the whole website immediately.

The provider of the chat room on our website had, at one stage and without our knowledge or consent, linked us through this facility, it seemed, to various romantic and pornographic chat rooms. Neither our web-designer nor I had been consulted; it had just happened. I checked the chat room facility, and found that it had been changed, and that now there were options to visit dating clubs. I did not investigate any further, that was evidence enough for me. I did not want those sorts of options to be available through the chat room facility on our parish website. Clearly I was willing to comply with the Bishop's wishes in this respect, and the next day we removed the chat room facility from our website. If the person, who had notified the bishop about this matter had contacted me directly, I would have been very grateful to him, and would have arranged to have had the problem sorted out as soon as possible. One needs to be vigilant if one is responsible for a website. The idea of having the chat room had been that it might be of interest to younger people visiting the site. They might find other young people wishing to discuss serious issues. It might be with regard to their feelings, both positive and negative, towards the Church. It could concern issues to do with searching for an appropriate morality and authentic spirituality. It might relate to sharing experiences of travel and living abroad, or maybe to do with serving in the Third World. They would have been able to discuss them by going online, so long as others were online at the same time.

However, I felt that to have the whole of the parish website closed down was an act of interference. It seemed to me to deny the right of freedom of expression. I felt it reflected an authoritarian attitude quite unworthy of leadership in the twenty-first century. The fact that his e-mail contained no reason for the position that he was now adopting did not seem in the least bit fair. It appeared to me that he had radically changed his mind from the viewpoint he expressed to me on 24 July 2001, two days after our website's launch, when he wrote, "I have had a quick glance at your website which looks excellent." Subsequently, after reading through a draft of the text of this book before its publication, he informed me that at that stage he was not aware that my articles were on the parish website, as he had made only a very cursory and fleeting visit to our site.

As the meeting began, it quickly became clear that the chat room matter, now that it had been dealt with, was not going to be the substance of our discussions. It was my articles on the Dean's page that Richard was clearly so upset about. He had been going through them with a fine toothcomb. It was far from a relaxed discussion between two people of liberal Christian outlook. When I had arrived to work in the diocese, almost five years previously, Richard Clarke had said to me that one of his chief concerns was that laypeople, for the most part, were so theologically illiterate. He wanted, he told me, to take the diocese "by the scruff of the neck" and introduce some serious adult education. It might have been thought that he would have welcomed my attempts to write some thought-provoking articles that challenged many a layperson's (let alone clergy person's) understanding of their faith. It seemed now that he had decided that I had gone too far. He was asking me how I could celebrate the Eucharist with integrity, and say to a communicant "take and eat this in remembrance that Christ died for you" and at the same time be writing in my articles that I did not believe that, in a literal sense, Jesus had died for our sins. This is such a crucial point that I take a separate chapter to expand further on it (see Chapter 19).

I got the feeling early on in the meeting that he had already made his mind up that some of the ideas I was expressing in my articles were outside the goalposts of Christianity. I was concerned about this, because I saw myself as joining in a worldwide debate about such central issues as the interpretation of the significance of Jesus within the Christian tradition. I considered that I had a legitimate place within such a debate. Furthermore, while such a debate remains unfinished, surely it is both undemocratic and anti-intellectual to remove someone from his or her position in the Church who clearly wants to participate in the debate? Indeed, some weeks previously, when a clergyman from Northern Ireland had complained to Richard Clarke about my theology, he had responded to this clergyman by saying that he knew I would welcome debate. He encouraged this person to contact me directly and engage in dialogue with me, which he then did.

I attempted, during our meeting, to draw Richard Clarke out so that he would allow me to question him about his understanding of the faith and his own theology, but I was not very successful. He was there to question me about my views, not to be questioned in turn by me. I was the one being investigated. He was the inquisitor. This was a mistake, to my mind, because the best way to have understood each other theologically was to share in open dialogue. I never felt fully convinced that he really understood my interpretation of the faith nor my reasons for it. He did not like what I had written about the Incarnation, but he would not tell me what he actually meant in twenty-first-century thought forms, when he had written in his book *And is it True?* that "Jesus Christ was the fullness of human-ness but also the fullness of divine-ness in a decisive and unique way" (p 117). In what sense can a human being be the fullness of divine-ness?

If Jesus were alive now in the twenty-first century, and we were to meet with him, would we not say that he came across to us as a remarkable, deeply spiritual, person? Would we not describe him as a brave and radical thinker and an activist on the side of the marginalized and the poor? I cannot imagine that we would be speaking about having just encountered the fullness of divine-ness. Perhaps we might say, as we talked with him, that we had a profound sense that human life is bound up with mystery. We might admit that our thoughts had been turned God-wards. Again, this does not seem the same to me as talking about someone who was the fullness of human-ness and the fullness of divine-ness. Furthermore, by what criteria would we judge that someone demonstrated the fullness of human-ness? I like to think that there is an important corporate side to our humanity. It is created through our relationships with others and depends on the quality of those relationships. I have never been persuaded that anyone in this life achieves a level of full humanity, whatever precisely that might mean. Most of us tend to think of our relationships as imperfect, and of our humanity as incomplete, battered, wounded, and to some extent depraved and deprived, no matter how positively we may also speak about ourselves and our sense of well-being. I would apply these points to the statement of one of my consultants, John Baker, who maintains that for Anglicanism, belief in the Incarnation is more than just a metaphor, and is non-negotiable. He wrote to me saying:

> Both the official and majority standpoints in the Church of England are that Jesus was divine, a position usually expressed in sermons by saying that in him God lived an authentic human life, or shared our human experience, or lived as one of us. This is non-negotiable in mainstream Anglicanism, not least because it is for many people the only way they feel they can call God good or loving in face of the evil and suffering in the world. Moreover this belief is not metaphorical. It is seen as crucial that it should be a fact, not a symbolic way of saying something about God's character. Clearly in this area you are radically at odds with most Anglican thinking. (see Appendix F)

The surprising, sinister, and shocking outcome of my meeting with my bishop was to learn that, as of that very day, I would not have his authority to do my work as a priest. He was imposing on me three months of enforced leave of absence from my ministry. The purpose of this was to give me time, over a period of not more than three months, so that I could reflect on the serious concerns he had expressed to me on issues of faith and belief. After which, if he remained unsatisfied with my understanding of Christianity, concerns about my future ministry in the Church of Ireland would be addressed by him. This sounded very ominous to me and I felt extremely threatened, even though I felt I could still work with integrity as a Christian minister. A letter would be in the post the next day to the Secretaries of the two Select Vestries of the Parish informing them of his action and he would also send a similar letter to all the clergy of the diocese.

He had suffered agonies over coming to his decision, but had been supported by the opinions of others whom he had consulted. He was concerned that the strain of serving the Church, given my theology, might be too much for me to bear, and it was his responsibility to keep these things in mind. He did not seem to understand that I had carried these burdens for nearly 30 years of hard and productive ministry. I had enjoyed good health during all that time, bar the normal times when we all get a bit down about our work or feel the strains it imposes on us weighing us down for a while; or when, for other reasons, we feel fed up with life in general. I was saying that I remained willing to do my work as a priest. I was prepared to continue to carry whatever burdens might be laid on me, as part of the consequence of seeking to serve the cause of truth, in all its diversity, and to serve the causes of love and caring also. He told me that he would not be entering into debate or dialogue with the media, and he suggested to me that it would not be helpful if I did either.

As I shook his hand at the door and said goodbye to him, he said something that I did not expect him to say to me. His words, as I recall them now, were "I am sorry to do this to you, you are a bigger person than I am." I did not reply, but gazed into his eyes to see if I could discern anything more about what lay behind this unforgettable meeting. Richard Clarke has contended, on reading this text prior to publication, that this statement is a fabrication on my part. So I doubt you will ever get the truth concerning whether his denial or my memory are correct. It is probably not of much consequence to you either way. However, I believe that it was this highly unexpected remark that triggered the recall of that heinous incident in Shakespeare's *Julius Caesar*, which I referred to in my Introduction. You may remember that I wrote that, as I drove away from the bishop's home, Caesar's anguished words "Et tu Brute" lay unspoken on my tongue. Richard Clarke approved of being liberal, but not my way. Where were his breadth and tolerance, let alone his courage? No minutes of this meeting had been taken. I never received a paper, written by my bishop, with his criticisms of my beliefs, nor did he publish a reasoned article in the diocese or in the media with his objections to my writings. I think I was entitled, and so was the Church, to a written response.

The next day I was preparing information regarding my pastoral work and administrative work to take with me for a meeting the following day, Friday 7 December 2001, back again at the bishop's residence. Still feeling very shell-shocked, I returned to the bishop's house to meet with Richard and with Pat Lawrence, the Archdeacon, who was given the task of taking charge of my parish by Richard. The main purpose of the meeting was to talk about practical issues in relation to the work in the parish over a busy Christmas period. However, during this meeting, Richard asked me whether I thought he would have instituted me to the Parish as rector if he had known then what he now understood to be my beliefs.

Given the attitude to my beliefs that he had seemed to express to me at that painful and unsatisfactory meeting just two days previously, I replied that I thought that he would not have done so. I want to make clear, though, that I still maintain that I believe that I was not mistaken to apply, in 1996, for the vacant position in my parish. I retain my sense of Christian identity within a cumulative and evolving tradition. I accept that when Richard was considering my application, he had a general perception of me as someone on the more liberal and radical side of belief, and certainly did not think of me as a person characterized by a strong fundamentalist faith. However, even if he had had, at that time, a fuller and more nuanced understanding of my interpretation of the faith, I submit that if he had turned down my application on theological grounds he would have, at the very least, betrayed a broad Church understanding of our faith.

A report in the media announced that as from December 5 2001, and for the next three months, I would be on enforced leave of absence from my work and would not have my bishop's authority to function as a priest during that period. On 15 December 2001, I issued this rather lengthy press statement. I wanted people to know my point of view and position:

A PRESS STATEMENT RELEASED BY ANDREW FURLONG,
DEAN OF CLONMACNOISE

The deeply attractive vision of a God of infinite love is, in my belief, (with all the problems and paradoxes it raises) part of the great and challenging mystery of the life we are caught up in. It is this vision that I reach out towards in a search to transform traditional forms of Christianity. Joan D. Chittister wrote in her book, *Heart of Flesh* p.172, "The revolutions that count come silently, come first in the heart ... Revolutions of this magnitude do not overturn a system and then shape it. They reshape thought, and then the system overturns without the firing of a single cannon. Revolutions such as this dismantle walls people thought would never fall because no wall, whatever its size, can contain a people whose minds have long ago scaled and vaulted and surmounted it."

Jesus of Nazareth lived in a very different world from ours today. He never drove a car, he never traveled by airplane, he did not hold a passport, he did not have a radio or TV or a mobile phone or a computer or a credit card or life insurance. Yet despite all the differences, he shares some fundamental values with those, who in one way or another, sense that they share some common ground with him. His religion was that of ancient Israel, and in Temple or in synagogue, he found vehicles to use to convey his worship to Israel's God. These vehicles may be quite different from those used in Christian worship, but what they transport is much the same: praise and gratitude, penitence and remorse, bewilderment and pain, trust and rage, dependence and responsibility. Many of the ethical and spiritual values of ancient Israel's faith are found in the Christian way of life too: peace, forgiveness, justice, compassion, hope, accountability, freedom, dignity, worth, love, and co-operation.

Jesus, it seems to me, was a self-effacing person who wanted to point people to the mystery of a God of immense tenderness, understanding, and concern. Such a remarkable member of the ancient community of Israel needs to have his place rediscovered within the Christian community that would not have come into existence had it not been for him.

With the deepest respect for others and their beliefs, to my mind, Jesus, and John the Baptist also, were mistaken and misguided 'end-time' prophets; Jesus was neither a mediator nor a savior, neither super-human nor divine. There is a sense in which the time has come to leave Jesus to his place in history and to move on. While at the same time I want to say that there is a need to rediscover his place in the totality of the Christian community as we understand it now. I believe that a new spirit of freedom will be sensed. People, nurtured in the Christian tradition, will no longer constantly be looking back over their shoulders to some allegedly complete and full revelation of divine love and human perfection, because they will not find such old beliefs credible any more.

The Anglican Provinces have never been strangers to tensions and conflicts within their membership. Out of such tension and conflict growth has come. There is a cost to being in a minority camp, as there is a cost to tolerating minorities within the main grouping. Grace, generosity, and goodwill are all required.

My bishop, Most Revd Richard Clarke, on 5 December 2001, withdrew his license, which authorized me to work as a priest; in his words "I am providing you with three months' leave of absence from any ministerial duties, in order that you may reflect on the serious concerns that I expressed to you ... regarding your recent public statements concerning faith and belief."

My most recent article: 'Pain and Integrity: reform from within', which was read at a Spirituality seminar at St Deiniol's Library, Wales on 3 November 2001, may be found in the Theology section of Anglicans Online www.anglicansonline.org and there are links there for other articles I have written.

I am deeply concerned about the disturbance caused within the parish where I have been working. The ideas and beliefs of people here are to be found on different places on the theological map of believing, thinking, doubting, and searching. Some people are evangelical, some conservative and traditional, some radical and liberal; some are still processing the faith they received in childhood in order to reach out towards a more credible adult faith.

I am sorry for the embarrassment and shock many people in this parish have felt and am very conscious of their varied thoughts and feelings. I am grateful for support both from within the parish and worldwide. I am sensitive to the weight of responsibility my Bishop, who is a personal friend of 30 years standing, feels.

I see this situation, once the dust has settled and all of us have processed our immediate reactions, thoughts, and feelings, as one which might provide both this parish and the Church of Ireland as a whole with an opportunity to affirm the extent of diversity of interpretation that exists in all of humanity's religions. I have tried to make our parish website, which has received worldwide acclaim (and where my articles had been published), a forum for diversity and conflict as well as a focus for cooperation and unity. Such a forum and focus can only be sustained in a spirit of tolerance, of broadmindedness, and with an awareness that living alongside unlike-minded people is the challenge given to us as we search for truth in all its complexity and mystery, and seek to shape a lifestyle reflective of our ethical values and religious vision.

One of the most positive aspects of my suspension is that it has enabled me to become more transparent about my present searching and beliefs. Up till now I had been living with a constant tension between saying what I really thought, and what it was more appropriate to say given any particular situation. I am aware in my life of both deception and cowardice, as well as of a search for integrity and of courage; I am sustained by both the support of others and a profound and mysterious conviction of being understood by God.

Richard Clarke's action was soon news around the world. The Dean of Clonmacnoise was presented as the Irish priest who did not believe in the message of Christmas as the coming of the Son of God into the world. It was a topical story, and received a mixed and predictable reception. I continued to feel very troubled and shaken. I have kept my bishop's letter, which he wrote to me following that awful meeting. It was dated 6 December 2001 and arrived the following day.

Part of it stated:

> I write to advise you formally that I am providing you with three months' leave of absence from any ministerial duties, in order that you may reflect on the serious concerns that I expressed to you yesterday regarding your recent statements concerning faith and belief. I also wish to confirm that as of 5 December 2001, you do not have my authority to exercise the ministerial duties of priest and deacon in the dioceses of Meath and Kildare. This situation will be reviewed no later than 4 March 2002, at which time, if matters have not been resolved to my satisfaction and approval, decisions concerning your future ministry within the Church of Ireland will be addressed.

The cost of seeking to serve the cause of truth, for me, could be very costly indeed: my livelihood, and all it meant to me and to others, was at stake; but so, I felt, was a credible vision of the Church for the twenty-first century. Profound questions surfaced again in many people's minds throughout the world. What freedom were the clergy entitled to in theological debate? If every ordained person and every lay person said quite transparently what she/he believed, how many churches would be able to handle such a situation? Had not doctrinal commissions in many parts of the Anglican Communion shown that there was considerable diversity of interpretation among theologians on key issues of the faith? Was there not deep debate over such issues as the authority and interpretation of the Bible, the significance of Jesus, and modern concepts of God? Did not theologians have diverse ideas about salvation, the development of doctrine, the role of the creeds, understanding symbol and metaphor, and the methods for historical research into the faith? Post-modernism raised questions about how we know anything, about the relation of truth to fields of discourse, and about the possibility of metanarratives. What significance did this have for Christianity and in what ways could it see itself as embracing pluralism? Did not the whole question of seeking for orthodoxy need to be debated? Were there new understandings of religion and of how it functions, that might help churches handle theological diversity in a constructive manner?

I felt myself to be a much-worried man as I reflected on what my bishop might have in mind if he felt he had to address the question of my future ministry in the Church of Ireland. Yet, despite my pain, I also felt strangely and curiously liberated. I felt like a bird that had flown away from its cage. Such are some of the contradictions of being human. What do I mean by a sense of having left a cage? I refer you back to my press statement, where I had written about my articles on the Internet: "it has enabled me to become more transparent about my present searching and beliefs. Up till now I had been living with a constant tension between saying what I really thought, and what it was more appropriate to say given any particular situation." Fear and freedom jostled with each other in the days to come. I might be as free as a bird in one sense now, but would I soon find the way back to my nest barred? Would I have to migrate and build myself another home outside what I thought of as a Church without walls? Some would undoubtedly say to me that I should have flown away long ago, of my own free volition. Indeed, that given my beliefs, it was incumbent on me that I find a different nest to be my base. They might further argue that any pain I suffered by staying on as an Anglican priest was self-inflicted. I had nobody but myself to blame for it, they would allege. On the other hand, might one not compare the Church with an enormous tree in whose branches many nests could be built? Wasn't that meant to be a characteristic of the Anglican Communion, the Church of Ireland included?

I accept that movement from one denomination to another for both laity and clergy is much more common in some parts of the world than in other parts. For example, there is a bewildering variety of Churches in the USA and quite commonly people move, or as they might say, escape from one, and try out another. The culture in the Anglican Church in Ireland and in England,

I think it would be fair to say, has been different. You may recall from Chapter 2 how at a very early stage of my ordained ministry I spoke to both my former Principal from my theological college in Cambridge and to my former Director of Studies at Jesus College, Cambridge University. I had wanted to consult with them about my doubts about my right to stay on as a priest of the Anglican Church. Both assured me that I was not alone, and that by staying in I might make some small contribution to a more liberal understanding of the faith. This then had been my *raison d'être*; in some sense I saw myself as a reformer. In my view, a religion that came out of a pre-scientific world needed updating, and I could play a minor role in the debates about how this might be done. Thus, for example, I had written my six-part dialogues for *The Church of Ireland Gazette*. I think, too, that some of the worldwide responses that follow after the Introduction catch this tension of being both for and against the church.

Being a member of the Church of Ireland and growing up within it was somehow more than simply about belonging to a Church, because of the distinctive social reality in which that Church exists and has existed. Being in the Church of Ireland was to be the inheritor of a certain political history within Ireland, though not a history that was monochrome, there had been a range of differing political viewpoints and aspirations within the Church of Ireland community since the Reformation in the sixteenth century. It was also a belonging to a particular culture that distinguished itself socially, in certain ways, from the culture of Roman Catholicism. As a small minority in the Republic of Ireland, about three to four per cent of a population of just over three and a half million, there was a sense of living in a social reality that defined itself in significant ways religiously, and not just in class or political terms.

We stuck together and networked closely. Our educational system was divided up on denominational lines. In my days at school and university, this meant that I was primarily mixing with the Protestant community, and had hardly any Catholic friends. I had plenty of Catholic neighbors around me, while growing up, and also when I worked as a curate in Dublin. At this time, between 1955 and 1983, if you went to a wedding between two Protestants, you would find that the majority of guests were also Protestants. Since then, thank goodness, things have moved on. If you had been born into the Church of Ireland, that is the Church you were expected to remain in until you died. Your family, your cousins, your close friends, maybe too many of your colleagues at work, were members of the same church. That was how it was in the Ireland I grew up in, and so there were other factors influencing me to remain within and loyal, in my view at least, to the Church of my birth and the Church I sought to serve as a priest.

Chapter 5

Facing deep uncertainty over my future

In the days following the withdrawal of my bishop's authority for me to work as a clergyman, which had taken effect from 5 December 2001, the news quickly got around the parish. People called to the Deanery, others telephoned, and others sent letters to support me. The media took an enormous interest in the case, and I was constantly giving live or recorded radio interviews, TV interviews, and newspaper ones too. I did not agree with Richard Clarke's view that it would be wise to keep my enforced absence from my work, and the reasons for it, away from the media, and I had never thought it would be possible to do so. Over six months my views received considerable attention from the media, and my story could be read in a dozen languages on the Internet. I was trying to give many journalists a crash course in theology, so that they would have some understanding of what my difficulties were all about. In most cases, I felt I got a fair and sympathetic hearing from the media and I enjoyed meeting these hard-working people. The story was traveling around the world and, as it did so, more messages of support arrived, often by e-mail. Naturally, some people who contacted me were against me; most, but not all of them, expressed themselves respectfully and politely. I had many sleepless nights during this time, as I lay awake thinking how I might best deal with the interview or program planned for the following day. I felt the stress of having my faith claims and ideas under scrutiny in the public domain and of the controversies that raged around them.

Within a fortnight of my being prohibited from working, with Christmas just a week away, it became clear, though, that a majority of the regular Sunday worshiping communities in Athboy and Trim were convinced that my position was untenable in the parish. As I describe below, at Select Vestry meetings in Athboy and in Trim, both before Christmas and in the following month, some of these parishioners proposed and voted on resolutions against me. Some parishioners were clearly very angry, and considered that if I had any integrity at all, I would do the decent thing and resign straightaway. As I acknowledged in my press statement, and in many media interviews as well, I was aware of and sensitive to the feelings of people both within and without the parish, both for and against me. I knew some people were shocked and startled, bewildered and pained, and embarrassed by the attention the parish was being given. I was conscious that others felt that what I was saying in the media was a breath of fresh air; they too longed for the modernization of their faith. It was reassuring to hear some of my parishioners, who, though critical of my views, nevertheless saying in media interviews that while they disagreed with some of my beliefs, they still looked on me as a fine pastor and admired me for that part of my work. They saw me as a person ministering to people with compassion and sensitivity, respect and concern. They valued my work, especially among the elderly and the young.

I had permission to continue to live in the Deanery, across the road from the Cathedral. I decided that I might inflame the situation more if, over the Christmas season, I went to worship in either of the two churches. I knew that for some people my face was like a red rag to a bull. Those who supported me in the parish recalled that, over the last few years, I had preached a number of sermons in which I had drawn attention to the fact that there was diversity among all religions and that Christianity was no exception. I had discussed a whole range of issues on which the ideas of Christians were at variance. I had included in these sermons matters such as the understanding and interpretation of the Bible, and the interpretation of the significance of Jesus. I had asked whether it is credible to conceive of God as an interventionist God. Should we pray for rain or fine weather for the farming community? Were requests by farming families for prayers for fine weather at harvest-time better met by remembering in prayer those who understandably felt very anxious at such a time, for their livelihoods depended on the results of the harvest? I had focused on a range of ethical issues, such as the morality of war.

There had been no strong reactions to these sermons. This in part had led me to think that perhaps most of the people to whom I was now ministering would be able to cope, if at some time in the future I were to become more transparent with all of my beliefs. The people who were my parishioners lived in a world in which, every day in the media, diverse opinions were offered about such matters as the crisis in health care, the state of agriculture, and the financial needs of teachers. They were used to pluralism and to taking a broadminded approach to the issues of the day, often realizing that they lacked the specialist knowledge to form a considered opinion. If they had been more aware, perhaps, that the theological world contained similar diversity, would they have taken a different attitude to my views or were they following the lead given by Walton Empey, our archbishop in Dublin, and his narrow line? He had pronounced himself as shocked and horrified by my views. It was a scandal for the Church, he had said, and he could not see how I could have a place as a minister in a Christian community. Was it just that this part of County Meath was a conservative, largely agricultural, community and very traditional in much of its thinking? How much of a difference would it have made if I had been the rector of a suburban parish in Dublin? How much of a difference would another style of episcopal leadership have made, both in Meath and in Dublin?

I mentioned above the meetings of the two Select Vestries in Parish. They each had about 16 members. In December 2001 both vestries agreed that the Parish website should be closed down forthwith. They did not wish my articles, to which they objected, to be available on the Internet on a website in the Parish's name. In January 2002, the two Select Vestries agreed that I should be called on to resign immediately as my position was regarded as untenable on account of my views, and that I must desist forthwith from issuing any statements to the media using the title of Rector of the Parish and Dean of Clonmacnoise. They further agreed on a resolution giving their support to our bishop and calling on him to remove me as soon as possible. Only one person had voted against the motions.

As a result of the closing of the parish website, I arranged to have my own site. In the meantime, however, Jim Adams, the Founder of The Center for Progressive Christianity, agreed to have my articles put on its website, which was a gesture I much appreciated. In fact, it has worked for The Center's benefit too, and it has decided to continue to keep my articles on its site, for the time being at least. As a result of doing so, it has attracted a very considerable number of hits. Undoubtedly, for some people who wanted to read my articles, this became their introduction to a Center well worthy of patronage and investigation for those looking for a balanced and intelligent approach to their faith. As far as the parish site was concerned, in almost five months of its existence, probably about 90 per cent of parishioners had never visited it; most were not computer literate or particularly interested in getting help at the local library where they could have viewed our site. The parish site, according to our statistical counter, had received over 3000 hits from people in at least 25 different countries in its brief and turbulent lifespan. I decided to take with me, not just the Dean's page, with my articles and its other contents, but also those pages on the parish site that had been my own particular 'creations'. I started a new page to be called 'Credo' (see Chapter 24). This would be a page for contributions from other people who wanted to share something of the place that their own questing to date had taken them to in terms of their beliefs.

Having this page was a way of saying, to the Church at large, that already there are many people who are reflecting on experiences in their lives and thinking for themselves. They will no longer accept, as adults, without questioning and examination, the way the faith is expressed in the ancient Church creeds that they were taught as children. The Credo page is a way of showing that it is the most natural thing in the world to expect diversity of reflection and experience as people seek to explore the mystery of who we are and why we are here. They undertake such reflection as members of an evolving Christian tradition. Some are interested in learning about some of the other great faith traditions of our world. I also look at life through Christian lenses, the Judaic-Christian tradition is the framework within which I think and meditate. I seek to gain insights from my own experience of life and that of other people, and extrapolate from them to build up my vision of God and my understanding of what it is to be human. Anyone familiar with the religious traditions of the world knows that there has been pluralism from the beginning, even though strenuous efforts have been made at times to impose conformity to one particular viewpoint, and to crush alternative ones. In the future, I think we are just not going to do that anymore. The Church, if it is still here, will try instead to encourage and affirm people in the uniqueness of their own personal search and insight into the multifaceted experience of being human. The Church needs to acknowledge that each individual has the right to describe the world, and to seek, if she/he wishes, to draw the outlines of a hidden and mysterious God who, to my mind, far exceeds our most sublime attempts to do so.

I was keeping in touch with quite a number of people in the parish, not necessarily those who agreed with me. However, it was proving difficult to be in the parish, living in the Deanery, and yet not in the churches each Sunday. It was hard not being permitted to take the funerals or weddings or baptisms. I was already beginning to grieve deeply. It was largely anticipatory grieving, but not entirely so, as I was now missing, each day, my ministry among people whom I had come to love. They had a special place in my heart, in my thoughts, and in my prayers. I could see that it would take a major change in many people's attitudes to me, if my ministry was to continue among them and that this was increasingly unlikely, though I still did not accept it would be impossible. I regarded the people of the parish, for the most part, as very reasonable people, and potentially open to the right sort of reasonable persuasion, if it came from a source that they would respect. I believed that a valid and credible case could be made that it is wiser for the Church to hold on to its radical thinkers. But would my Church hold on to me? I was very concerned about my employment.

In January 2001 I had had a telephone call, out of the blue, from a barrister (attorney), Joe Revington, who had been with me at secondary school as well as at Trinity College, Dublin. He had heard through the media about how my bishop had stated that I did not have his authority to work as a priest for a three-month period and that I was on an enforced leave of absence. We had not been in touch for 30 years and it was good to hear from him, and to learn from him that he had been concerned for me. I called him back a few days later and said that, especially since he had considerable experience in cases where a person's employment might be at stake, I would be very grateful to have his advice over a number of issues, if he would be willing to give it, which fortunately he was. I began to discuss with him my status as a priest in relation to employment law. It is a very unclear matter, it would seem. In some respects, it looks as if a priest's work comes under what is called a 'contract for service', but in other respects it would appear to come under a 'contract of services'. Would one of these forms of contract imply that a member of the clergy had more freedom as she/he did her/his work, including theological reflection, teaching, debating, and preaching, than the other form?

If someone loses a job, perhaps through redundancy, he or she may find another similar job using the same skills, and hopefully at a convenient distance from where he or she lives, perhaps with family too. A new job would not necessarily mean a different home, nor necessarily mean leaving the community and parting from neighbors, though it would mean no longer having the same people around at work. For me, though, as I considered the 'worst scenario', it could mean much more. It was in this sense that I was experiencing some anticipatory grief as I thought about what it would mean for me if I were not permitted to resume my work in the parish. It would mean the loss of the home in which I was so settled, and where friends and family loved to come and stay. It would mean the loss of the garden that I had worked so hard to improve and transform. I, and many others, had enjoyed it.

It would mean the loss of good neighbors, whom I was very fond of. I thought of the loss of the town community that I had come to value greatly. It would mean parting from my friends from within that community. I appreciated much that went on in it, such as the drama and musical productions. It would mean leaving behind those who had become good friends at the local Catholic presbytery. It would mean the loss of my job, and parting from all the people whom I had come to love and care about. It would mean the sadness of knowing that those who most wanted me to stay as a liberal dean and rector would be disappointed deeply. It would very probably mean, in a Church of Ireland context at least, the loss of my profession. In addition to all this anticipatory grieving, I was carrying the uncertainty of not knowing what decision would be made about me. If I was not allowed to work again in my parish, or elsewhere in Ireland, how I would support myself in the years to come, until I would be entitled to draw on my Church pension?

I constantly counted my blessings, among which were nearly 30 years of work, not by any means all faultless, in the ordained ministry, and the enrichment that many people's lives had brought to mine. No person brings to the ordained ministry all the human gifts that can be used within it. I was deeply grateful that on account of the qualities I was born with, and because of my upbringing and my professional training, I seemed able to offer a ministry to people that was often greatly and sincerely appreciated. While I did not set out to elicit compliments, it was very affirming to receive them. For example, a particular person might say to me that, in her or his opinion, I was in certain ways quite exceptional as a priest. Another person might mention that my ministry on some occasion, which might have been a sad or a happy one, had been enormously appreciated. I was aware that the symbolic value of my role – as pointing to the mystery of an awe-inspiring God who held human life to be of sacred worth – had an importance that far transcended any sense I might have had of my own significance or usefulness. I was conscious too, in this post-modern age, of people who had lost any sense of God. Some of these people believe that the universe is all there is. Others think there may be more. Perhaps there is an origin outside the universe and a meaning to life that cannot be entirely expressed in our human and finite words. Their old sense of God has gone, and nothing has yet replaced it; there is a void. In talking to both these groups of people, I found my bridge to reach them was over the river of my uncertainties. I could not claim that I knew there was a God; what I did claim was the uncertainty of my speculation.

The winter and spring months of 2002 were proving to be a stressful time. Would I find meaningful and useful work to do for the next 10 years or so, until I reached 65 years of age, if I had to leave my present post? Where would I find to live? I owned no home. I had been deeply grieved after leaving Zimbabwe in 1994, after 11 years there. I had missed the people and the country so much that I was heartbroken at the time. That year had been exceptionally hard, compounded as it was by the stress of waiting for a broken marriage to be dissolved through the courts and with the beginning of a new job at one of the coal faces of suffering in a large hospital trust in Leeds. However, I do not think that, even then, I had felt so stressed and distressed as I did in those last months in the Deanery in Trim, beginning in December 2001, and continuing on into the following year. If I thought, at any stage in those days, that I was beginning to get a handle on any of my griefs or my anxieties, it seemed to shift and turn, so that I was then quickly presented by another of their many facets. I had never been so overwhelmed by so many different grieving and worrying experiences at the one time. But I was determined to survive. For much of the time, in public, I was able to keep a brave face on things. There were not many people who knew what my deepest feelings were, and what this time was meaning for me as a person. I was always conscious that there were countless people who had far tougher battles to fight than mine.

I knew that people had been writing to Richard Clarke, and indeed to Walton Empey (the Archbishop of Dublin) and to Robin Eames (Archbishop of Armagh), because they had sent me copies of these letters. Such people were seeking to persuade these ecclesiastical leaders that the Church was better to hold on to its radical thinkers than to get rid of them; it needed them. There had to be a place for an Andrew Furlong and his beliefs. Did these letters, though, have any influence on their thinking? I did not know.

Chapter 6

In dispute: doctrine and diversity, identity and boundaries

At the end of February 2002, thanks to two well-wishers' generosity, I was assisted with the cost of traveling to attend the Jesus Seminar of the Westar Institute, in California. This Institute was formed in 1986 as an advocate for religious literacy. It is staffed by professional theologians who are also, or have been, full-time academics in Universities and Colleges, mainly in the USA. They have done much good work in bringing modern insights and knowledge from differing fields to the study of the Bible, with a particular focus on the stories about Jesus. It has many associate members, from many walks of life, who are interested in exploring further a more open and liberal understanding of our faith. I had been looking forward very much to this seminar, and to meeting Bob Funk, its founder, and other scholars too, and to learning more about their important work. They gave me a wonderful welcome and were very sympathetic to my situation. I met other people at the seminar who had stories to tell similar to mine. On the final evening, at the dinner, Richard Holloway, a former Primus of the Episcopal Church in Scotland and Anne Primavesi were made Fellows of the Institute, as Don Cupitt had been the previous year. I received a Westar award and citation; it was a humorous gift, but an affirming one too. The citation reads:

> The Fellows of the Westar Institute and the Jesus Seminar proudly present The Millstone Award to Revd Andrew Furlong for Bravery and Courage in the face of tradition and its defenders. "Those who entrap one of these trusting souls would be better off to have millstones hung around their necks and be drowned in the deepest part of the sea." Matthew 18:6, Scholars' Version, voted 'black', Robert W. Funk, President and Director, March 1st 2002, Santa Rosa, California'.

Voted 'black' means that the majority of the Fellows of the Westar Institute and the Jesus Seminar agreed that this was not an authentic saying of Jesus. The gift was an imitation millstone on a leather rope, presumably so that I could wear it round my neck. Was I being given a choice between a guillotine and a millstone?

A few weeks before I had left Ireland to fly to California, I had had a letter from Richard Clarke asking me to attend a meeting with him on

Monday 4 March 2002 at 8pm. In fact, he re-set the date for the meeting to the following day at 3pm, when I informed him that I would only be returning from the Conference and arriving at Dublin airport at 5pm on 4 March. He had declined my request to hold the meeting at the end of that week, when I would feel more rested. In fairness to him, he had made it clear in December 2001 that my case would be reviewed no later than 4 March, so he could protest that I need not have gone to the Jesus Seminar, if it meant that I would only return that day jetlagged. In the letter that had advised me of the meeting in March, Richard had also stated, "Patrick Lawrence [the Archdeacon] will be present, and if you wish to be accompanied by an individual, this would be appropriate."

I had invited Professor Andrew Mayes, Erasmus Smith Professor of Hebrew at Trinity College, University of Dublin, who had been giving me considerable and valued support, advice, and friendship since December 2001. I had remembered him from my undergraduate days in Trinity, when he had just embarked on his academic career. In the weeks leading up to this next crucial meeting with my bishop, I constantly had in mind the letter I had received after he had withdrawn his authority for me to work as a priest, as of 5 December 2001. Part of it had included this ominous statement, "This situation will be reviewed no later than 4 March, 2002 at which time, if matters have not been resolved to my satisfaction and approval, decisions concerning your future ministry within the Church of Ireland will be addressed." I drove to Maynooth, a mile from the diocesan office, which was opposite the bishop's house, where the meeting would take place. Andrew and I had arranged to meet for lunch and to talk together about how best to approach the meeting with Richard. As I still felt very jetlagged, I asked Andrew Mayes to keep some notes of the meeting, as I might well not recall everything said, apart from the fact that it would be a good idea to have the important points of the meeting recorded. As it turned out the Bishop had not arranged for any official minutes to be taken.

It was an unsatisfactory meeting with Richard Clarke. Robert Townley, the Dean of Kildare was present, in the place of Patrick Lawrence who was ill that day. The four of us were crammed into a very small office. Once again I was arguing that it was legitimate to state in an academic article my reasons for not believing that, in a literal sense, Jesus had died for our sins; however, in the Eucharist, I believed that I could still say with integrity to a communicant: "Take and eat this, in remembrance that Christ died for you." I was understanding those words metaphorically and symbolically to mean: "You are found loveable, forgivable, and reconcilable by God." I emphasized the importance of accepting that God transcends human thought. God is unknowable to us in this life. Theology, however profound, is based on personal experience and conjecture. I was making the point that if Jesus had not come into the world we would not have our present ways of speaking of

God in his/her relationship to the world. I meant by this that, for example, Jesus' parables gave us distinctive ways to speak about how God may be envisioned as relating to us. He is like the father in the parable of the prodigal son or the shepherd who leaves the other sheep to search for the lost one. I asserted that I saw my interpretation of the faith as a legitimate one.

When asked by Richard to confirm to him that my articles, both on my website and in the media, were representative of my views I neither affirmed nor denied this. I did say that my articles would have to be understood properly. I thought of myself as a Christian and was not engaged in any form of deception as far as that part of my identity was concerned. (See Andrew Mayes' second letter in Appendix D). I found it hard to work out what Richard Clarke was making of the things I was saying. I did not feel as if I had got onto his wavelength nor did I feel as if I had been really listened to. The meeting concluded after about an hour. Neither Andrew Mayes nor I felt that there had been a real meeting of minds. This was the last occasion on which I spoke with Richard Clarke, though in time, I am confident we will heal our relationship. I returned home with a distinct feeling of apprehension. I had a sense that the affirmation of pluralism in matters of belief and its formulation that had been so evident at the Jesus Seminar in California, just a few days previously, would be disturbingly absent from whatever conclusions my bishop might now be drawing from this meeting with him. He would be considering, from his perspective, the future of my ministry within the Church of Ireland. And what of my parishioners? Some had been encouraging their bishop to get rid of me as soon as possible; others, I knew, although they were in a minority, wanted my ideas to refresh and liberate their church.

The postman, who was a supporter of mine and enjoyed a chat at the door about how my situation was going, came at his usual time of about 10am on Friday 8 March 2002. I went into my study and, with a tremble in my hands, I opened the letter that I guessed was from Richard Clarke. I was alone in the house. I felt as if my face must have gone very pale. It was an invitation to resign as Rector of the Trim and Athboy Group of Parishes and from the position as Dean of Clonmacnoise. Part of the letter, dated 7 March 2001, stated:

> Following our meeting on Tuesday 5 March 2002 I have reflected further on the situation. My conviction remains that the views you have expressed – in particular on your website, but subsequently restated in the media – which deny the central place of Jesus Christ in the Divine Scheme of Salvation are in direct contradiction with your ministerial task, including liturgical functions, as a priest in a parish. With genuine sadness I therefore believe your position as Dean of Clonmacnoise and

Rector of Trim and Athboy is untenable. I must in consequence invite you to resign these offices. I am truly sorry that matters have reached such a sad conclusion. However, if I have not received your resignation in writing on or before Thursday 14 March 2002, I believe I will have no option but to bring the matter to the Court of the General Synod. If this situation were to arise you would, of course, be kept informed of all the details of the process.

Richard's letter expressed his sadness in coming to his decision that my position in the Church was untenable. To have resigned after almost 30 years of service and ministry was likely to be highly traumatic. Where was the caring and compassionate, and generous face of the Church? For there was no mention of assistance towards having counseling, if I were to agree to resign and consider, in the months to come, that I needed it. There was nothing in his letter, if I consented to resign, about a retraining grant that would be available from the Church's Sustentation fund to assist me, nor what the situation would be in regard to my pension. He had given no detailed reasons of a theological nature setting out, on paper, his objections to my theology. His letter did not indicate whether, if I agreed to resign from the parish, he would explore the possibility of a different post within the Church, such as the post of canon theologian, where I could continue my explorations, reflection, and study.

I consulted with a number of people and then replied to Richard Clarke that I would not be resigning. I would go to court. By refusing to accept my bishop's invitation to me to resign, was I also breaking the oath I had sworn to him at my Institution, on 20 March 1997, as rector of my Parish, "I will render all due reverence and canonical obedience to Richard, Bishop of Meath and Kildare, and his successors, Bishops of Meath, in all lawful and honest commands"? I saw the need for many issues to be raised in the Church's highest court, such as the right and duty of clergy to reflect theologically and to freely critique their faith. I wanted the whole question, in a post-modern age, of the appropriateness of the concept of orthodoxy discussed. I felt strongly about arguing the case for an understanding of religion as a human creation. In my view, this does not preclude the belief that we have both our brains and minds, and our spirits and hearts, as God-given gifts to use in the search for an authentic spirituality. I wanted to share my approach to Christianity as a lifelong quest for meaning and truth – a journey characterized by uncertainty, provisionality, pluralism, tolerance, and the constant need to re-interpret the faith for a new age.

Many people gave it to me as their opinion that I stood little chance of winning my case. For, as they said, you are up against the Establishment, and it is one of that Establishment who is bringing you to court. Furthermore, they contended, the Church of Ireland traditionally has been quite conservative doctrinally. Others pointed out that a court was hardly the place for nuanced theological reasoning. They reminded me that some judges of the Court would be bishops, while others would be legal professionals who were lay members of the Church of Ireland and not theologically trained. I was asked whether I could be sure that the judges of the Court, and in particular the lay judges, but not just necessarily them, would fully understood the intricacies of the theological debate between myself and my bishop? How would I be able to ascertain if this were so or not, they enquired of me?

I was torn between fighting my case to the end, raising all the issues that I and many others thought needed to be brought out into the open, and the knowledge that the Church of Ireland had authority to make grants towards a person's retraining, if she/he left the Church, on what might be regarded as grounds of conscience. The Church of England had made arrangements, in the case of the ordination of women, to provide a financial package for priests who felt that they must leave the Church because of the decision to ordain women. I did not know whether such a retraining grant would definitely be made available to me if I went to trial and lost. Indeed, I did not know, for certain, if one would be offered to me if I simply resigned straightaway, before the trial began. As noted above, my bishop's letter, inviting my resignation, left me in the dark as far as the possibility of such a grant was concerned. How could you make your mind up without all the facts before you? Joe Revington, my barrister, certainly thought that there was a strong possibility that the Church would not be inclined to be helpful if I went to trial and lost. It was an unknown. I thought that they probably would still help, but the matter of legal costs still had to be kept in mind. They could easily escalate if at some point it were necessary to go from the Church Court to the High Court of the State, perhaps to have a judicial review of my case.

My letter dated 12 March was very brief and to the point since I was feeling very angry.

Dear Richard,
I have received your letter, of 7 March 2002, inviting my resignation as Dean of Clonmacnoise and Rector of Trim and Athboy. I do not accept that invitation. I await to hear from you.

Yours truly,
Very Revd A. W. U. Furlong,
Dean of Clonmacnoise and Rector of Trim and Athboy

Now that a hearing of the Court of the General Synod was to be the next step, my barrister's help would be essential. He did not know much about theology, but then the professional skill of a barrister is that she/he has to learn about all sorts of specialized subjects, from the workings of a railway signal box to the scientific details of blood transfusion, depending on the case in hand. Joe Revington did not think, though this proved to be mistaken, that a hearing of the Court would take place for a couple of months, as the normal pre-trial work took some time and second, if there were to be any attempts to complete an out-of-court settlement, this too would take time. He did not think that the Church authorities would really want a high-profile media trial that many people would regard as a medieval way of going about solving this situation. Heresy trials smacked of a different age. He advised me that a great many cases involving a person's employment never in fact came to court at all, and were settled out of court. I would need a solicitor as part of the team. Then the initial work of pre-trial communications, which normally covered a wide range of issues, could begin with the bishop's solicitor and barrister. Joe soon discovered, when he telephoned my bishop, that Richard intended to represent himself in court. He would be prosecuting his own case; Joe understood this to mean that he was not going to have the services of either a barrister or a solicitor. There would therefore not be any people, from the legal world, for my team to do the preliminary pre-trial work with, such as voluntary discovery of documents.

On 15 March, three days after writing my letter to my bishop declining his invitation to resign, I received an e-mail from Richard Clarke saying that he had just filed a Petition against me with the Registrar of the Court of the General Synod, and that the Registrar would send me a copy, by registered post, of this Petition. Richard Clarke also said a Press statement was being released, which stated:

> Following a meeting with the Very Revd Andrew Furlong, Dean of Clonmacnoise, the Bishop of Meath and Kildare, The Most Revd Richard Clarke, invited the Dean to resign as Dean of Clonmacnoise and Rector of Trim and Athboy as the Bishop believed Dean Furlong's position as Dean and Rector to be untenable in the light of the doctrinal views held and expressed by him. The Dean has decided that he would not accept the Bishop's invitation. The Bishop has therefore now referred this matter to the Court of the General Synod.

I awaited my summons and, while I did, from day to day, many questions and thoughts filled my mind. Were there no other alternatives to the course of action that Richard Clarke had embarked upon? Was this the way in which all other bishops in the Church of Ireland or in other provinces of the worldwide Anglican Communion would have handled a similar situation? What about the ways other denominations might have dealt with a matter like this? As well as requiring people to undertake a course of theological education before they become ordained as clergy, do we not encourage them to continue to keep up with the new developments in theological thinking and to follow the debates? If a person finds during his or her ministry that his or her thinking has changed radically, are there some areas of thought where such change is acceptable and others where it is not? For example, most people would accept that it was permissible and indeed a good thing that many clergy changed their minds about the position the Anglican Church had gradually abandoned during the twentieth century – that only men could become priests. They had been free to debate the topic without fear of repercussions, although it created significant tensions in many parishes and dioceses, and between laity, clergy, and bishops. Many Anglican theologians in the universities ceased in the mid-twentieth century to believe in the Incarnation in a literal, historical sense. They were free to write books arguing their viewpoint, emphasizing the symbolical and the metaphorical approaches to faith. Laypeople might read their books and come to the same conclusions.

Some academics, such as Hans Kung, John Hick and Lloyd Geering, came up against the ire of their Church authorities. But most scholars have not suffered persecution over recent decades. Like laypeople, they have enjoyed freedom of speech without fear of repercussions. A priest, though, might read a book such as *Honest to God* by Bishop John Robinson or *The Myth of God Incarnate* edited by John Hick. He might come to similar conclusions to those of many laypeople and academics who also had read one or other of these books. However, he was expected to keep quiet about his new convictions for fear of persecution. What sort of Church is this? Is it fair to have one attitude toward academics and laity and a different one toward clergy? Is there not a better way to construct our life within the Church? Does it not mean taking a new attitude toward our theological thinking? For, given the unknowability of God, it is inevitably conjectural and speculative; and given the diversity of human beings, and the differing cultures and social realities in which the Church exists, is it not understandably and inescapably pluralistic?

Chapter 7

Summoned to court – a Christian course of action?

PETITION
In the Court of the General Synod
The Bishop of Meath and Kildare, Petitioner
And
Very Reverend Andrew William Ussher Furlong, Respondent

I, Richard Lionel Clarke, of Bishop's House, Moyglare, Maynooth, Co. Kildare a member of the Church of Ireland and bishop of the Dioceses of Meath and Kildare in the said Church do hereby charge that Andrew William Ussher Furlong, now of St. Patrick's Deanery, Loman Street, Trim, Co. Meath being Dean of Clonmacnoise and incumbent of Trim and Athboy Parishes in the diocese of Meath in the said Church, did in or about the month of November 2001 and thereafter publish or cause to be published in electronic format and subsequently within the print and broadcast media, beliefs contrary to the doctrines of the Church of Ireland as contained and expressed, inter alia, within the Historic Creeds and the Book of Common Prayer, in particular by his denying of the divinity of Christ and of the efficacy of the sacraments. Further, the actions of the Respondent reject his subscription to the declaration for subscription which he made at ordination and at institution.

I desire that the said Andrew William Ussher Furlong be charged as aforesaid and duly brought to trial.

Scheduled to this Petition are a number of articles of the type described above which on the 5th day of March 2002 the Respondent confirmed to me were articles on a website he maintained and statements made in the media which were written by him, and representative of his views.

I solemnly declare that I believe the charge hereinbefore made to be true.

This Petition was signed by Richard Clarke, and dated 15th day of March 2002, and sent to -

The Registrar of the Court of General Synod Church House, Church Avenue, Rathmines, Dublin 6
And
Very Reverend Andrew William Ussher Furlong, St. Patrick's Deanery, Loman Street, Trim, Co Meath

A registered letter arrived at the Deanery, in Trim, after St Patrick's Day weekend, on Tuesday 19 March 2002, sent to me by the Registrar, Canon Victor Stacey. It contained this Petition and copies of three articles that I had written, to be found in the Appendices, 'Pain and Integrity: reform from within', 'Treasure in Earthen vessels: reflections of a reformer', and my article from the 'Rite and Reason' column of *The Irish Times* of 8 January 2002 called 'Why the Church must be willing to alter the path it follows'. I duly sent copies to both my barrister and my solicitor.

In the Petition, it states: "Further, the actions of the Respondent reject his subscription to the declaration for subscription which he made at ordination and at institution." Here are these Declarations, which I subscribed to when I was instituted as rector of the Trim and Athboy Group of Parishes:

I, Andrew William Ussher Furlong, do hereby solemnly declare that –

1. I approve, and agree to, the Declaration prefixed to the Statutes of the Church of Ireland, passed at the General Convention, in the year of our Lord One Thousand Eight Hundred and Seventy.

2. I assent to the Thirty-nine Articles of Religion, and to the Book of Common Prayer, and of the Ordering of Bishops, Priests, and Deacons. I believe the doctrine of the Church of Ireland, as therein set forth, to be agreeable to the Word of God; and in Public Prayer and Administration of the Sacraments I will use the form in the said Book prescribed, and none other, except so far as shall be allowed by the lawful authority of the Church.

3. I have not made, by myself or by any other person on my behalf, any payment, contract, or promise of any kind whatsoever (save that I will faithfully perform my duty) touching or concerning the obtaining of the Benefice of Trim and Athboy Group of Parishes; nor will I at any time hereafter perform or satisfy, in whole, or in part, any such

payment, contract, or promise, made by any other person, with or without my knowledge or consent.

4. I declare that I do not hold office as an Incumbent, Rector, Vicar, or Licensed Curate, elsewhere than in Ireland, and that I do not hold any other Ecclesiastical Office which I have not made known to the Bishop of Meath and Kildare.

5. I will render all due reverence and canonical obedience to Richard, Bishop of Meath and Kildare, and his successors, Bishops of Meath, in all lawful and honest commands.

6. I promise to submit myself to the authority of the Church of Ireland, and to the Laws and Tribunals thereof.

7. I subscribe the above Declaration, to be instituted to the Benefice of Trim and Athboy Group of Parishes.

This 20th day of March, 1997

The next communication from the Registrar was dated 22 March 2002 and informed me that the sitting of the Court of the General Synod would be at 10am on Monday 8 April in Church House, Rathmines, Dublin. It was going to be held much sooner than my barrister, Joe Revington, had anticipated. The letter stated that the Primate (Robin Eames) had ruled as chairman that he would permit no more than two persons to support the case of the Petitioner and the Respondent. I was asked to send the Registrar the names of those who would accompany me as soon as possible. Having consulted with my barrister, Joe Revington, I e-mailed the Primate as follows, sending a copy to the Registrar's office:

Dear Primate,
I have received a letter from Canon Victor Stacey, dated 22nd March in which he informs me that the Court of the General Synod will sit on Monday 8th April.
Please note the following:
I shall be represented at the trial by Joe Revington, Barrister-at-Law.
I am not at this stage able to furnish the names of my witnesses.
I am reserving my position on the ruling to allow me no more that two witnesses
Please note that this is a serious matter for myself and the Church, and I require an adjournment to allow me fully to prepare my case,

consult with my advisors and witnesses and adequately instruct Counsel. You might advise me as to what procedure I should use to make such application for an adjournment and perhaps you might nominate a lawyer with whom my counsel might discuss this and other procedural matters.

Before I had received a reply to this e-mail, a further letter arrived, dated 25 March, from the Registrar. It included the following:

Dear Dean Furlong,
The Primate has instructed me to notify you of the following:

The Court of the General Synod

8th April 2002
Church House, Dublin at 10 a.m.

PROCEDURE

Presentation of the Petition.
Presentation of the defence.
Opportunity for questioning by either or both parties.
Opportunity for questioning by the judges.
Opportunity for concluding statements by either party.
Adjournment of the Court.
Publication of judgement in due course.
Note: The Court will expect the Petitioner and the Respondent to present their case in person, but either may call on no more than two persons to speak in support. Names of those involved in this respect should be communicated to the Registrar one week in advance of the Court.

I received a reply to my e-mail to the Primate from the registrar dated 27 March 2002:

Dear Dean Furlong,
As Provincial Registrar responsible for the arrangements of the Court of the General Synod of the Church of Ireland, I refer to your Email dated 25th March (received 26th) to the Primate.
The question of any adjournment of the Court scheduled for 8th April is a matter for the judges appointed for that occasion. Consequently it is not possible for me to respond to your request which should be made to the Court on 8th April.

The Procedure for the Court will be as contained in my notice to both parties dated 25th March.

The Registrar sent a copy of this letter to my barrister, who e-mailed the Registrar on 3 April 2002, sending me a copy. Everything seemed to be happening in a rush.

Dear Canon,
My thanks for copying to me your reply to Dean Furlong.

I note [In the Constitution of the Church of Ireland] that under the heading 'Ecclesiastical tribunals' [Chapter 8] Rule 52 states *inter alia* ... "Until further rules shall have been made in pursuance of this section, and subject to such rules, the rules, orders, forms and fees of the Diocesan Court and registries, dated 9th of May, 1935, shall be the rules, orders, forms and fees of the Diocesan Court and registries, and of the Court of the General Synod and of the registry thereof respectively"....

It appears to me therefore that the rules the Court will be held under will be the Rules of 1935. If I am correct in this you might let me either have a copy of the rules or let me know where I might get same.

You might also note that we do not agree with the document entitled Procedure, which you kindly copied to me. I shall make a further submission on this matter when I see the rules of 1935 referred to above.

You might also note that I am now instructed by WHITNEY, MOORE & KELLER, Wllton Park House, Wilton Park, DUBLIN 2.

You might also note that I shall be applying to Bishop Clarke, this a.m. for further and better particulars of the charge brought, voluntary discovery of all documents in his possession which touch on the matter in issue and shall be serving a notice to produce. These forms would normally be exchanged between the respective lawyers for each side, but as I understand Bishop Clarke will not be nominating a lawyer we shall be obliged to serve them personally on him and shall copy same to yourself unless otherwise advised ...
Yours Sincerely,
Joe Revington

In 2002, Good Friday fell on 29 March and Easter Day on 31 March. Whether the judges spent Easter Monday, a public holiday, reading through the charge and my three articles in preparation for the hearing the following Monday, I do not know. It was stressful waiting for the day of the trial to arrive. Joe

Revington was seeking to reassure me that there was no chance of the full hearing taking place on 8 April; it would have to be adjourned, and that for good reasons that he was preparing to present. But was summoning me to court a Christian course of action? I doubted it. For at the very least there were better options available. Would not the Christian course of action have been to have tried those ways? I explore this further in Chapter 11.

Chapter 8

Preparing for the trial with my legal advisor

Who were my judges going to be? There would be seven of them. Some would be bishops and others would be members of the legal profession. What were the sentences that they might hand down to me, if they judged me to be guilty of the charge as presented? The Rules for Ecclesiastical Courts, and the sentences that they may hand down, are found in Chapter 8 of The Constitution of the Church of Ireland. This chapter stipulates that in the case of a charge relating to doctrinal issues the panel of seven judges must be made up of three bishops and four laypeople. Every three years, the Standing Committee of the General Synod elects its panel of ten lay judges, who are all members of the Church of Ireland, and who fulfill the necessary criteria for election. From this panel four lay judges had been chosen. They were The Honourable Mrs Justice Catherine McGuinness, a Supreme Court Judge, His Honour Judge Gerald Buchanan, a retired Circuit Court Judge, Mr Ronald Robins, Senior Counsel and Mr Kenneth Mills, Senior Counsel, who had been a former history teacher of Joe's and mine at St Columba's College many years ago. The ecclesiastical judges were to be The Most Revd Robin Eames, Archbishop of Armagh (President of the Court), The Right Revd John Neill, Bishop of Cashel and Ossory, and The Right Reverend Harold Miller, Bishop of Down and Dromore.

> Rule 29 states, "The ecclesiastical judges to constitute a Court of the General Synod shall be the three or two, as the case may be, members of the House of Bishops, first in order of precedence, who may be able to attend."

The Most Reverend Walton Empey, the Archbishop of Dublin, had expressed in public his criticism of my beliefs and did not sit as a Judge of the Court in this case.

> Rule 58 states, "The Court of the General Synod shall have power to pronounce sentence of admonition, or of suspension *ab officio* or *a beneficio*, or of deprivation, or of deposition from holy orders, subject to the provisions of Section 35; and shall have power to inhibit any person charged from the exercise of his office *pendente lite*."

Rule 35 states, "The decision of the majority of the members of the Court of the General Synod shall be the decision of the Court; but in every case which involves any question of doctrine, or the deposition from holy orders of any clergyman, the concurrence of two at least of the ecclesiastical judges shall be requisite for a judgment adverse to the clergyman charged, and, in every case, the sentence shall be pronounced by one of the ecclesiastical judges."

As far as these various sentences are concerned, an admonition would have meant what it says, and a suspension from my work would have been for a specific period. I might have permission to live in the Deanery and receive my stipend, but without any work-related allowances. A deprivation would have meant that I would have been removed from my positions as the Rector of the Trim and Athboy Group of Parishes and as the Dean of Clonmacnoise. Somebody else would in due course be appointed in my place. If that had happened, I would have been free to apply for another position within the Church of Ireland. However, it is very unlikely that given the Court's judgment, any bishop would have issued me with his license to work as a priest, even if, for example, those representatives from a parish chosen to interview me had been keen that I come to be their rector. If I had been sentenced to deposition from holy orders that would have meant that I would not have been regarded as a clergyman any more within the Church of Ireland. The Constitution does make provision for an appeal to be made to the Court requesting that a rehearing be considered. Even if I had received the sentences of deprivation or depostion, there is nothing in the Constitution that would have prevented me from seeking work elsewhere in the world within the Provinces of the Anglican Communion. Some liberal bishops and members of their dioceses might be glad to avail of my services. Although, if I had have been deposed, and so removed from holy orders within the Church of Ireland, I am not sure how another bishop from a different part of the world would have proceeded. Likewise, nothing in the Constitution prevents me applying to join another denomination, though whether they would employ me as a minister is another matter.

On my barrister's advice, as noted in the previous chapter, I had informed the Primate that we wanted an adjournment. Joe Revington did not agree with the procedure laid down for the Court hearing. It was drawn up on the assumption that the Petitioner and the Respondent, my bishop and I, would not wish to be legally represented. I had not been consulted about this and had simply been presented with a *fait accompli*. Joe was expecting to have to cross-examine Richard Clarke and any witnesses who spoke on his behalf, as a barrister would do in a civil court. He did not agree that the Petitioner and the Respondent should be restricted to no more than two witnesses each;

this would not happen in a civil court, and the rules governing a Church court were based on civil law. There had been no pre-trial work done, such as the voluntary discovery of documents. It was important to establish that we were not prejudiced in the sense of not being privy to relevant information that my bishop, or, for example, the House of Bishops, had that might affect the case. Furthermore, he did not think that adequate time had been given for preparation of such a case where my 'job' was at stake. As I will describe below, I could possibly lose my job, my income, the house I was living in, my reputation, indeed, perhaps too, my profession.

In his letter to me of 7 March 2002, Richard Clarke had said that if a Court of the General Synod were to be called then I would be kept advised of all the details of the process. A most important 'detail' was the Rules for the Court hearing. Only in the week before the hearing was due, did Joe Revington receive a photocopy of the Rules from the registrar, though as we later discovered this photocopy only included a part of the Rules. I went to the Representative Church Body Library, in Dublin, to enquire if the Rules were available in a book to borrow, and was given a copy.

Joe was very confident that on 8 April 2002 the judges would agree to the Court being adjourned, and that I need not to worry that I did not have all the witnesses I might need ready to speak in support of my case. There were a number of people with whom I had been consulting and to whom I felt very indebted. These included: Professor Andrew Mayes, The Erasmus Smith Professor of Hebrew at Trinity College, Dublin; David FitzPatrick, a layman within the Church of Ireland; Professor Maurice Wiles, a former Regius Professor of Divinity at Oxford University; and Right Revd John Baker, a former Bishop of Salisbury. In connection with my 'case' Andrew Mayes had written a number of letters to the Press, including a letter to *The Irish Times*, published on 9 January 2002, and a second letter published in the *Church of Ireland Gazette* on 1 March 2002 (see Appendix D). David FitzPatrick wrote an article, 'The Dean in Context', for the newsletter of his parish of St John the Evangelist, Sandymount, Dublin (see Appendix E). I asked Maurice Wiles and John Baker, both of whom had served on Doctrine Commissions of the Church of England, if they would respond to the three articles cited in the Petition by Richard Clarke, in the light of my forthcoming trial at the Court of the General Synod. I also sent them some tapes of interviews I had had with the media. Their responses are reproduced in Appendix F.

My barrister had been very busy with his normal practice in Munster, and usually came to Dublin just for the weekends. It wasn't until the day before the hearing that I met him, although we had been talking on the phone frequently. It was the first time we had seen each other in over 30 years. As students in Trinity College, Dublin we had both worked in the summer holidays in Glencolumkille, County Donegal, at a work camp for

European students. Father James McDyer had been instrumental in having the work camp arranged. Over a three-week period, our task had been to dig trenches and lay water pipes for homes that had no tap water. I had been to the camps for two summers in the late sixties and really enjoyed them. One of my photographs shows Joe standing in a trench with that friendly smile on his face, that I remembered from both our school days together at St Columba's College, Dublin and our student days in Trinity College.

I arrived at the hotel at Dublin Airport where we had agreed to meet. Driving up to Dublin, after playing in a golf competition at my club at Headfort, Kells, I had been focusing my mind on my meeting with Joe and preparing myself for whatever the next day would bring. I knew people all around the world were watching and waiting to hear news of this trial. Despite the passage of time, we recognized each other instantly; it was good to see him again. I expressed, once more, my appreciation of the help he was giving me. A few minutes later, Andrew Mayes arrived; he had agreed to be one of my witnesses. I had not asked David FitzPatrick, who had also agreed to be a witness, to come to this meeting. He was going to be involved in his surgery the next day, but would be available to come to the hearing if required.

Joe went over the procedures with us as he imagined the business of the Court would be conducted. He had never acted as a barrister in a Court of the General Synod before. He expected that, after the formal beginning, he would be called upon to state his reason for an adjournment, he would also tell the Court what were the objections which he had both to the procedure for the Court hearing that the Primate had decided upon, and to his ruling on a maximum of two witnesses. I gave Joe the copy of the 1935 rules for the Courts of the Church of Ireland, both for Diocesan Courts and for the Court of the General Synod. On comparing them with the photocopied Rules he had been sent by the registrar, he discovered that these photocopied sheets did not cover all the Rules as per the book I had just lent him. Later that evening, as he read through them, he noticed that the date set for the Court hearing was too early. I had been given up to 14 March to respond to Richard Clarke's invitation to me to resign. He had lodged his Petition on Friday 15 March with the Registrar, who had then posted me a copy of it on that same day. I had received my copy of the Petition after the St Patrick's Day weekend, on Tuesday 19 March; the previous day had been a bank holiday and no post had been delivered. A minimum of three weeks had to elapse, after my receipt of the Petition, before a trial could begin and on 8 April that period would not be up.

Joe told Andrew Mayes and me that he would be pointing out to the seven judges that this case could take a considerable amount of time; it would be a substantial trial covering several weeks, in his opinion. There were issues not just of doctrine, but also of my employment. It would seem clear that by restricting the witnesses to two on both sides, the Primate might have been envisaging that this trial would take four or five hours at most.

Andrew Mayes wanted Joe to be sure to make the point that we were challenging a statement within the Petition that related to the meeting which he had attended with me on 5 March 2002 with Richard Clarke, and with Robert Townley, the Dean of Kildare in attendance (in place of Patrick Lawrence, the Archdeacon). In the Petition it states: "Scheduled to this Petition are a number of articles of the type described above which on the 5th day of March 2002 the respondent confirmed to me were articles on a website he maintained and statements made in the media which were written by him, and representative of his views." In fact, I neither affirmed nor denied that the articles were representative of my views, but said that they would have to be understood properly. We would dispute in Court the phrase in the Petition "The Respondent confirmed to me".

After an hour and a half, we had said as much as was needed, and set off for our respective homes. I would be staying in Dublin that night with my brother. We all agreed that Richard Clarke had not handled this matter from the beginning in the way it could have been handled. Withholding his authority from me to work as a priest was the first step in a series of unhappy events; the matter should have been handled very differently. Even if a full hearing of the Court were to eventually take place and Richard Clarke were to lose his case, what would happen to him and what would be the reaction of the people in the Trim and Athboy Group of Parishes? The Court of the General Synod was their highest authority too. Would they accept me back again or would half or more of the parishioners leave and go to join neighboring parishes; if so, how would the Trim and Athboy Group of Parishes survive financially? About half a dozen parishioners were to come the next day to the hearing of the Court. None of them were in support of my position. They supported the bishop.

Chapter 9

On trial – Andrew Furlong or his Church?

On the morning of the trial, I arrived in good time at Church of Ireland House in Rathmines, Dublin, where the Representative Church Body has its offices and where the Court would be convened. The hearing of the Court was due to begin at 10am and was open to the public and the media. I had no idea how many people would turn up, but I guessed at least 70, in fact there were more. There were two people from the media standing waiting in the car park, one with a TV camera, the other with a camera for ordinary photographs. I drove into the car park and sat alone thinking to myself about the day ahead. I knew that the Court of the General Synod of the Church of Ireland was its highest ecclesiastical Court. At my ordination, nearly 30 years ago, I had made a solemn oath, "I promise to submit myself to the authority of the Church of Ireland, and to the Laws and Tribunals thereof." I was aware of my aloneness, as I often am. I knew my friends and family would have me in their thoughts on this particular day. Some had offered to take the day off work to come and be there. I had dissuaded them; the hearing would be adjourned, almost certainly, after about half an hour, so there was no point in coming, although I was grateful for their offer. Others began to arrive. Andrew Mayes came and we talked briefly together. Richard Clarke was accompanied by Michael Burrows, the rector in Bandon at the time, and a good friend of Richard's. Michael was to be a witness for Richard. I saw John Neill and Harold Miller, two of the ecclesiastical judges of the Court chatting together; what would they have thought as they had read through my articles cited in the Petition in preparation for my trial?

A small room had been reserved for me and my legal team and witnesses. About 9.40am I decided it was time to go into the building. I had just seen my solicitor, Peter Hayes, arrive. I went over to greet him. The photographers came towards us and we waited for a moment or two as they took the shots that they wanted. I was calm and quiet; I felt embarrassed that my Church, which I had sought to serve to the best of my ability, had come to this point. I did not think that history would judge us kindly. We were offered cups of coffee and shortly afterwards Joe Revington arrived in the room set apart for our use. Then Joe was called out. At the last minute Richard Clarke had decided to have legal representation. His team would consist of Richard Nesbitt SC, and William Prentice, a Dublin solicitor, who was the Chancellor for the United Dioceses of Meath and Kildare. It was too late now to begin the normal pre-trial communications. Joe returned with this information and went over with us the points he would be making.

It was time to go into the room set aside for the use of the Court. It was the boardroom that was used for meetings of the Standing Committee of the General Synod and, sometimes too, for the meetings of the House of Bishops. At a quick glance, it seemed to me that there were at least 70 people in the room; it appeared full. There was another room available as well, where other people were seated, able to listen to the Court hearing relayed through loudspeakers. In the boardroom, close to one of the walls, was a row of seven chairs for the judges placed at a long table, at whose end was another chair for the Registrar. Facing the judges were tables and seats for the Petitioner and the Respondent and their teams. As there was not room for Andrew Mayes, he sat behind Joe, Peter, and me. Joe was in the middle. I could see where the media were seated, about 20 people I estimated. A stenographer was present too. On coming into this room, I had noticed several of my parishioners and I nodded towards them in recognition of their presence. They looked stern and serious.

Just after 10am the seven judges and the Registrar came in and the Court rose. The Primate was in the middle seat. As I looked at their impassive faces, they were seated as follows, from left to right as I was looking at them: Harold Miller, John Neill, Gerald Buchanan, Robin Eames, Catherine McGuinness, Kenneth Mills, and Ronald Robins. The bishops were wearing their purple cassocks, but none of the lay judges were robed, as they would be for their normal work in a civil court. The Primate opened the proceedings in a somber tone of voice. He announced the purpose of the trial and said that the Court had a serious matter before it, and that the business of the Court must be conducted in a fair and just way. He introduced the judges, and the Petitioner and Respondent and their legal teams. He announced that he and one of the other judges knew the respondent. He said that some considerable number of years ago, he and I had worked together in the same parish where he had been the rector; he mentioned that Kenneth Mills had once taught me. He asked whether anyone had any objections to the panel of judges. Mr Richard Nesbitt SC for the Petitioner (my bishop) replied that his side had no objections. My barrister said:

> At this stage, your Grace, I would reserve my position. I reserve my position because I wish to know at some stage any negotiations or discussions that may have taken place between the Petitioner, who I understood was prosecuting his own case today but now apparently is not, and members of the hierarchy, and I would be seeking at a later stage an order for discovery of notes or memoranda in power, procurement or possession of the Petitioner in respect of conversations or meetings that might have taken place between him and any member

of the Court, so until that matter is resolved I cannot give you a definitive answer, however for today's purposes we have no objections.

The President:

Do I take it that the two disclosures that I have made do not enter into that particular objection?

To which my barrister replied that there was no objection. Joe then went on to explain that the Rules stated that three weeks needed to elapse from the date on which I received my summons to come to court and the date of the trial. That time had not yet elapsed he said, and that would be one ground on which he wanted an adjournment. But more importantly he went on to explain:

This is a very serious and substantial matter and I think your Grace has already referred to that. My client had spent his entire life working in the Church ... and as such he now comes before this Court in jeopardy for his good name and his livelihood. He is not a person of independent means; he has no income other than that provided by his office at the moment. In those circumstances we would ask your Grace and the Court to allow us to call however many witnesses we feel is appropriate to prove our case and in that context I would say to your Grace that I would see this Court lasting some weeks rather than some hours or some days, and it would be our intention to call senior members of the Anglican Communion worldwide to consider the question of theology. But entwined with the question of theology is the question of my client's constitutional and employment rights in this country.

My barrister reminded the Court that the Rules governing the trial allowed for a special case to be stated. He argued that if,

Bishop Clarke was in a position to withdraw his Petition and we could then agree on the form of a case stated and the words to be used by reference to the Court for a question of theology, then we would be in a completely different position. The employment issue would be taken out of the hearing, for the time being at least.

Richard Nesbitt replied:

I have had the opportunity to take instructions, President. I don't think there is any rational reason for attempting to divide what is a straightforward Petition, this is a Petition concerning the office that the dean holds and either the dean will be found wanting in the matter of the Petition or he won't.

If the bishop had agreed to a special case stated, and if the Court had agreed to this too, it would have meant, as I explain in Chapter 11, that the Court would probably have set up a theological commission to investigate my views in relation to the teaching of the Church of Ireland. It would have meant that during such an enquiry, which would have provided a much better environment for detailed theological reasoning, the threat of a sentence being imposed upon me would not have entered into the matter at that stage. As the judges did not have the full Rules in front of them, but only a photocopy of part of the Rules, Joe was asked to give them the Rule book I had supplied to him and they were then able to read the relevant Rule No 39 in relation to a special case for themselves. I was surprised to see the business of the Court being conducted in this fashion. My barrister, then, gave another reason why it was important to have voluntary discovery, as there was an important factual matter in dispute between the parties. In the Petition it had stated:

> Scheduled to this Petition are a number of articles of the type described above which on the 5th day of March 2002 the respondent confirmed to me were articles on a website he maintained and statements made in the media which were written by him, and representative of his views.

Joe explained we would dispute the statement "The Respondent confirmed to me". This statement referred to the meeting on 4 March between the bishop and myself at which Andrew Mayes and Robert Townley had also been present. He told the Court,

> That is precisely because of that matter that we are so determined to get discovery of the notes that were taken at that meeting. We have a copy of notes, contemporaneous notes, which were taken by Andrew Mayes, Dr Andrew Mayes, who will be giving evidence, and he went home and wrote up his notes …to this interview. And I understand that the bishop had somebody else attending at the meeting who also took notes, and I will be seeking an order from the Court that those notes be produced and discovered to us, I think … it is a matter in dispute, a factual matter in dispute.

The Primate said that the judges would now leave the Court to consider the various points that had been made. The two teams went to their respective rooms. Would there be an adjournment granted? Would the restriction on not more than two witnesses be lifted and, if not, would that mean that we would have to consider appealing this in the High Court and, if so, at what expense? Some difficult decisions might have to be made very shortly.

I was still feeling calm. However, at the same time, I was conscious that I must be suppressing many emotions in order to achieve this inner peace. I was aware, though, in addition to my inner calmness, of a considerable sense of strain and pressure from outside, and I could see strain on other people's faces too. If the judges agreed that I could have more than two witnesses, then whom might I invite? I would almost certainly have to look outside Ireland. I was still not sure how many clergy within the Church of Ireland would support my position, but I was aware that in the light of what was happening to me, many of them would fear to do so. I did not think that my witnesses necessarily had to be Anglicans. I was trying to think, to begin with anyway, of suitably qualified people within the worldwide Anglican Communion, who might feel this was a sufficiently important matter not just for me, but for the Church as a whole. I would be hoping to find people who would be able and willing to travel to Dublin and speak on my behalf. Was I prepared to draw on what savings I had to pay for their travel and accommodation bills? Joe and Peter spoke to us of how they thought the four lay judges would have reacted to the points that Joe had made in the Court a few minutes earlier. They were both confident that they would be advising the three ecclesiastical judges that an adjournment must be granted, and that it was not just to restrict the Petitioner and the Respondent to no more than two witnesses each.

After about 40 minutes, we were informed that we needed to return to our seats in the courtroom. The judges came in and took their seats. In an even more somber tone of voice than he had used at first, the Primate began:

> I declare the Court in session. You will recall that the judges were asked to consider several points and we now have the decisions of the judges.

What was to follow? Were they turning down our appeal for an adjournment? Had D-day in fact arrived? I did not feel properly prepared if this was the case and Joe was certainly not properly prepared for his cross-examination of Richard Clarke. Would we have to call in David FitzPatrick, my other witness? How would the day proceed? The Primate was speaking slowly and deliberately, no doubt conscious that the media were writing down everything he was saying. The Court had his full attention, or most of it; if some, had other thoughts going around in their minds too. What was Richard Clarke thinking at this time?

Firstly, regarding the application for an adjournment, with great reluctance, bearing in mind the seriousness of the issue not only for the Respondent but for the whole Church of Ireland, we have agreed to an adjournment until 10am on Friday 10 May [2002].

Secondly, we cannot imagine that it is helpful for the Court to have before it witnesses or evidence other than that strictly relevant to the doctrines of the Church of Ireland as referred to in the Petition.

Thirdly, as voluntary discovery has been agreed between the two parties, we believe that it is reasonable to ask the parties to comply with this within one week from today.

I would just like once more to assure the Court that the judges are taking it extremely seriously and also ask the parties and their representatives to accept that we are approaching our task with the utmost care. The Court stands adjourned.

The strain in the air was palpable. A person sitting behind me was clearly exceedingly angry and frustrated, and both Andrew Mayes and I heard him whisper in a voice surely intended for my hearing, 'He is just a greedy little man, out for more money.'

As I gazed across the room at Richard Clarke, I realized that anyone would recognize from the expression on his face that he was feeling upset. I could feel some sympathy for him as I imagined that he had thought progress would have been made that day on a matter that had been weighing heavily on him over the preceding months. Many people wanted to see him vindicated by the judges, which would happen if they upheld his charge against me. No doubt he too was hoping and expecting to be vindicated by the judges' decision. He would have to carry on waiting. I decided it would not be wise at this point to go over and talk with him. Anyway, I had my own feelings towards Richard. A few people had told me that they had met Richard on various occasions over the last five months and that he had often looked tired and strained. We both should have worked out a plan about how we would explain my ideas to my parishioners, most of whom were completely unaware of modern Christian scholarship, its divisions, and the debates going on between theologians worldwide. Like so many other laity in the parishes, they had been indoctrinated in the faith as children, and what they had learnt then became the interpretation of the faith that nearly all of them would adhere to as adults. Potentially it was a great opportunity for adult education. We should have planned to try to update them on this situation and explain that it was inevitable that not only academic theologians, but also laity, bishops, and other clergy, would not always agree on today's interpretation of the Christian story. If a mediator in conflict resolution was necessary, then he or she should have been brought in to help.

There are congregations around the world where some of the congregation agree and some disagree with their rector's conservative or radical interpretations of the faith, as the case may be. Surely people can live with the fact that they are aware of what they interpret the orthodox position to be, and that the line that their rector takes may be different in certain ways. They may not always like it, but they respect their rector's freedom and integrity to search and explore, to question and think for himself or herself. Similarly, some of the laity have critiqued their own faith, examined the interpretation of the faith as they were taught it as children, and worked out their own credible faith for life as an adult. They may say that they go on changing their minds as their thinking develops about a range of matters to do with their faith: same sex relationships, remarriage of a divorced person, euthanasia, global issues of justice and poverty, and a vision of God.

Later, the same week as the trial, Robin Eames traveled to Canterbury to meet with other Primates of the Anglican Communion for one of their regular meetings. At the end of their week-long meeting, and to everyone's surprise, they issued a statement on a doctrine of God. In it they stated: "We believe that God the eternal Son became human for our sake and that in the flesh and blood of Jesus of Nazareth God was uniquely present and active. All claims to knowledge of God must be brought to Christ to be tested. Through Christ alone we have access to the Father." Had the issuing of this statement anything to do with my heresy trial? Was it meant to give backing to the seven judges, especially if high-powered members of the Anglican Communion were to come on 10 May, when the Court would sit again? I suspected that this might be so, but I may be completely wrong. In *The Church Times* (UK, 26 April 2002) Keith Ward, the then Regius Professor of Divinity at the University of Oxford, wrote a scathing article about the Primates' statement on a doctrine of God.

> As an obedient theologian, I bow before the Anglican Primates' unexpected declaration ... that they still believe in God. But why did they make it, and why is it so very defensive and unadventurous? It is easy to see what they are afraid of. There is horrid post-modernism, with its denial of 'universal and abiding truth' ... There is the pestilential view that resurrection might be based on "the subjective experience of the apostles". The Primates do not attempt to grapple with these actually rather old and well-discussed views. They just say: "They really are very, very horrid, and we are not having any of it." Why shouldn't they say just that? The reason is that it just confirms the

widespread impression that the Church is a defensive reactionary organization, which turns its back on modern thought … [I]n an age when inter-faith relations have become vital and exciting, they say: "Through Christ alone we have access to the Father." Hard luck, Muslims and Jews: you just don't have the right access code.

There may be some way in which Jesus gives a unique form of access to God, but it needs careful and sensitive spelling out, not just blunt – and offensive – assertion … Why don't the Primates address the question of what makes the idea of God as a bearded male potentate, becoming human just to save a minority of the human race … so unacceptable to so many? Why don't they rejoice in the exciting work done by many contemporary theologians to recover a sense of the mystery and infinity of the divine being, and to undermine the ridiculously limited and literal views people often have of the reality of God? … One of the best modern poets, R. S. Thomas, himself an Anglican priest, wrote in a well-known poem, 'Via Negativa': "God is that great absence in our lives, the empty Silence within." Is R. S. Thomas a naughty post-modernist? … We do need a doctrine of God for today … but the old words will not do any more.

I will not forget Monday 8 April 2002 for a long time. This, the day of the trial, was a tense day. Who or what had been on trial on this sorry day? Was it I? Or was it the old institutional church and its prescriptive theologies? Had not a new era arrived, and did not the Church need to catch up as quickly as it could? Or perhaps history will show in the years to come that it tried, but did not succeed? Or perhaps the Church's own historians will gratefully record that it did transform itself and that the evolving tradition continues to develop in unexpected directions.

Chapter 10

A reluctant resignation and an opportunity lost

I did not hang around Church of Ireland House for too long after the trial. A journalist wanted to know which people from the worldwide Anglican Communion I was thinking of inviting: would I invite Bishop Richard Holloway, and would I invite Bishop John Shelby Spong. I replied that I was still turning the matter around in my mind and had not decided on anybody to invite yet. I had indeed wondered whether either Richard Holloway or Jack Spong would be willing to help me, but at that stage had made no definite decision. It was a good guess, though, by Kieron Wood of the *Sunday Business Post*. I passed a few of my parishioners in the car park who were chatting together and one or two acknowledged me. None of the members of the parish who supported my views was able to be present. It was those who regarded my position as untenable in the parish who had come to the trial. Revd Bill Bowder had come over from London for the trial. He had followed Paddy Semple and become the Rector of Dunlavin Parish, County Wicklow in 1997, but after a few years had returned to journalism and was now working for *The Church Times*. I agreed to have lunch with him, as he wanted to do an interview with me, so we found a pub nearby. The interview was published in *The Church Times* on Friday 12 April 2002 and appears in Appendix H.

I got back to the Deanery in Trim about 4pm and then the shock and the exhaustion set in. Had I really been before a Court of my Church on account of my beliefs? It seemed as if I was in a different time frame. Could this really be the twenty-first century? Didn't people know that a worldwide debate was still going on about how to interpret the significance of Jesus and how to evaluate the power and meaning of 'his story'? Why did so many people still have to take it all so literally?

I made my evening meal and had some wine. The telephone rang several times as family members and friends kindly rang to see how I was and how the day had gone. I walked around the big back garden at the Deanery; you could fit four tennis courts into it, I had once estimated. About 60 yards away stood a very large 250-year-old house where clergy of the parish had lived until the middle of the twentieth century. Like so many clergy houses of that era it had had about 15 acres of land around it, including a large orchard and vegetable garden. Adjoining my back garden was the old coach house. I fed the goldfish in the pond, and watched the water thrown up by the little fountain in the center of the pond fall gently back onto the surface, sending ripples in all directions. A dog would have sensed my mood; the goldfish gave no indication that they did. I enjoyed watching them swim around for a few minutes. There was plenty of food in the pond for them to survive on. It did not matter if, for several days, they missed out on the 'supplementary feeding' that I was giving them. I loved this garden – its sounds, its privacy, its peace, its beauty, and its space.

I felt drained when I awoke the next morning. The stress and strain of the previous day was having its effect on me. But now I had to think. I spoke to Joe who said that, at present, he would not be doing anything. "Let the hare sit" was his advice. He expected that Richard Clarke's legal team would be in touch with my solicitor in the next couple of days in connection with the voluntary discovery of relevant documents. The best thing was for us to wait. The pressure was on the Church authorities. Did they want the media to turn the matter of a bishop bringing his dean to court into a high-profile heresy trial? Our colleagues in the Roman Catholic Church in Ireland were, understandably, under fierce examination by the media over child abuse sex scandals, and the credibility of their Church and its leaders was, in many minds, losing ground. What would a heresy trial in the twenty-first century do for the image and 'ratings' of the Church of Ireland? By all means, Joe said, think about which people to approach about being witnesses and see what their response might be. The Court was due to sit again in just over four weeks; there wasn't that much time to find suitable and competent people to act as witnesses, assuming, that is, that the case went ahead.

I was in touch with Andrew Mayes again in the next few days. He was aware that more attempts were being made to persuade Richard Clarke to suspend his Petition and to allow more time and space to see if there might be alternative ways of handling the controversy. He was not found to be persuadable over this issue. Andrew was becoming more doubtful that, given the context of the Church of Ireland, I actually stood a good chance of winning my case. However, he would still be a witness, and speak on my behalf, if I decided to carry on and fight my case. David FitzPatrick too was still willing to be a witness; he believed that the Church of Ireland was broad enough to hold within it people of a wide range of interpretations and beliefs. I was constantly thinking about my case myself. I read again the responses (Appendix F) that I had received from John Baker and Maurice Wiles, both of whom had served on Doctrinal Commissions of the Church of England. Their arguments against my position might be just the sort of reasoning I would have to face in the Court on 10 May. I considered in my mind the sort of responses I would wish to make. They were both well versed in the current academic literature about the interpretation and significance of Jesus, and each had written well-respected books on the faith in the modern world. As I expected, John Baker had replied that while he agreed with much that I had written, it was, to his mind, a non-negotiable part of Anglicanism that belief in the Incarnation was essential. He thought I should resign. Maurice Wiles was more concerned about whether I had enough positive things to say about Jesus to warrant my continued place within Anglicanism. He could only give me very qualified support, which would depend on my developing some of the positive things I had to say about Jesus and expanding on them. When later approached about being a witness, Maurice Wiles declined both for the above reason and on grounds of health.

I also approached Richard Holloway. He replied that he would like to help, but unfortunately when I gave him the date of 10 May, it turned out that he had engagements already made that would prevent him coming to speak in Dublin on my behalf. He was, however, of the mind that I would probably lose my case. The Church was in a state of transition in a post-modern world; a paradigm change in relation to how all religions were to be understood was taking place, but in the meantime the Churches held to the old orthodoxies, and I had moved beyond this position. Such was his verdict. Dr David Hart of Derby University and a leading member of the Sea of Faith Network, which I had joined in November 2001, did express willingness to be a witness for me when I spoke with him.

The days were going by, a week had passed from the hearing on 8 April. I talked with Joe again. Voluntary discovery was meant to have taken place, but nothing seemed to be happening. I continued to turn the situation around in my mind. It was increasingly clear that the parish would break up if I was to return, and that would only be possible if I were to continue with my case and win it. Supposing, though, I did do that and won the case, where then would I go, if it proved impracticable to return to the Trim and Athboy Group of Parishes? I could not imagine any other parish accepting me in Ireland. So, whether I won or lost, it seemed to me that I would not work again within the Church of Ireland in an ordained capacity. Was anything to be gained by continuing with the case? My mind was gradually coming to the point of view that perhaps it was better for the Church as a whole, and its future, if the seven judges were not asked to make a ruling on my theology. Leave the question open as to where the boundaries are to be drawn, do not risk the situation that might arise, of the judges deciding on a too narrow version of orthodoxy. Even though the days of orthodoxy counting for very much might be coming to an end, it might take another generation or two for such new thinking to have wide effect. I was advised again by some people, who knew the Church of Ireland much better than I did, that it was important not to damage the liberal cause. A verdict against me, it was thought, would strengthen the fundamentalist wing and weaken the liberal position. The issues I had raised about the need to modernize a religion that had begun in a pre-scientific and pre-critical age were not going to go away: they would have to be faced again. The issue of literalism could not be swept under the carpet either.

If Richard Clarke had not withdrawn his authority from me to do my work as a priest, perhaps we would never have got into this situation. But that was now water under the bridge and there was no going back, or so it seemed. Perhaps the best thing was to accept this and move on. What would I do and how would I earn my living? Where would I go and live?

My legal advice is that I cannot go into further details with the way my story developed, other than to say that on 7 May 2002 I went to Dublin and entered the offices of Whitney Moore and Keller where my solicitor, Peter Hayes, worked. In his presence and that of William Prentice, who was the bishop's legal adviser and our diocesan chancellor, I signed my signature and in doing so effected my resignation. A Press statement would be released saying that following the resignation of Andrew Furlong as Rector of the Trim and Athboy Group of Parishes and as Dean of Clonmacnoise, the Bishop of Meath and Kildare had withdrawn his Petition to the Court of the General Synod.

It was over.

I held my chin up as I went out of the door of my solicitor's office. I had to continue to be brave. What, however, would I do next? A part of me felt dead but I was walking, so some part of me must be still alive. I was a free and independent human being with my own vision of life. I would find another way to seek to live it out. That evening I issued my own Press statement.

STATEMENT FROM REVD ANDREW FURLONG   7 MAY 2002

Christianity comes out of a pre-scientific and pre-critical world. As Bishop Richard Clarke has written in his book *And is it True?* (p.119) "the language of the creeds is that of Greek philosophy. It is not a mode of thought or expression which is understood fully today ... If we were to write creeds today, they would be vastly different, both in language and in the concerns addressed." Both Bishop Clarke and I are concerned to re-interpret Christianity for a modern world in which we no longer believe that God 'sends' earthquakes, disease, or other disasters. There is an undercurrent around the world which is moving the Church, and other religions too, to face up to the fact that faith needs to be expressed in the terms of the twenty-first century, bearing in mind our current understanding of the universe in which we live. It means that theologians are expressing provisional viewpoints as they seek to find ways to say something significant about the God of the twenty-first century universe, and how such a God may be imagined to be connected with such a world as ours.

Theologians like myself are engaged in a discussion and a debate, and we go on developing and modifying our views and positions.

I had hoped that the Church of Ireland, in recognizing that my ministry in the Athboy and Trim Group of Parishes was regarded as untenable by the majority of the members of this parish (none of whom would claim to be theologically literate) would have found alternative work for me, such as the post of canon theologian, where I could continue my reading, debating, listening, and writing and communicating. As this has not happened, I have decided to resign. But the issue of modernizing Christianity will not go away.

I regret that my bishop imposed a five-month silence on himself, because right from the beginning I think it would have helped immensely if he had said much more openly in the parishes of this diocese and in the media that he has long recognized the need for Christianity to be updated; he could have gone on to say that my statements should be viewed like his, as well as those of other theologians, as provisional statements, as we all explored the mystery of being human and belonging to an evolving religious tradition which had always contained diversity of conjecture, speculation, thought, and belief. He emphasized to me on my arrival to work in this diocese five years ago the need for adult education, for more theologically literate laity. He knew for over 25 years that I held what are regarded by many as liberal and radical views.

I regret that Archbishop Empey in stating that he could not see how I could have a leadership role in a Christian community did not appear to be aware that he was excluding, by these remarks, a significant number of members of the Church of Ireland who recognize that the Church contains a variety of viewpoints: evangelical, conservative, traditional, liberal, and radical. Part of the role of an archbishop is to represent the comprehensiveness and breadth of his or her Church.

The people of this parish remain embedded in my heart; I have sought to serve some of them through times of great personal tragedy, I have shared with others times of uncertainty, and with others times of joy. I remain conscious that the last five months have been a difficult time, in differing ways, for many of them. I apologize for hurt caused to them for which I am responsible, and wish all of the people well for the future.

In the following days, editorials about my resignation appeared in *The Irish Times* and in *The Church of Ireland Gazette* (see Appendix G for both of these editorials). It was reported widely in other parts of the media too. CNN and other major media channels carried the story around the world. The statistics for hits on my website still record that the busiest day so far was the day after my resignation. On 8 May 2002 my website had 7608 hits and I received hundreds of e-mails. Not all the messages were in support of my views, though the majority were; quite a number were from the members of the other faith traditions who were intrigued to hear about my story. They had read "Irish priest resigns because he does not believe that Jesus was the son of God."

There was some speculation in relation to my resignation in Church of Ireland parishes. The *Church Review of the Dublin and Glendalough Diocese* of June 2002 has these sentences written by the rector of the evangelical Crinken parish:

> The Church as an institution with its power structures and dignitaries exercising control from remote places is crumbling at this moment before our eyes. The principle focus is on the Roman Catholic Church, but there is enough controversial activity in our own Church to keep us from adopting a superiority complex. The settlement with the Dean of Clonmacnoise, insider sources have revealed, is two years' salary and provision of accommodation, which perhaps rounds up at around £200,000 and all of it coming out of the pockets of people in parishes.

However, in July 2002, Crinken parish announced a clarification in the *Church Review*

> The widely circulated 'guesstimate' of the settlement with the Dean of Clonmacnoise on his resignation and reported in this column last month has been challenged by Archbishop Walton Empey. He says the settlement is 'an absolute fraction' of the £200,000 figure and none of it will come from parish giving. This clarification is welcome in the absence thus far of any official statement from the central bodies of the Church.

I had come back to Ireland in 1997 after being in other parts of the world for 14 years. It had been my desire to put my roots down again and stay in Ireland for the rest of my life. I would reconnect with old friends and make new ones. Perhaps I would marry again, if I were lucky enough. So the thought of applying to work in other parts of the Anglican Communion was not what was on my mind. Maybe I could find work in the USA, in the UK, or in New Zealand as an Anglican priest; I was sure there would be a bishop whom I could find who would be willing to give me a license so that I could resume my ministry. However, if I did so it would mean uprooting myself again, moving to another country, trying to re-root myself in a new community and seeking to make new friends. I did not feel ready for that at this stage. I would need my family and my friends around me, as I sought to come to terms with what had taken place.

I sat down at my desk in my study in the Deanery in Trim one morning in mid-May, just about a week after my resignation. I turned on my computer. I went online in order to surf the net. I wanted to look up the Peace Studies degree run by the Irish School of Ecumenics, now incorporated into Trinity College, Dublin. I found out that there is a one-year, postgraduate MPhil. Degree, and that applications had to be in before the beginning of June. I decided to apply for a place on the course.

I had been trying to think of a way to integrate some of my former experience into whatever the next chapter of my life would be. I had lived for 11 years in the Third World, and had not lost touch with the part of it I had known best. I read news every day about Zimbabwe by e-mail and invariably it was sad and disturbing. To take a course in Peace Studies was the best idea I could come up with. A number of people to whom I spoke thought it was a good idea to apply and see if I would be offered a place. Richard Holloway thought it sounded good and certainly, he told me, it would be mind stretching. Others thought that the course would be helpful to do, and the year doing it would give me time to network with others in the field. It would also give me time to process all I had been through, as I sought for a new identity and role in my life. In July 2002, I received confirmation that I was being offered a place. I contacted one of the administrative staff and found, to my delight, that there would be students from 14 different countries on the course with me. It would be a real international mix of people who would bring a wide range of life experiences with them. How exciting! I stood to learn so much. There would also be another international group of students, sharing the same seminar and lecture rooms, and the same library. They would be studying the Ecumenics course. They were bound to be an interesting group of people too, I felt sure. I would make new friendships that would enrich my life in many ways.

So now, as I begin to write the chapters for this book, in my current home in Dalkey, about eight miles from Dublin, I also spend part of the day reading some of the Peace Studies course books in preparation for beginning it in September 2002. I find it so stimulating to engage in issues to do with international ethics and international politics. I read about the different contested theories there are to explain what it means to be living in a globalized world. I study books about peace and equality, about development and inter-generational justice. This is not a completely new field for me. I see it as a vast and important area of study. It will cover stories of hope, but also stories of war, hunger, genocide, injustices, the exploitation of women and children, the imbalances of power, the Third World debt burden, and the precious ecosystem of our planet and our abuse of it.

I will also be studying gender issues, conflict resolution and non-violence, human rights, the United Nations (how it needs be strengthened and reformed), the European Union (how it will continue to grow), contemporary Islamic politics, conflict in N. Ireland, the politics of peace and conflict, social constructivism, cultural diversity, and much more too. The post-Cold War era and the primacy of the USA as the sole superpower will be a focus for much discussion. What will its real interests be? How can its government and people be persuaded to sign up to several of the key international treaties that so far America is not party to? How will it continue to come to terms with 9/11? How well will it come to better understand its own domestic problems, and how well will it achieve insight into the antagonism it arouses and the admiration it evokes throughout the rest of the world? The moral challenge of being human in such a battered, wounded world will be strongly presented on my Peace Studies course. We only come this way once, or so at least I would want to claim. Can I still use my life for good, to make a difference in some small way to enhance the lives of others? If theology has conflicting theories and diverse viewpoints about a whole range of beliefs, the social sciences, and political and economic studies, seem to have far more.

I live now in that part of greater Dublin where I had grown up as a child and as an adolescent. My elderly mother lives in a nursing home nearby and I rent her small home from her, which helps to pay her bills. I will need to work next year, but I can draw on my funds and survive financially this year as a student. It is strange to be living here in Dalkey, so close to the two homes I had grown up in. I like this area very much. Dalkey is beside the sea, it has two tiny harbors and three old Norman castles. It looks out on Dublin Bay and Vico Bay. The coastline is very pretty with the Dublin and Wicklow mountains not far away. I so enjoy being back beside the sea. Zimbabwe was a land-locked country and I missed seeing the sea and feeling myself close to it. Although, having said that, I would also want to record that one of my great joys in Zimbabwe was having situated, at the far end of my parish, 150 miles from the other end where I lived, the beautiful Lake Kariba. On the journey there, at least once a month, I invariably passed by animals close to the road. As I traveled, I never saw a lion, a leopard, or a cheetah, but they were there, unseen, not far away. However, I often saw elephants, buffaloes, zebras, impalas, monkeys, waterbuck, baboons, giraffe, warthogs, eland, and kudu and, at the lakeside itself, crocodiles and hippos.

I never know from day to day, now in Dalkey, what memories will come back to me of those days growing up here with family, neighbors, friends, kindergarten school, church, shopkeepers, and other residents. As a boy, then, I had no idea of the chapters of my life that lay ahead, nor can I now see what further ones there will be. Whatever they may hold, I hope they will meet my deep needs for seeking to be of service, for meaning, community, intimacy, autonomy, and growth. Here is a part of my current 'Credo' (see Chapter 24) that I wrote for myself – not for you! – for you perhaps have your own Credo yourself. Maybe it is a provisional one like mine, always there waiting to be changed and deepened. It is never completed. As Auden said of poems: they are never finished, just abandoned.

> The destiny of this risky adventure of life lies over the horizon, in eternity; the meaning of life continues to grow. Let life be developed and used, be open-minded, courageous, and humorous, seek to adore.

Chapter 11

The Bishop's crook – a better way?

When a person is consecrated to work as a bishop, he or she is given a crosier or pastoral staff that is meant to resemble a shepherd's crook. This is a symbolic emblem of a bishop's leadership. It is suggestive of pastoral leadership. The shepherd, and his or her sheep, are not good twenty-first-century models for a modern democratic Church, where participation and responsibility need to involve as many people as possible. However, what a person is not given at his or her consecration is a garden hoe! I mention this with the parable of the wheat and the tares, ascribed to Jesus, in mind. The tares growing in the midst of the wheat are to be left until harvest time. This might suggest that a bishop is not to use his or her pastoral staff or crook as a hoe. She/he is not to try to solve problems by taking out the 'tares', whatever or whoever the 'tares' may be considered to be.

Rather, the crook is a reminder that a bishop, as a leader, is there in a Church context to be a pastoral agent. He or she is meant to be about the task of building and maintaining human relationships. In my case, this would have meant coming amongst unlike-minded people to enable us to go on working and worshiping together and to continue to trust and respect each other. It requires a person with real human leadership qualities. The challenge is not to use the crook as a hoe and weed out the 'difficult person', but to come alongside a group of people, who are faced with a major challenge as to how they are going to continue to relate to each other, and to help them to find solutions to their problems. This is the pastoral solution that Richard Clarke to my mind never attempted. I am suggesting that withholding his authority from me to work as a priest for three months was not the right way to have handled this situation. There is no doubt that other people, working as bishops, would have acted differently.

However, once Richard Clarke had imposed a period of leave of absence on me, and then withdrawn into his 'ivory tower' for the next five months, refusing to engage in public debate and discussion, a very different situation and climate had been created. Some people rejoiced in what they saw as the actions of a tough and decisive bishop. It might take a few months, but then the Dean would have gone. People of a fundamentalist or conservative outlook, all around the Church of Ireland, and in other Churches too, would be delighted; it would increase their power and influence. A liberal bishop had played into their hands. It is very rare for a person to have their authority to work withdrawn by their bishop on account of their theological research. If a person were charged with some crime, that would be a different matter. The Bishop seemed to be perceived to be saying that there was only one way to understand Christianity and that the Dean must go. While a minority within the parish strongly disagreed with the bishop's actions, the majority of regular Sunday worshipers agreed with him. Much as they may have liked me and would miss me as a person, my continuing ministry would no longer be tolerable to them, unless a suitable intervention helped them to see that pluralism need not threaten them and could be welcomed for the richness it brings.

But surely it wasn't necessary. In one of her interviews for her book, *C of E: The State It's In*, Monica Furlong talked with Archbishop George Carey, whom she quotes as having said:

> I'd like to argue, you know, that the broad Church that we are now is probably a foretaste of what is to come. If we want to think about the coming great Church, then it is going to be one in which we have to accept huge differences within the family, and we are not going to have final answers this side of eternity. Living with differences, I think, is actually the genius of Anglicanism. (p. 162)

One might think of William Temple, who though publicly doubting the Virgin Birth, became an Archbishop of Canterbury, at a time when the majority within his Church still did believe in the Virgin Birth. Alternatively, one might point to Bishop John Shelby Spong and the theses he published at the Lambeth Conference in 1998. In them he stated:

> Theism, as a way of defining God, is dead. God can no longer be understood with credibility as a Being, supernatural in power, dwelling above the sky and prepared to invade human history periodically to enforce the divine will. So, most theological God-talk today is meaningless unless we find a new way to speak of God.
>
> Since God can no longer be conceived in theistic terms, it becomes nonsensical to seek to understand Jesus as the incarnation of the theistic deity. So, the Christology of the ages is bankrupt.

Richard Clarke was not, in this case at least, prepared to even try to fight to maintain the "genius of Anglicanism". The odds were not only stacked against me, but an opportunity was being lost. The Church used to be seen, by some people at least, as a community of hope for a divided world. In the Church you could find tolerance and broadmindedness; people found ways to live with their conflicting viewpoints and faith claims, as they sometimes did in other religious traditions too. Though, it must be said, the Church's record is far from pure in this regard. But was the Church, as people like

Richard Clarke seemed to want to shape it, likely to be a place that the world might look to for inspiration? For as members of the human family in the world, we face the enormously difficult moral challenge of finding ways to live, with all our diversity, at peace and not at war. We need good examples, we need inspiration, and we need the spiritual and moral resources to construct a peaceful tolerant world for us all to live in.

My bishop would say in the months to come that he thought I should become a Unitarian or a member of Judaism. This to my mind was seeking to evade the problem of how unlike-minded people are to live together, not that they don't share much in common, for they do. The debate about the interpretation of Jesus and the shape of Christianity in a modern world was ongoing and, not unsurprisingly, hotly contested. The Church of the future should not be a Church seeking to push people with controversial views beyond its boundaries (see Andrew Mayes' first letter in Appendix D). It needs to accept that serving the cause of truth, and particularly in the context of religious claims, means inviting people to persevere, if they are willing, in a difficult task – that of helping a religious tradition to evolve given the best insights and innovative thinking available. It implies accepting the need to live with what may appear, at the time, to be views that cannot be reconciled. Isn't the most important feature of the Church that it has a vision of love as the ultimate reality in life, and that those who seek to be its members are struggling in their own lives to respond to that vision, in the ordinary events of the world, with the imperfect love of their own inner beings?

So what other alternative courses of action might have been considered in 2001? What strategies might have been discussed, earlier in the year, when I had sent my bishop the text of a controversial article that I hoped that *The Irish Times* would publish? Later in 2001, in November and December, when the media started to publicize my liberal beliefs, and people began to complain to Richard about them, what other ways might there have been of dealing with this controversy? Could it have been addressed as both problem and opportunity? Were there alternative courses of action that my bishop might have taken after his meeting with me in March 2002 or that the House of Bishops might have taken? Did I have other choices and courses of action open to me? In what follows I ask more questions, than provide answers. I am aware that many Churches and other bodies, such as the Sea of Faith Network, are struggling to address these issues. How are we to look on issues concerning what has traditionally been perceived as the boundaries of an organization and its identity? Where does democracy come in? What are the issues concerning power and authority? Whose interests are being served? Whose voices are not being heard? Who decides about membership? Under what conditions can a person become a member and under what circumstances should they relinquish their membership or be asked or compelled to leave? Are there limits to doctrinal diversity? Who decides, and should we care?

As I have already written, in Chapter 2, I think that in April 2001, Richard and I ought to have discussed together what was the likely result of *The Irish Times* publishing an article such as 'A Faith Fundamentally Flawed?'. How would it affect my work in my parish? What would be the responses from within and without the Church of Ireland? Was it the right course of action to take, through the medium of a national newspaper, to try to engage the public in a debate about Christianity? Would people welcome a public debate through the letters columns? Was such a forum a good place for me to speak more transparently than I had done in a parish setting? Was there some way to prepare the people of my parish for what would come as a considerable shock to them? What consideration did I need to give to the rest of the diocese, or to the Church as a whole? Should I have resigned first, before speaking transparently and openly about my struggles to find a credible faith as part of a lifelong quest in search of meaning, purpose, and truth? Yes, the issues I was discussing had been debated in the media for 30 years or more. Television documentaries and radio programs had been produced about the life of Jesus, and a variety of views had been put forward. Many books had been written. Many others before me had said nearly all of what I was saying. In April 2001 my bishop had said in the course of his letter to me, after receiving the article 'A Faith Fundamentally Flawed?', that he was not in doctrinal agreement with Cupitt or Spong. If he had said to me, then, that he was also not in doctrinal agreement with me over certain areas of my interpretation of the Christian faith, we could have begun the task of further dialoguing together. But the months slipped by and this did not take place.

When, finally, he did tackle me on my beliefs, it was in a very different atmosphere and context. It was clear he and I had some deep conflicts over our ideas about what authentic Christianity is. I believe that Richard Clarke should have called in a skilled and experienced facilitator who would have helped the two of us to work together towards conflict transformation. It was clear to me that our conversations about belief, in December 2001 and March 2002, were inadequate, and certainly left me feeling dissatisfied, because I did not feel that we had shared in a true dialogue or that I had been truly listened to. I did not feel that we had reached a sufficiently deep level of analysis to understand our conflicting views properly. I also felt threatened by the power of his office and the way he might use his power.

I further think that some attempt at conflict resolution with a facilitator was needed in the context of my parish. At the very least some sort of healing of relationships might have been achieved. The people of my parish for the most part loved me, and I loved and cared deeply about them. I remain convinced that, probably after a process of conflict transformation which I might have engaged in with them, a suitably gifted and able person, who had won our respect and trust, might have persuaded them, for they were reasonable and mature people, to accept me back after my enforced leave of absence as their Rector and their Dean. That of course was never tried. I did invite everyone in the parish to my home in the Deanery, before I finally left, to say goodbye to them, and they very kindly made me a presentation to show their appreciation of my work among them. However, that occasion, good as it was, was insufficient to mend some of the cleavages that had opened up in the preceding months. Furthermore, there were people who felt too strongly against me to come and say goodbye; I would have liked to have had the opportunity to draw closer to them again. One TV reporter, Joe Little of the Irish television company RTE, when announcing that I had resigned, said the matter left a sour taste in the mouth. I have that feeling inside myself too. I think the Church needed to do better, for human relationships are a significant part of what we are meant to be about.

When Richard Clarke had written to me saying that he did not think my beliefs made it tenable for me to remain in ministry in my parish, he indicated that if I did not accept his invitation to resign, he believed that he would have no other recourse but to take me to the Court of the General Synod of the Church of Ireland, its highest court. I disagree with him that there were no other alternatives, and I want to suggest what they might have been.

First of all, before or instead of imposing a three-month period of enforced leave of absence on me, he could have initiated a debate. This would have been to take a different route from the one that he chose – of withdrawing his authority from me to do my work as a priest. That, together with the very strong criticisms Archbishop Empey made of my beliefs, created a situation in which many people came to feel that even if they were sympathetic to some form of pluralism in the Church, their leaders, and especially Archbishop Empey, were quite adamant that my views made it impossible for me to be a minister within the Christian community. On one occasion Empey had stated that Bishop Robinson and Bishop Jenkins of the Church of England, however radical were their beliefs, never denied that Christ is Lord. "But this is exactly what Andrew Furlong has done," he fumed. I never heard him unpack what he thought the metaphor of 'Christ as Lord' might mean in twenty-first-century terms. I consider that what both Archbishop Empey and my bishop missed out on was the opportunity for debate.

They have both claimed that adult Christian education is important and that they would love to see more adults, as members of the Church, better educated theologically. Here was a golden opportunity. There was immense interest in the case. Richard Clarke, I think, should have arranged with me to debate together. He could have brought in other theologians more expert than either of us. There could have been panel discussions with laity, bishops, and clergy asking whatever questions they wished. Walton Empey could have done the same in the Dublin diocese. We could have gone on radio and television and held our debates and discussions through these media. The fact that Richard Clarke never wrote an article arguing his case as to why he was imposing three months' enforced leave of absence on me, and withdrawing his authority from a senior member of the clergy to do his work as a priest, was a further missed opportunity for engaging in reasoned argument in the pubic domain. Yes, undoubtedly, public debate would have brought forth strong passions. In his letter to *The Irish Times* (see Appendix D) Andrew Mayes gives strong support to the need for debate. He wrote, "Mr Furlong's views, or at least the public expression of them, require further clarification and debate ... In any case, the discussion should continue, and continue especially within the Church."

In the political sphere, as the debate about going to war against Saddam Hussein and his country was conducted in many countries around the world, it was evident that people held their positions with immensely strong feelings in many cases. There were differences over the moral and legal aspects of the situation;, there were contested views about what the real interests were of the USA, or of the UK, or of the countries who asserted that they would veto a second resolution at the United Nations Security Council. At the time the following questions, and others too, were being asked. Should the UN arms inspectors be given more time? Was the UN going to be severely damaged, if no second resolution was sought for or won, and Iraq was attacked? Had sufficient planning been done so that immediate humanitarian aid would be available once war ended, if there was going to be a war? How possible would it be to deliver food and medical aid during the war? Was this issue so serious that it deservedly became a resigning issue for certain politicians and diplomats?

I ask now why, if such serious debates can take place in the public domain over these issues, is the Church so frightened about debating more publicly its contested interpretations of the faith?

Another course of action, which the Rules of the Court of the General Synod permit, is for the bench of bishops to put a question concerning a doctrinal issue to the Court for its deliberation with the expectation that the Court would set up some sort of commission to consider the issue and to report back. I do not know whether this course of action was discussed by the bishops or not. It was not acted on. This would have taken the burden off Richard Clarke's shoulders of pursuing the matter, at least originally, by himself. It could have meant framing a theological question on whether views such as those expressed by me were heretical or acceptable within the concept of a broad view of the Church of Ireland and presenting it to the Court. It would have set up a commission of theological experts to examine the issue and report back, before making its judgment. Then my case could have been further addressed according to the judgment given.

A considerable number of people, both within the Church of Ireland and outside it, are aware that in the House of Bishops, which is made up of the 12 bishops of the Church of Ireland, there is quite a degree of theological pluralism regarding interpretations of Christianity. Some of them quite definitely find their ideas in relation to the significance of Jesus on the theological map of searching, questioning, doubting, and believing in a conservative section, some in an evangelical area, some in a fundamentalist corner, and some in a liberal wing. How difficult, at times, they find it to work together because of this diversity, I do not know. I am not aware of them publicly acknowledging the pluralism and conflicts that exist between them on account of their differing beliefs.

Are not similar situations found among the senior leadership of a great many Churches worldwide? Such diversity certainly exists in the higher echelons of political life and of business enterprises. It should be noted that sometimes in the Church of England the bishops themselves have dealt with contentious doctrinal issues by setting up a Doctrine Commission, which then reports back about three to five years later. The report, though, is not always acted upon and may just sit on the shelf gathering dust. It was said to me, with some degree of seriousness, that if a person is going to be a bishop she/he must realize that she/he will be expected to have the capacity to fudge issues, to leave them alone, and not attempt to sort them out. The same might be said of politics or other areas of life. Perhaps sometimes it may be a wise policy or a pragmatic policy to follow, but surely not always?

An alternative course of action, which Richard Clarke and Walton Empey might have followed, would have required that my bishop present a Petition against me to the Court of the General Synod, as he did, but then Empey would first have set up a commission of enquiry to see if there was a *prima facie* case for bringing this issue as a doctrinal charge to the Court of the General Synod, as he was entitled to do as our archbishop. This would have involved inviting some theological experts, both lay and clerical, to investigate the case. It would not have been a rushed process and both sides would have had the right to have legal representatives and witnesses. If such a case had been established, then the charge would have been placed before the Court. Such an enquiry, properly conducted, would have allowed for dialogue, so that all parties would have felt both genuinely heard and listened to and their views understood. Again, I do not know whether or not these two leaders discussed such a course of action, and it was not acted upon.

Another course of action was attempted during the hearing of my case on 8 April 2002. My barrister pointed out to the Court that as it stood, in his opinion, the charge was more than one of a theological nature. It involved issues of employment. As such I stood to lose not only my present position as dean and rector but my income and my home. He reminded the Court that the Rules governing the trial allowed for a special case to be stated. As Joe said to me, some months later, to have proceeded by way of a special case stated would have meant that the gun would have been withdrawn from my head. The discussions would have taken place in a very different atmosphere as a result.

The final way to have proceeded was to have tried to find a means for the Church to catch up with modern thinking. It certainly became more and more clear that the views that I was expressing through my articles on the Internet were proving highly controversial. The following astute observation of Richard Holloway offers the correct diagnosis, in my view. I alluded to it in the previous chapter:

> Those people who believe that the Christian Faith is a prepacked and unalterable teaching will find this book dangerously subversive. But the author is not out to replace the traditional faith with another, more modern version: he is saying that the day of purely official theology is at an end. What Andrew Furlong is demonstrating in these pages is the vitality of a theology that allows, indeed celebrates, a number of different approaches, including his own. He is telling us that the day of prescriptive doctrine is over – it's just that the Church has yet to catch up with the fact.

At Newgrange in County Meath, Ireland, across the River Boyne from the great burial chamber, there is an interpretative center in which you can learn about the Neolithic community, of 5000 years ago, who built the burial chamber. As they worked to build it, it is very unlikely that they stopped to think that some day their culture, religion, and civilization would be no more (except for those burial chambers that might survive the ravages of time). Some day there may be similar interpretative centers for the culture, religion, and civilization known as Christianity. On the other hand it could evolve, be transformed, and modernized. Is the attempt still worth making? One person who wrote to me thought so:

> What I have understood is that you have been suspended for daring to question some of the long held and cherished doctrines of the Church and like all those before you who have dared to rock the boat of orthodoxy you are being punished. One hoped that martyrs in the western world were a thing of the past, but not so. What we do know, of course, is that this is the action of a frightened minority group – the Church in Britain and Ireland surely has to be called that – and they are reacting as all those who fear they have everything to lose and nothing to gain have always reacted, with bigotry and sententiousness.

I observe that Don Cupitt in Britain has also tried to raise issues and to approach faith in a spirit of honest enquiry. 'They' would like to silence him too ... All power to your elbow. If we do not raise these issues now our children certainly won't as there will be no Church about which to raise anything, not even a regret!

As I wrote in the Introduction, the Sea of Faith UK Network began a study in 2002 into the allowability of doctrinal diversity within Christianity. It has a fascinating page on its website dedicated to this study. Here is a summary of what this study is about:

The Sea of Faith UK AGM, at its 2002 meeting, passed the following resolution:

The Sea of Faith UK AGM takes note of the recent resignation of Andrew Furlong as Dean of Clonmacnoise and expresses concern regarding the pressure to conform to traditional doctrinal beliefs that led to this resignation. At the same time, the AGM recognizes that a religious tradition, like any organisation, has a legitimate interest in defining its identity and that the appropriate balance between tradition and diversity within this identity is complex and subject to change over time.

The AGM therefore asks the Steering Committee to initiate a study on the allowability of doctrinal diversity within Christianity, in the context of religious faith as a human creation. The purposes of the study are to inform the Network's views on this subject and to assist the Network in defining its position regarding situations where a religious tradition formally questions the acceptability of the views of one of its members or representatives. The study should include both research and consultation with SoF members. The results of the study, along with proposed statements of policy, which may be adopted by the membership, should be presented to the 2003 AGM.

This paper defines the terms of reference for the study, which will be called 'The Sea of Faith (UK) Enquiry into the Allowable Limits of Ecclesiastical Diversity in Matters of Christian Doctrine', or simply 'The Diversity Study'. The terms of reference define the purposes, responsibilities, tasks, available resources, and time lines relevant to the study.

The Churches have done immense good, and stood for good, in a thousand ways. However, at the level of the mind, the Churches need to realize that, in a free civil society, they have been, to some extent, its unrecognized prisons. In terms of what to believe, the prisoner has not been permitted to scale a wall and to transcend a boundary has been forbidden; she/he has been told what to believe. They had better believe, it used to be said, for fear of damnation. How often has it been said, "This is the ruling of the Church, the faithful must accept it." No longer can belief be prescribed; no more will people accept being told what to believe. The Churches have to make way for far more participation by all members and for the democratization of belief. Every person has the right to name and describe her or his world and to give it meaning. Every human being has the right to search for her or his own spirituality. If she/he chooses to do this by inter-reacting with the Christian tradition, then she/he will bring her or his own unique and differing insights to such a lifelong quest.

Part Two:

LET THE CHRISTIAN TRADITION EVOLVE

Both the Introduction and Part One give considerable insight into how I interpret my faith today. In what follows here in Part Two I expand on my thinking about some key areas within Christianity. The last chapter of this section contains the beliefs of others placed alongside my provisional 'Credo'. Our faith, understood symbolically, is rich and diverse. If your interpretation of faith is different to mine, it does not follow necessarily that they are in opposition. One may enrich the other. Both are human perceptions of what is profoundly mysterious. Those who journey, as Don Cupitt pointed out, often know the destination to which their journey will take them. Their journey is a pilgrimage to a fixed, well-known holy site. On the other hand, journeys also are made by those who are explorers, adventurers, or questors – who do not know the destination – they only know that a well runs dry and they must search for another one. There is something inside them that entices them to travel on into the unknown hopefully.

Chapter 12

The Bible – deconstructed and re-evaluated

What are we to make of the diverse writings contained in the Bible? Do its images, metaphors, and symbols, which change their meaning over time and in different contexts, still speak powerfully? There is a range of different attitudes to the Bible within the membership of the Churches, and outside it, characterized by some of the following feelings: respect, puzzlement, antagonism, alienation, gratitude, joy, uncertainty, and love. What authority can the Bible have for today's radical believer? While Churches have given a revered place of authority to the Bible in their Church constitutions and doctrinal statements; do not some people question that today?

Like most people of my generation within the Church, and like most Christians of previous generations, I grew up accepting that the biblical accounts of a God who had talked to a range of different people were about something that really had happened. I learned of the God who had talked to Adam and Eve in the Garden of Eden, who had spoken with Noah, and who had called Abraham to go forth and sacrifice his only son, Isaac. I was taught of the God who communicated with the boy, Samuel, by night in the Temple and who at the baptism of Jesus was heard to speak from out of the clouds. As I was growing up, I do not remember hearing a sermon questioning these matters of conviction and belief. The theology of the Bible was not examined critically either. The Bible recorded the election of the people of Israel to be the special people of their God, people whom he favored above all others. I was then taught that the Church took the place of Israel, because Israel failed to recognize Jesus as the Messiah, sent as savior by this God. The question was not asked whether the biblical writings are human faith claims, which have nothing to do with the decision-making of this God, whose thoughts anyway are inaccessible to us.

I now see things very differently, though many Christians understand the Bible otherwise. As far as the Jews are concerned, and I am thinking primarily of the Old Testament of the 'Christian Bible', the story of the people of Israel, to my mind, cannot be the story of how their God sought them out to be his chosen people. Rather, their theology is their own creation developed over many generations and centuries. I realize many Jews would disagree with me. I see it as the story of their own search both for an understanding of the divine and for their own identity in relation to the divine. It has its roots in a time when all the tribes around them had their own gods and their own theologies. Part of the people of Israel's story is about the reason why they felt entitled to their land: they alleged that their God had given it to them. On the basis of their beliefs, they could claim that their conquests of other tribes were legitimate. They believed that their God himself had given them their ethical code and decreed many laws about how they should live. In fact, their ethics were something that they had developed themselves, and their justification for invading other tribes and taking their land was their own self-made justification.

As their religious tradition evolved, there is evidence of the influence of other cultures and beliefs, such as the belief in an afterlife, which came to them in about the fifth century BCE, probably from Iranian philosophy. Their creation stories show similarities to those from Babylon. Their liturgy and other cultic practices were often a reaction to those of the other tribes with whom they mingled, did business, fought against, or made alliances with against more powerful nations. Their religion is a human creation as are all the other undertakings of humankind, whether in the arts or in the sciences. Like other societies they had their sacred events, which were particularly important to them. They had their holy days and places for worship. They had their religious leaders and objects of special religious significance, such as the Ark, the Tabernacle, and the Temple. They had their holy writings, which came out of the mists of history when stories were passed from generation to generation by word of mouth. They were reinterpreted in the telling and often added to and embellished.

In my view, they did not have a hotline to their God nor did he constantly tell them what he expected of them and what their place was in the world. In their theological thinking they developed a degree of sophistication that not many other peoples achieved. They became clear in their minds that if there was a God, it was more credible to believe in just one such a God and to describe his nature as good, even though this left unresolved many of the problems posed by the existence of evil. At their best, they acknowledged that their God was inscrutable and beyond their fathoming. They faced mystery and could only trust that it was love that lies at the heart of life. They had been created in love, for love, and by a God of love: such, to my mind, was their faith.

Their religious tradition belongs to a pre-scientific and pre-critical world-view. It reflects beliefs common at the time. Then, gods were seen as interventionist gods, controlling many of the forces the people, at that time, did not understand. The gods would send good weather as well as foul, bless them with health and punish them with disease, destroy them in floods and earthquakes, and rescue them, at times, from the storms at sea or the lightning and thunder on land. They would fight on their side in battle against their enemies. One of their constant pleas was for peace and the reestablishment of their nation in independence from the powerful empires that ruled over them. Some day, they came to hope, their God would come and save them. They needed his help for they were a small nation in the face of much more powerful ones. He would drive away their enemies, and establish a lasting peace in a world of justice in which the victims of the past would be vindicated. Perhaps at such a time there would be a special divinely appointed leader, a Messiah, who would be strong and successful, as their stories told them King David had been. Some of them claimed this to be the plan and the will of their God, but, in my view, this was simply speculation on their part. They had no privileged access to the mind of their God. Those who thought of the dead waiting in their graves for this time to arrive believed that they would be raised to life and judged: some would enter the new kingdom of peace and justice, others would go to hell. Their God never fulfilled these human dreams, which some of them believed had been inspired by him.

Though there were diverse and conflicting views within their tradition, the idea of a national savior, a Messiah/Christ, appointed and blessed by their God, remained in many minds as a powerful hope for a different future. Little did they realize that some day the world would recognize a new religion. The one in whose name it would be founded would himself be one of their own. His followers, initially all Jews too, would find in their scriptures what they then took to be many prophetic allusions to the person they now proclaimed as Christ and Lord. They interpreted his life, and their own, through the lenses of Jewish faith. They were part of a religious tradition that they did not then recognize to be a human creation.

Jesus of Nazareth belonged to this pre-scientific and pre-critical world. He too interpreted life, and constructed his sense of reality, through wearing Jewish lenses. The Jewish framework was an unconscious part of many of his assumptions and much of his thinking. He believed that supernatural miracles could take place and that sicknesses were caused by demons. He believed the community of Israel to which he belonged was the chosen people of their God. He had expectations in relation to what he believed to be the coming kingdom of this God. It was arriving and making its presence felt in some new way, he claimed, as he interpreted what was taking place as a result of his interactions with other people and his relationships with them. The utopian dream of independence and freedom for his people, following the long-hoped-for intervention by their God (the day of the Lord) was imminent, he seems, to my mind, to have thought. Both the interpretation of the purpose and meaning of his death and the claims about his resurrection, in my view, have to be seen as belonging within a particular framework of belief – what is called Jewish eschatology. His disciples preached that his death had been predicted by the prophets and planned by their God. His resurrection was linked with their own imminent entry into a new realm beyond the powers of death, and with the resurrection of those already dead. A judgment of the dead would soon take place. Jesus of Nazareth, now believed to be a divinely appointed Savior, would shortly return and, rather than live in a peaceful kingdom here on earth, they now proclaimed that he would bring them, and his other followers, to a new life in heaven.

An illustration of how these Jewish lenses influenced the construction and telling of a story may be found in St Matthew's Gospel. He wrote, "And Jesus cried again with a loud voice and yielded up his spirit. And behold the curtain of the temple was torn in two, from top to bottom; and the earth shook, and the rocks split; the tombs also were opened, and many bodies of the saints who had fallen asleep were raised, and coming out of the tombs after his resurrection they went into the holy city and appeared to many" Matthew 27:50-53. In my view, Matthew is not speaking literally here, he is writing symbolically. He is drawing on the Jewish expectations of how the dead would come out of the ground or out of their tombs when God entered human history to restore the fortunes of Israel and give it independence once more. He is wearing Jewish lenses. He is telling those listening to his Gospel that the 'end-times' have come. Similarly, St Paul wrote, also wearing Jewish lenses. He saw Jesus' proclaimed resurrection as the first fruits of a general resurrection of this 'end-time', and he expected it to take place in his own lifetime.

We know today that none of this happened. The world has gone on its way; it has not ended. Nor was there any miraculous divine intervention; no kingdom of justice and peace was established. Nor were the Jews as a nation set free from the rule of the Roman Empire. They did not become independent again. Once we can remove the lenses from our eyes that the biblical writers were wearing, whether for writing the Old or the New Testaments, we will see the history of the people of Israel, the life of Jesus and the beginnings of the Church in a very different perspective. One of my consultants, John Baker (see Appendix F), wrote

> I myself believe that scripture has unique authority, because it is an archive from the historical process by which a people was prepared by God to be the one in which the Incarnation could happen ... Without the Bible we cannot put Jesus in his faith context, or understand and interpret his significance.

I agree that we need the Bible to act as a main source for an understanding of Jesus both as a member of the ancient community of Israel, and as the one in whose name a new religion came into being and began to evolve. If Jesus had not come into the world we would not have our present ways of speaking about God in his/her relationship to the world. However as I do not believe that God came into the world to live a human life in the person of Jesus, in a historical sense, as John Baker does, I do not accept that God was preparing a people to be the one in whom the Incarnation would take place.

With great respect for others who do not see the Bible in the same way as I do, I must still ask this question. So what is left of the Bible after it has been deconstructed? Many of us today can no longer read it, or listen to it being read, as once we did. Our world-view is radically different in important ways. We are much more aware that our religion is a human creation and that it continues to evolve as it is interpreted from one generation to another, from one culture to another, and as fresh thinking and insights are brought to bear on it. In so far as the Bible speaks of the mystery of an elusive, unseen and inscrutable God, if there is a God at all, it can remind us of this aspect of our faith. The pluralism in the Bible, and the conflicting views of God and God's nature, are a clear testimony to the way in which a religion evolves from generation to generation as it reflects on the past, re-expresses it and adds creative insights or introduces what will for a future generation appear to be incredible ideas. The attempt to characterize God needs to encompass the great heights and depths of human experience, as we try to envisage a God responsible for all we know and experience. I affirm the spirituality found in parts of the writings in the Bible that indicate that awe and worship, reverence and humility, gratefulness and penitence, confidence and questioning are fitting attitudes to have in relation to the divine mystery. Many of the moral values found within it are values that we esteem and prize too, though many of the situations to which we would apply them now are new.

The human search for meaning and purpose, found in many of the writings of the Bible, contains wisdom worth holding onto. Some writings acknowledge an acceptance of the unfinished task that a human being leaves behind them, when death takes them from this world. I still think that the Bible, like much other literature, can function as both mirror and microscope. We can identify with some of the great stories included in the Bible because of our own life experiences. It acts as a mirror to us in which we see how we are or how we have been or what we have done. It may be conflicts within families, such as those between Jacob and Esau or between Joseph and his brothers; it may be the adultery of David in taking Bathsheba to himself, or it may be the suffering of Job. The Bible acts too as a microscope, because we may find, as we identify with these ancient stories, that our lives too are being examined through the lenses of truth and justice. The message of the Bible is also one of mercy, and of that we are all in need – both as a resource within to give to others who have harmed or hurt us, and to receive from those who have become the victims of our selfishness or depravity.

There is much that we can no longer connect to or in some cases approve of. I think of the animal sacrifices, the treatment of those suffering with leprosy, the hygiene laws and food restrictions, the regulations relating to purity and impurity in men and women, the institution of slavery, the interventionist God. In many ways the Bible represents a world we have left behind. We can recognize both its achievements and its failures. We can see it as the product of human endeavor and creativity, and of inadequate thinking and delusion. We can hear the cry for justice and peace, as well as the terrible cry to go to war. We can admire the heights to which people have ascended and acknowledge the depravity to which they have sunk. We can empathize with their reaching out for hope and consolation. We can identify with them as they found themselves both to be attracted to the goodness of God and also in rebellion to their God. So we may value the Bible, but we need to do so in a critically aware way, always remembering that religious language is metaphorical and symbolical, and that God, if there is a God, is unknowable to us in this life. Some people believe strongly in Revelation, they claim that God does choose to reveal himself, and has done so in the past, indeed that the Bible is essentially the story of the self-revelation of God and especially in the life of Jesus, his death and resurrection. As perhaps is clear, I see these things otherwise, and refer you for my view on Revelation to Appendix A.

To my mind, the Bible's authority is not the authority of a God who was once claimed to have written it: its only authority is the authority of the spiritual and moral truths we believe we find within it. Though we can never prove we have found such moral or spiritual truths. Modern democratic voting does not mean that the majority has found the truth either. We can only try to make our judgments, according to our best lights, and at times we may be right and at times we may prove to have been mistaken. In a transformed Christianity there is no longer a good reason why the Bible should have the same dominating position as it has been given up to now. It may very well be that the writings and reflections of other authors will help to give contemporary life more meaning and significance than the biblical authors can do today. However, to my mind, because of its antiquity, and the resonance still felt within it, there is a sense in which the ethical values, the vision of a God of love and mercy, and some of the great symbols and images take on a timeless quality which adds to their appeal. In newly constructed liturgies, as well as having biblical material, I would want to see much non-biblical material: poetry, fiction, drama, non-fiction, film, video, and material from the Internet. A good contemporary liturgy not only provides a satisfying and challenging vehicle for worship, for reaching out towards the mystery of life, but also for giving expression to who we believe we are, and from whence we opine that we have come, in so far as we can understand ourselves. In a relevant liturgy we will find the opportunity for experiencing the joys and pains of life, for affirming our worth and values, and for reminding ourselves of our immense responsibilities on this precious planet as we struggle towards a lifestyle of sustainable development and inter-generational justice.

I have been challenged by Maurice Wiles in relation to my assessment of the significance for us today of the biblical imagery and symbols (see Appendix F). He wrote:

> If symbolic language is as central to religious faith, as I think we both believe it to be, is it not possible for more of the traditional imagery to serve the spiritual quest to which you want to contribute?

He noted that contemporary poets still draw powerfully on such imagery. I agree with him about our poets. I think, for example, of an ancient symbol, such as fire, found not just in the Bible. God is spoken of as a consuming fire, something quite terrifying. Hymn writers refer to the fire of love. T. S. Eliot took up the theme of fire in 'Little Gidding':

> The only hope, or else despair
> Lies in the choice of pyre or pyre –
> To be redeemed from fire or fire.
>
> Who then devised the torment? Love.
> Love is the unfamiliar Name
> Behind the hands that wove
> The intolerable shirt of flame
> Which human power cannot remove.
> We only live, only suspire
> Consumed by either fire or fire.

Did R. S. Thomas have the symbol of fire in his mind in his poem 'The Presence', from *The Laboratories of the Spirit*?

> and seen the reflection
> in an eternal mirror of the mystery
> terrifying enough to be named love

The Bible is full of symbols – light, water, fire, earth, cloud, darkness, bread, wind, and storm – to mention just some of them. I am sure that Maurice Wiles makes a valid point in referring to what is rooted in the past. As he implies, poets go on giving the 'old' fresh expression. But a part of me is not quite satisfied. I can see the value of the familiar and the tradition-bound images and symbols. However, I need too the images and symbols that were not dreamt of long ago, and that come out of our present and very different world. Wiles also wrote in his response to me:

My own view is that the sense of a surrounding mystery of love that we call God, strong enough to shape and inspire our attitudes to the world and to one another, needs particular images that are rooted in the past, have grown over time and thus have deep resonance in the tradition to which a person belongs. (Rahner has been a significant influence here.) So for me the stories of Jesus and 'the myth of God incarnate' are not, despite all the problems they raise, alienating in the way you describe; rather they have the potential, appropriately understood, to serve as powerful symbols of the spiritual realities that you want to affirm.

Chapter 13

Jesus of history – credible and elusive

To my mind, all religious traditions are pointing to the ineffable and the indescribable and contain questions about meaning and purpose (the meaning of both our own lives and that of the universe). They all evolve over time and contain much diversity of thinking and believing; they are continuously in need of re-interpretation. The historic creeds of Christianity, as well as the documents that came to form the New Testament, were formulated in thought forms that belong to a very different age to ours. In my articles and in media interviews I have been trying to express, in contemporary language, the meaning of faith from within the perspective of an evolving Christian tradition. I have joined a discussion and a debate that has been going on since our modern era began and in which there have been many conflicting viewpoints expressed.

The Shoah (the Holocaust), as well as the assumptions on which our modern scientific understanding of the world are based, are commonly cited as reasons for questioning belief in an interventionist God. Does this mean, therefore, that it does not make sense to understand, in a literal way, the story of the Son of God being sent from heaven to be the Savior of the world? Does it mean that we cannot rationally take this story to refer to something that happened as a historical event? If it is not true as a historical fact, can the story be true in some other way?

Two other issues concern me, which relate to life both in Ireland and throughout the world. It seems to me that the implications of believing in a non-interventionist God affect dialogue between members of the Christian faith tradition and those of other faith traditions. In the past Christians have seen their tradition as having a superior position in relation to others, because of their doctrine of the Incarnation (for which belief in an interventionist God is required if incarnation is held to be more than metaphor, relating to something true historically). Second, the image of God in the Christian tradition comes across as primarily male (think of the doctrine of the Trinity: one God, Father, Son and Holy Spirit or the Lord's Prayer: 'Our Father'). While there have been female images of God in Christianity's evolving tradition, e.g. 'mother' in Julian of Norwich's writings, they have never had a sufficiently important place, to my mind. As the implications of believing in a non-interventionist God are worked out, it seems to me that there can be much greater emphasis put on the notion that God transcends gender and is not to be thought of as primarily male. I believe we need far more symbols and images that come from the feminine world, as well as to hear more frequently the female voice speaking to the world, in both compassion and fury, in the name of her God. And whether speaking in the name of God or not, we certainly need far more women in places like the United Nations Security Council and in other key areas where men dominate, such as peace commissions, human rights organizations, and ecology forums.

We need to begin at the Enlightenment.

The Enlightenment, usually dated from c.1650-1780, saw the end of the pre-scientific medieval world-view. Beliefs such as volcanoes and avalanches being acts of God or famine and disease being punishments from God or a person being capable of wielding supernatural powers belonged to that old world-view. So did belief in an interventionist God. The Enlightenment heralded the new age of Reason. Since the seventeenth century both the understanding of history and the methods of historical investigation have developed very considerably and continue to do so. It has put theology and the 'beliefs of the faithful' into crisis.

For theologians it has meant trying to distinguish between the 'Jesus of history' and the 'Christ of faith':

> The distinction between the two figures is the difference between a historical person who lived in a particular time and place and was subject to the limitations of a finite existence, and a figure who has been assigned a mythical role, in which he descends from heaven to rescue humankind and, of course, eventually returns there. (*The Five Gospels*, p. 7, eds. Robert W. Funk, Roy W. Hoover, and the Jesus Seminar)

The ground-breaking work of scholars such as Hermann Samuel Reimarus (1694-1768) and David Friedrich Strauss (1808-1874), in what is called the first quest for the historical Jesus, was succeeded by Albert Schweitzer (1875-1965) in the second quest for the historical Jesus. These two quests have been built upon by scholars from around the world. Irish scholars, such as Sean Freyne, have made significant contributions. Today's scholarship is called the third quest for the historical Jesus:

> The question of the historical Jesus was stimulated by the prospect of viewing Jesus through the new lens of historical reason and research rather than through the perspective of theology and traditional creedal formulations. (*The Five Gospels*, p. 2, eds. Robert W. Funk, Roy W. Hoover, and the Jesus Seminar)

It was seen that the documents of the New Testament, and other Christian writings of the same era, contain the stories of the 'Christ of faith' and that it requires considerable 'detective work' to find the 'Jesus of history' behind and within some of those stories. The vast range of differing interpretations of Jesus and of his significance and meaning that has emerged over the last 250 years has been affected by the stage that modern historical methods and self-understanding had reached and by the current dominating philosophical climate of the day. It has also been influenced by the socio-economic, political and cultural backgrounds of the scholars and by a variety of other factors that relate to hidden assumptions and motives, values, personality and gender differences and psychological and spiritual development. We will never be able to reconstruct the whole story of Jesus, and it would always be a reconstruction. None of us knew him in person; we do not have that sort of knowledge. However, with all the new information available today, we can reconstruct his story better than scholars could 100 years ago.

The search for the historical Jesus has been aided by new knowledge about the socio-economic conditions under which he lived, the extent of Hellenization in first-century Palestine and the nature of provincial life in that part of the Roman Empire, together with archaeological findings. Over the last 50 years there has been an emphasis on the Jewishness of Jesus, of the Jewish culture that shaped and conditioned his mind and thinking, his outlook and attitudes. The discovery in the twentieth century of the Dead Sea Scrolls and the Nag Hammadi manuscripts (including the *Gospel of Thomas*) has also contributed to a fuller understanding. However, to my mind, a major factor has been the methods developed to assess the probability of the words of Jesus, as recorded primarily in the Gospels, being his authentic words. One eminent Fellow of the Jesus Seminar estimates that about 50 per cent of the words ascribed to Jesus in the Synoptic Gospels (Matthew, Mark, Luke), John's Gospel, and the *Gospel of Thomas* do not contain the authentic words of Jesus. Each age and culture, no matter how modern the techniques of historical investigation used, will to some extent find its own 'Jesus of history', who will relate to the social reality in which the Church of the day finds itself. A range of criteria has been developed and refined over the last 200 years to aid scholars in finding the words most likely to have been said by Jesus. If he only spoke in Aramaic, then with a few exceptions the best we have are the Greek translations of those words. These criteria fall into a number of main groups:

It is possible to see how one writer has altered the text of another writer (for example, the authors of Matthew or Luke have changed the text of Mark's Gospel).

Jesus used a distinctive language and oral style found in aphorisms and parables.

Sometimes the needs and problems of the Church were addressed by words of Jesus put on his lips by the Church.

The beliefs of the Church about the significance of Jesus were expressed by Jesus himself through the construction of sayings and speeches put on his lips.

This is but the briefest summary of a complex area of scholarship over which there is diversity of opinion.

Chapter 14

Christ of faith – symbol and archetype

There are differences as well as similarities between my current thinking about the Jesus of history and that of the Jesus Seminar and their founder, Robert Funk (see both *The Five Gospels*, *Honest to Jesus* and *A Credible Jesus* by Robert Funk and *Re-Imagine the World* by Bernard Brandon Scott). They would see Jesus as a wandering sage (or teacher) and John the Baptist as an eschatological prophet. I, too, see Jesus as a wandering sage, teaching through remarkable parables and unusual aphorisms. I also see both Jesus and John the Baptist as 'end-time' prophets who expected a supernatural intervention by God to restore the fortunes of their nation. God would give back to them both independence and peace in a kingdom ruled by him. We agree in thinking that the first generation of Christians thought that Jesus would return within their lifetimes to usher them into a new kingdom, now envisaged as being in heaven.

The ancient community of Israel was a small nation by comparison with the much bigger ones who dominated life in the Middle East over the period beginning 1000 years before the birth of Jesus. The members of this community believed that their God was intimately involved with their history, out of his love for them as 'his own people'. They developed a way to understand their defeats and misfortunes as expressing both the anger of their God and his punishment on them for their disobedience to him and his laws. After their experience of exile in Babylon (beginning in 586 BCE), and in the centuries following, some of them developed a hope that some day their God would drive their enemies away forever. Their fortunes as a nation would be restored.

For this strand of Judaism, it was a nationalistic and religious utopian vision. Their God would reign in power and glory. This new kingdom, which would follow on after the resurrection of the dead and the judgment of all, was thought by various groups in first-century Judaism to be around the corner. The Essene community living at the Dead Sea expected it at any moment and John the Baptist saw it as his mission to warn people about it. According to John the Baptist the judgment would be fearsome. The group called the Sadducees, who did not believe in the resurrection of the dead, would not have agreed with this vision.

What some Jews assumed at this time, in the development of Israel's religious tradition, were a number of beliefs. First of all, they did not think of people when they died as going 'straight to heaven' to enter an eternal dimension of life. Rather, they thought of their dead as waiting in some shadowy existence below the ground for the arrival of the judgment day. Before the exile they had not believed in an afterlife at all; it was a relatively recent belief for them to have adopted. Second, they seem to have thought that God would appoint an agent for the task of bringing in the new kingdom (a Messiah, several Messiahs, or a Son of Man figure?). Third, they appeared to believe that there would be a time of tribulation and trial before the day when the new kingdom would dawn (see the book of Daniel and the Gospels).

Whether Jesus of Nazareth was a wandering sage or rabbi, or an 'end-time' prophet like John the Baptist, his aphorisms and parables are part of his continuing legacy. Pontius Pilate probably sentenced Jesus to death because he appeared to be looked on by some of the volatile pilgrims, who had arrived in Jerusalem for the Passover festival, as a Messiah. Neither Pilate nor the Jewish leadership wanted civil unrest fired by deep religious beliefs and nationalistic hopes.

We will never know for certain what triggered the disciples' claims that God had raised Jesus to new life beyond the grave. I am inclined to think that their claims were triggered by visionary experiences, which were interpreted by people wearing the lenses of Jewish eschatology. I do not believe in a physical resurrection, even one in which the body of Jesus was alleged to have unusual properties. One thing is clear to me. Believers in God agree that the existence of God cannot be proved, although in the Christian tradition attempts have been made to do so by many distinguished theologians through the centuries, including Anselm and Aquinas. If God's existence cannot be proved, then I believe it follows that the disciples needed faith to believe in Jesus' resurrection, for only God could bring back to life someone who had died. If the disciples met Jesus, after his death, in a way that did not require faith, then his resurrection would be a proof of God's existence. So for me this means that Jesus' resurrection belongs to the faith stories that emerged about him after his death, a point not always (I think) clearly appreciated. These stories belong, with others, to what are called the stories of the 'Christ of faith'. We have noted already another related belief: that he would come back again to usher in the new kingdom. Very soon after Jesus' death his followers ceased to think of this kingdom as an earthly one; it became a heavenly kingdom. In fact, Jesus has not returned as they expected, and the world has continued on its way.

The various interpretations of the meaning that the first generation of Christians found in the death of the Jesus of history also came to form part of the faith stories of the 'Christ of faith'. Their scriptures were hugely influential in the task of drawing out the meaning of his life and death as they were now coming to perceive it. He was believed to be the one who had destroyed human death, which had come into the world as a result of sin. Second, they believed he had borne, through accepting death, the punishment that should have been faced by the rest of the human race (those already dead, those who were alive, and those not yet born). Third, his death was believed to have been a sacrifice made to God.

Many people (though not by any means all who subscribe to the Christian faith) recognize difficulties in these interpretations of what Jesus' death was believed to have meant or achieved. Some of their objections are these:

From science, death is a natural process and not (as traditionally believed) a punishment for sin and a power needing to be defeated (e.g. Romans 5:12: "Therefore as sin came into the world through one man and death through sin, and so death spread to all because all men sinned").

From ethics, an innocent person (claimed to be Jesus) should not bear the punishment of the guilty (e.g. Romans chapters 5 and 6).

From theology, to require for the forgiveness/salvation process a human death and sacrifice suggests divine sadism (e.g. Hebrews 9:11-14: "But when Christ appeared as a high priest of the good things to come, then through the greater and more perfect tent (not made with hands, that is, not of this creation) he entered once for all into the Holy Place, taking not the blood of goats and calves but his own blood, thus securing an eternal redemption. For if the sprinkling of defiled persons with the blood of goats and bulls and with ashes of a heifer sanctifies for the purification of the flesh, how much more shall the blood of Christ, who through the eternal spirit offered himself without blemish to God, purify your conscience from dead works to serve the living God").

Whatever one may think of these objections; it is clear that for the first generation of Christians the human Jesus of history became in their faith stories a Savior and a Mediator. The Christ of faith was growing in meaning and significance for them. The faith stories, whether they are his birth stories or the theological discourses put on Jesus' lips in St John's Gospel, all help to portray who the Christ of faith was for Christians of the first century CE. Some of the stories would speak of him as God's pre-existent Son and of the Word made flesh (John 1:1: "and the Word was God").

Theologians today examine the Mediterranean world of this first century, in which the Gospel was formulated and preached. They know of its many other religions, especially those that speak of a dying and rising God. It was a world very different to ours in the twenty-first century. People then believed in interventionist gods; in some of the stories they told, these gods might procreate children of human and divine parenthood. In Acts 14 we read that some of the people of Lystra could say of Paul and Barnabas: "The gods have come down to us in the likeness of men!" (v 11); "Barnabas they called Zeus, and Paul, because he was the chief speaker, they called Hermes. And the priest of Zeus, whose temple was in front of the city, brought oxen and garlands to the gates and wanted to offer sacrifice with the people" (vs 12-13). It was a world where, for worship, animal sacrifice was common, as in the Temple worship of Judaism in Jerusalem. It was a time when the Roman emperor was sacrificed to as another god, a world where there was a strong belief in the supernatural and where many miracles were believed to have happened. It was held that special people could perform supernatural actions.

The Jesus of history, believed to be risen and alive, believed to be the Savior of the end-time, was now being interpreted and believed to be a divinity as well. The title 'Lord' suggests a belief in divinity. The Christ of faith and the stories of what was believed about him continued to grow; there was much diversity and pluralism. In the centuries leading up to the formation of the historic creeds of the early Church most attention related to doctrines of the Incarnation and of the Trinity. The chief reason for the creeds was not because the Church of the day simply wanted to produce a contemporary statement of faith, but because there were so many interpretations of Jesus and theories about the nature of God. There was a good deal of conflict within the Church over these issues. Diversity and pluralism are far from new. All of this was taking place in a pre-scientific world in which interventionist gods were believed to be continuously at work. If it was possible then to believe, in a literal sense, in a person who was both fully divine and fully a human being, it is very difficult to do so in the twenty-first century. This is a part of the controversy in which I am engaged. One of my consultants, Bishop John Baker (see Appendix F), claims that Incarnation is a non-negotiable doctrine of Anglicanism and that it means that God became a human being in the life of Jesus. He does not think that Jesus had two minds, a human one and a divine one, as was once thought. He believes Jesus was fully human and like any other person was limited in his thinking by the knowledge and conceptions of his day. He accepts that as a human being Jesus would not and could not have been conscious of being divine. For me, the problem with this belief is that I cannot see how, if someone had met Jesus, they would have established a claim that he was more than human, in the sense required if one is to believe that God became a human being. To my mind, all one would have been able to say was that one had met a remarkable, extraordinary, and deeply spiritual and loving person. I say this now against the background of nearly 2000 years of Christian history during which the stories of Jesus Christ have rooted themselves deeply in millions of people's psyches. The subject of those stories has become both symbol and archetype. In Christian literature and art – in paintings, music, drama, and sculpture – the creative imagination has soared to extraordinary heights, as it has pondered the symbol and the archetype, in an endeavor to catch something more of what the words of faith struggle to suggest and to convey.

Chapter 15

Distinguishing the Jesus of history from the Christ of faith

What are the connections, as I see them, between the Jesus of history, whose story lies behind and within the stories of the Christ of faith found in the New Testament and in other early Christian writings, and the stories of the Christ of faith and the mysterious God we reach out to, seeking to adore and serve him? I referred briefly to the parables and other sayings of the Jesus of history. In these he speaks of his belief (as a member of the ancient community of Israel) that God can be trusted to be both infinitely loving and endlessly forgiving. The Christ of faith, believed to be both savior and divine, embodies these values of love and forgiveness. There would have been no Christ of faith if there had not been, first, a Jesus of history. However, if the stories of the Christ of faith are not to be taken in a literal and historical sense, they can still have another sort of truth.

The Christ of faith stories point to the mysterious God of infinite love and endless forgiveness, whom both Jesus and his followers had believed in, and who is still believed and trusted in today. The stories of the Christ of faith say that we are found to be loveable, forgivable, and reconcilable by God. This is what is believed to be true. It is this same faith-claim that is metaphorically referred to in the Pauline saying, "In Christ God was reconciling the world to himself" (2 Cor. 5:19). The stories of the Christ of faith, telling of his birth, death, and resurrection, are metaphors of faith that transcend the literal and point us to what are claimed to be realities beyond our normal range of knowledge.

Confusing the stories of the Jesus of history and the stories of the Christ of faith has caused immense trouble for the Churches. It has not been easy for many people to make the distinction between them, particularly since the Christ of faith stories (about the coming and return of a Son of God as savior, mediator, and divine person) are intimately connected to the stories of the Jesus of history, the man from Nazareth. One example would be the stories of Jesus' resurrection appearances. Many Christians would still see them as historical reports, albeit of an unusual and unique event. Mary, so the faith story goes, met the risen Christ and saw him with her own eyes; here was the man she had come to know and love over the last few years and who had been put to death by crucifixion on the previous Friday. Other faith stories tell of how the disciples had a meal with the risen Christ; again he is the same person that they had shared supper with on the previous Thursday evening. As was noted earlier, only God can raise someone back to life after he or she has died.

If the resurrection stories really were descriptions of historical events, then it would prove the existence of God, a proof that believers do not accept as possible. We believe God exists, we do not know it. So this means, to my mind, that the resurrection stories are faith stories and belong to the Christ of faith stories, stories whose truth is not dependent on them being taken literally, as descriptions of historical events, but rather is dependent on a metaphorical and symbolic interpretation: they point to what we believe to be true about God and his love and forgiveness. Indeed, even to speak of historical objectivity is to use a post-Enlightenment concept and, therefore, to introduce a reverse anachronism to the first century. Many scholars consider that first-century writers were primarily concerned with expressing meaning rather than historical literalism in the modern sense.

I believe that Jesus would be both amazed and horrified if he were able to come back and meet us today. As a practicing Jew, he would have had no idea that a new religion had been founded in his name, of the beliefs formulated about him, or of the forms of worship in which his name and his story figure so prominently. In my view, he would be most surprised to discover that a 'Christ symbol' or archetype had been created that has sunk deep into many a person's psyche. He would be taken aback to learn that many people speak of their relationship with the mystery of God as a relationship with this Christ figure. To my mind, he might soon learn that this symbolic figure is pointing both to the mystery of a suffering and loving God and to the potential for human beings to become more 'Christ-like' in qualities of vulnerable love, self-sacrifice, and goodness. He would feel very remote from our world and culture. It goes without saying that he lived in a very different world from ours today. Yet despite all the differences, he does share some fundamental values with those who sense that they have some significant things in common with him.

Is there a way to understand the metaphor of incarnation that takes us away from having to use the Greek and Latin philosophical concepts of the first five centuries CE, which suggested it was plausible to believe that in the one 'person' there could be both a human person and a divine person? I share with others a belief that the Church is in transition as it continues to move from the pre-scientific, supernatural world in which its creeds were formulated to a modern world. Space needs to be provided for fresh thought. This is how the Church's intellectual life has progressed in the past. There are many examples of how, over differing issues, some members' thinking went ahead of the 'corporate faith' of the Church as an institution and then later on the 'corporate faith' caught up with its membership.

Theologians do their work of thinking about God, as do 'ordinary believers', by using a range of different analogies, metaphors, and symbols. Two of the ways in which the relationship between human beings and God has been imagined involve thinking in both personal and non-personal analogies. Using a non-personal analogy we can think of God as like an ocean: we, and all the rest of her creation, are the waves on the ocean. Speaking like this, we can state a belief that we live in God or say that God is in everything. Using the images of ocean and wave poetically we can say that God (as ocean) knows the life of the wave from the inside: God is in the wave. Here is a way to express that the divinity of God was intimately connected with the humanity of the Jesus of history, that God knew human life and experience from the 'inside', by being so connected to Jesus. Clearly, however, such a connection is unique only in the sense that each human being's life is believed to be unique.

On the other hand, to use personal analogies is to think in terms of an 'I-Thou' relationship, as Martin Buber described it. Here, God is thought of as like a person. We stand before such an all-embracing God as beings who have been created as moral beings, held accountable and responsible. While some theologians, such as Harry Williams, have sought to use incarnation as a metaphor in this way, my own feeling is that it is better simply to speak of immanence and transcendence. So the metaphor of ocean and wave speaks of the immanence of God, while the 'I-Thou' relationship speaks of transcendence. It is not a question of one or the other metaphor; they need to be held together in tension. It is not 'either-or' but 'both-and'.

While a considerable number of the members of the Christian Churches no longer find it credible to believe in an afterlife, and might interpret concepts such as 'resurrection' in terms of this life's experiences, I find myself still believing in life after death. A life after death is not something that I can prove, any more than I can prove the existence of God. However, because I believe that we are infinitely precious to God, and loved and valued beyond our imaginings, I still find it plausible to believe that there is meaning beyond death in a new moral universe, which we cannot begin to conceive. It is highly mysterious, but such is the goodness of God that I believe and trust that all evil will finally be vanquished – but in that deeply demanding way of 'overcoming evil by doing good'.

We are social beings whose humanity is significantly dependent on our relationships, not just with each other but with the cosmos and its Creator. I find it appalling that so many of us, particularly in the so-called developed world, go on daring to live lifestyles in painful contradiction to our professed beliefs and values: we live in a global village full of the horror, humiliation, and neglect of others' basic needs as people. The sociologist, Francis Fukuyama, in his book, *The Great Disruption*, on the transition from an industrial age to an information age, wrote that he thinks that the mainline religions will see a decrease in the importance of the creedal aspects of their evolving faith traditions (see Chapter 22). He has suggested that people will go on joining the mainline Churches for several reasons. They will want to belong to a community with a value system that their children can be brought up in. They will want a community with rituals, rites, and resonance that connect deeply with the past. He believes that there will be more emphasis on orthopraxy (right practice) and much less on orthodoxy (right belief); the creedal aspect of religious traditions will be recognized for what it is: a rational wrestling with mystery where there can legitimately be considerable diversity in the speculation undergone.

A point that he does not make is that the stories both of the Jesus of history and of the Christ of faith will almost certainly function like the great plays of someone like Shakespeare. For generations, people have found that a production of *Hamlet*, *Macbeth*, or *King Lear* has spoken with power and meaning to them and has helped them understand a little more of the mystery of what it means to be human. So too, in all probability, the Christian stories will continue to speak with power and meaning to our human condition, so long as ways are found to interpret them for our culture and world-view.

Even in the pre-scientific age of interventionist gods, people were aware of the hiddenness, silence, and mystery of such gods. In our modern age, this hiddenness, silence, and mystery are more apparent. The sense of the silence, absence, and unknowability of God has pervaded the modern era, fills the poetry of someone like R. S. Thomas, and was reflected on deeply by Simone Weil. It raises the question of who are we in the face of such mystery.

I have written elsewhere of religions as being like motorways that are constantly in need of another lane (Appendix C). In other words, I am saying that it is normal for there to be much diversity within an evolving religious tradition. Some will travel along a conservative lane, some down an evangelical lane, some down a liberal or radical lane. As new understandings and interpretations emerge, more lanes are required to accommodate those journeying with fresh ideas. Ultimately, to live with faith is to admit that we do not know for sure about God or indeed about the rightness of our ethical commitment. God may or may not exist. We remain problematic to ourselves and life retains its mysterious quality. Part of our identity, wrote John Caputo, is that we do not know who we are. W. H. Auden thought that one good way to live with this sense of the mystery of who we really are is by laughter, which is both a protest and an acceptance.

> When we truly laugh, we laugh simultaneously with and at. True laughter (belly laughter) I would define as the spirit of carnival … [It] celebrates the unity of our human race as mortal creatures. We are all in the same boat. We come into this world, depart from it without our

consent. We are problematic to ourselves. Carnival's solution is to laugh, for laughter is simultaneously a protest and an acceptance. During Carnival all social distinctions are suspended, even that of sex. Young men dress up as girls, young girls as boys. The escape from social personality is symbolized by the wearing of masks. (*Forewords and Afterwords*, p.471)

The broad Church, which I believe it is important to maintain, will continue to contain diversity of thinking and believing as the stories of Christianity, preserved and interpreted within the Christian community, are passed on to the next generation. In particular, I believe the understandings of the Christ of faith stories will continue to require to be received with tolerance, broad-mindedness, generosity of spirit, and mutual respect, as believers remain mindful that nobody knows for certain when it comes to the things of God.

Chapter 16

Leaving Jesus to his place in history

Christians wrote the Gospels from the perspective of faith. They believed that Jesus had been raised from the dead and now sat at his Father's right hand in glory waiting to return, at any moment, at the end of the world as divine Savior and Judge. I have explained already why I do not see the historical Jesus of Nazareth as also to have literally been the 'Christ of faith' of the Church. I do not believe, in a literal sense, in the presence of the Risen Christ: "Lo, I am with you always to the close of the age" Matthew 28:20.

I have studied the books of New Testament scholars who have attempted to 'discover' the historical Jesus, what he said and did. For those not familiar with the principles of such historical research, an excellent introduction is the book, *The Jesus Seminar and its critics*, by Robert J. Miller. In it he describes what he calls the third principle:

> The third principle is this: all history is reconstruction. The events of the past are gone forever. They can influence the present and, strictly speaking, the present is created by the lingering effects of the past. But past events in their 'pastness' can exist only in memory and imagination. Since we have no memories of events earlier than our own childhoods, the historical Jesus has to be reconstructed. It has to be pieced together from the evidence left behind, much as archaeologists reconstruct ancient buildings from the few pieces left on the ground. (p. 41)

One of the implications of our modern understanding of history is that it may mean that the significance of a person or an event may only become apparent over time. People sometimes will say that 'we are too close now to the events to be able to judge them with any real objectivity.' This is not to suggest that we do not bring some interpretation to the reconstruction that is history writing, for we always do. My statement about leaving Jesus to his place in history needs thinking about. None of us knew him; he lived and died nearly 2000 years ago. His story is constructed and told in different ways, depending on people's beliefs and interpretations. For me, his story lives on, but because I do not believe him to have literally been our Savior nor now a divine presence with us always, he comes across to me as, in many ways, an alien figure from a distant and a very different culture.

His story does not dominate my life, though there are parts of it that remain a continuing inspiration, a challenge, a help to me in constructing my vision of what I hope God is like. His teaching about loving one's enemies stand as a permanent challenge to the human race, as does his call to give special attention to the marginalized and the poor in society. Speaking for myself, I need, though, spiritual inspiration and ethical challenge from more contemporary sources too – from the ordinary and the extraordinary people who share life with us now in this century.

We have no photographs or paintings of how Jesus really looked; we know very little about his childhood, his psychological development, his teenage life and interests or his young adult life; we do not know his sexual orientation. We do not know the sound of his voice; we do not know his tastes in food. We do know that his world-view and culture were very different from those of the twenty-first century and we can be fairly certain that, were he able to come and experience ours, he would feel very alien within it.

The real historical person, Jesus of Nazareth, never thought about the many problems that concern us in our day and he simply could not have done so. He never exercised his mind on issues to do with genetic engineering or United Nations Security Resolutions; it would never have occurred to him to think about over-population, threats to the environment, or nuclear war. To my mind, though others will disagree, in an evolving religious tradition, as Christianity is, the significance of Jesus' ideas diminishes.

It is one thing to recognize this, it is quite another matter to actively diminish the constant references to the imaginary figure, Jesus Christ, the Lord of the Church. This figure of faith has entered into the psyches of Christians in every generation and will be hard to extract. Not that most Christians contemplate such action. Every time Christians meet to worship, this imaginary figure of faith inhabits the world of their worship. It will take huge radical change, as I have been arguing in other chapters, to make significant changes in this regard. The point was made to me that at the Reformation the Protestant Churches gave up devotions to Mary, the mother of Jesus. Will there be another reformation when people will give up their devotions to Mary's son?

In the epilogue to his book, *Why Christianity must change or die*, J. S. Spong wrote:

> Is my reformulation of Christianity adequate for our new world? I would be surprised if it is judged to be so. It is at least the best I know how to offer at this moment, given when I live and how far into the future I can see. But if I were asked to bet on what will happen tomorrow, my best guess would be that my approach will prove to be

not too radical, as my critics will claim, but rather not nearly radical enough. I suspect that the next generation might even dismiss me as an old-fashioned religious man who could not quite cut the umbilicus to the past in order to enter the future. (p. 227)

There is a clear sense that Spong feels it important to go on holding onto Jesus; he remains the 'God-bearer'. By contrast, people like myself see a need now "to leave Jesus to his place in history and to move on" and want to take the scissors and cut the "umbilical cord" between ourselves and Jesus. Or, to put it in another way, Jesus no longer functions as an archetype for us. Monica Furlong wrote: "One of the symbols Jung cited was that of Jesus as the 'archetype of the self' that is to say the symbol which helped us as individuals or as groups to become what is in us to become." (*C of E: The State It's In*, p. 96)

Preachers, especially of an evangelistic outlook, will ask their congregations whether they truly love Jesus, their divine Savior and their Lord. They believe Jesus, in a literal sense, to be God – come to live a human life. Have they placed their lives into his hands and surrendered their hearts to him? For me, it would be impossible to preach like this. I do not think you can have a real relationship with a person from another era, even if you believe that such a person is alive in heaven. H. A. Williams wrote: "Or as the preacher puts it in John Steinbeck's novel, *The Grapes of Wrath*: 'Don't you love Jesus?' Well, I thought and thought, and finally I says, 'No, I don't know nobody name' Jesus. I know a bunch of stories, but I only love people.'" (*Poverty, Chastity and Obedience*, p.118)

Not every person who has some sympathy with my position will feel drawn to being quite so radical, and some may feel happier with the current position as described above by John Shelby Spong. Likewise, there are liberal Christians, such as those associated with The Center for Progressive Christianity, for whom Jesus is still clearly very important. In the Eight Points by which they define Progressive Christianity they state:

> By calling ourselves progressive, we mean that we are Christians who proclaim Jesus Christ as our Gate to the realm of God ... understand our sharing of bread and wine in Jesus' name to be a representation of God's feast for all peoples.

They do not accept the doctrinal 'savior' language codified in the fourth-century creeds, such as Jesus being the sacrificial Lamb of God.

I am indebted to William Shakespeare. If asked to choose one line from his plays, it would be from *Hamlet*: "To thine own self be true." I like that quotation from *Hamlet* very much, because it resonates with integrity and authenticity – important values for me. If asked to choose from among Jesus of Nazareth's teaching, what I liked best, it would come from the parable of the Good Samaritan. Though if you pressed me, I would admit that I cannot be 100 per cent certain that this parable, as it is found in the Gospel of Luke, actually records the very words of Jesus (in translation, of course). As the Samaritan made his journey, he came across the injured victim, and the parable says: "He came where he was" (Luke 10:33). Those words have underlain my pastoral ministry over nearly 30 years. I cannot stand completely in other people's shoes and share their experience fully. However, in both suffering and joy, and perhaps especially in the former, I have tried to come compassionately to where people are in all their hurting and pain, with their anguish, tears, and questions. It is a matter of trying to get onto their wavelength and trying to see and feel things as they are doing. It is a costly exercise of both the heart and mind, as well as a rare privilege. If Jesus had told no other story but this parable, with those significant words, "He came where he was," I would still remain in his debt and be grateful for them. It does need to be pointed out, of course, that the words, as Jesus meant them, described a physical action, but it was an action inspired by concern and compassion. The door was already open for a spiritual interpretation of these words. So I do not mean that I have no place in my life for the story of the historical Jesus; there is a place, but it is certainly not as big a place as it seems to be in many other people's lives, but then we interpret his significance differently.

Chapter 17

An interventionist God in question

I find it rather terrifying to have to admit it, but I do not believe in an interventionist God. One of the consequences of not believing in an interventionist God is to accept that such a God would let us annihilate ourselves in a nuclear war, or in some other way. We, as human beings, and other living beings too, would all disappear from the face of this precious planet. There would be nobody to mourn our passing; there would be no grief. The millions of other galaxies would continue on their way and our own Milky Way would not miss us either. The story of the ending of the human race would go unreported. It could happen. I belong to the generation born after the invention of the nuclear bomb and have lived with the threat to our survival that it poses.

Our modern understanding of the universe in which we are privileged to live makes the old belief in an interventionist God implausible and incredible. In their prayers and liturgies, people of various religions still use words that would suggest that there is a protector God out there, waiting to intervene when necessary. If people started to pray as the second plane came straight for the Twin Towers in New York on 11 September 2001, it made no difference to their safety. No God miraculously changed the flight path of that plane, with its pilots bent on destruction and death. Nor did prayers prevent bombs reigning down on Baghdad in the horror of its destruction. No God has stopped flooded rivers from breaking their banks; no God has prevented an avalanche from crashing down on top of an Alpine village; no God has reduced the power of a major earthquake so that it simply sends a gentle tremor through the surface of the earth. No God intervened to prevent or speedily halt the Holocaust or the multitude of other instances of genocide, the cruelties of torture or of other wars.

The main religions began in a very different world, when it was commonly believed that the gods constantly intervened in the affairs of the world. The gods were responsible for both good and bad events happening in the world. They sent famine and flooding, earthquakes and disease. It was believed, then, that they used these terrible methods to express their displeasure with their human subjects. It was accepted that they also sent good harvests and empowered people with good health, and in doing so expressed their approval and benevolence. In Greek mythology the sons of the gods came down to earth and had intercourse with the daughters of men. In some of the old religions such relationships were not seen as incredible and implausible. People believed in the stories that spoke of such events.

If you are taking a more literalist approach, then you will claim that at the heart of a Christianity, in which Jesus is believed to be literally divine and literally the Savior of the world, is a belief in a unique action by an interventionist God. This God became a human being. The belief may be put in its traditional form by saying that God the Father sent his Son into the world to live a human life. The person claimed to be both human and divine was Jesus of Nazareth. He became the Savior of the world, it is claimed, by dying on the cross, and then was raised to new life again; soon afterwards he returned to heaven to his Father. When I was studying in preparation for working as a clergyman, I came to think that such beliefs were no longer credible. I began my working life in 1972 and was requested by my bishop to resign in 2002. For many people, this has meant that I have been a hypocrite and a heretic, a person guilty of a major deception, for 30 years. I deserve neither respect nor sympathy.

The position that I subscribe to in this book is that I do not understand religious language in a literal sense. I understand it in a metaphorical sense, and in a symbolical sense too. If statements are going to be made such as: "Jesus is our savior," then this needs unpacking. We need to ask what is its metaphorical meaning. Is it not stating the conviction that "we are found loveable, forgivable, and reconcilable by God"? Is it not also a statement of belief about ourselves: that we see ourselves in the sight of God to be people who are loveable, forgivable, and reconcilable? The symbolical meaning takes us beyond words and points us to a realm that words fail to describe. In so far as religions continue to support belief in an interventionist God, I consider that they are in need of radical modernization if they are to survive as credible belief systems.

The challenge to Christianity is huge. In a radically reformed Christianity, Jesus of Nazareth would no longer be proclaimed to be the savior of the world in a literal sense; he would no more be understood to be both human and divine; he would not dominate the liturgy of the Churches; there would be no more Mass or Eucharist.

It seems to me evident that religions evolve and develop over the period of their existence. We accept that scientific subjects will go on developing and evolving. What physicists knew 100 years ago is much less than what is known today. Arts subjects, such as history or philosophy, also change and develop. One generation of scholars builds on the work of previous ones, assessing and critiquing their achievements and failures. In some of the monotheistic religions, it is clear that at an early stage of their development people believed that each tribe had its own god. It was only later on that such beliefs came to be dispensed with, as people moved on to a belief in one Creator God. In many other ways too, they have evolved and changed.

People familiar with the history of Christianity will know that from the beginning there was much division among Christians about how to interpret the significance of Jesus of Nazareth. Was he just a great prophet, perhaps the Messiah? Fundamentalists need to ask themselves the question if he was divine, then in what way was his being divine related to his being human as well? Could he have had two minds: a divine one and a human one. If so, how would they both have been related to his brain? Was there any interaction between these two minds? There was an element of contingency and of political pressure in the decisions of the great Councils, out of which came the historic Creeds that were seen to define orthodoxy. It was the dominant theology of the day that held sway. Had the debates and conflicts, which have always been characteristic of religions, worked out differently, then the face of Christianity might be very different today. Perhaps many of the wars fought between Christians and those of other faiths might never have taken place. Anti-Semitism might never have flourished and festered in human hearts.

Part of the challenge for believers today is to try to think of new concepts of God. We need new metaphors, new symbols, new analogies, and new images. Religious traditions record the impossibility of the human mind understanding the infinite. In the case of trying to think about God, there are the problems of God, if there is a God, being both unseen and not open to observation and being big enough to account for the universe in which we live. Our thinking about God is speculation; religious history teaches us to expect diversity of thought. Nobody knows for sure what God is like. We are faced by mystery. It is important, though, to understand that the ways in which we think about God relate to our own self-understanding. Is it helpful today, for example, to use an image of God as a 'father'? Does it not imply that we are 'children' in relation to this God? Given the immense responsibilities that we need to face up to in order to create a sustainable form of living on this precious planet, is it a good idea to have being 'children' as a part of our self-image and identity? Do we not need to emphasize our adulthood and all the responsibilities that we need to assume for the sake of ourselves, our world, and its future? If there is no interventionist God, the weight of responsibility on us is all the greater.

If God is characterized by a love that is all-embracing and inclusive, is there not some sense in which the active loving of God makes a difference to that dynamic reality to which God and Creation, time and eternity, and the visible and the invisible belong? I believe there must be. That is why this chapter has the title 'An interventionist God in question'. I have my reasons for not finding it credible to believe in an interventionist God in many ways, but when it comes to the total reality, which in faith we claim exists and that we belong to, then I want to allow space for the hidden mysterious undetectable action of God.

Chapter 18

The absence of God and the mystery of God

In the liturgy of the Churches, phrases like these are common: "The Lord is here; His Spirit is with us." I was at a Church conference where, a number of times, the leader said: "Let us celebrate God's presence among us now." At one level I can agree with these statements of belief. Part of the meaning of the concept of God is that God is present everywhere. God's love is an all-embracing reality. However, in another sense, I feel uncomfortable with these statements. I do not have any sense of the presence of God. I have never had any sense of God supporting me, guiding me, strengthening me, loving me, forgiving me, or correcting me. If there is a God, as I believe there is, then I take it on trust that such a God is loving, forgiving, tolerant, patient, tender, and compassionate. However, I do not experience these things for myself.

Poets such as the Welsh Anglican priest R. S. Thomas, struggled with a similar sense of the absence of God. In one of his poems, 'The Absence', he wrote:

> It is this great absence
> that is like a presence, that compels
> me to address it without hope
> of a reply. It is a room I enter
>
> from which someone has just
> gone, the vestibule for the arrival
> of one who has yet to come.

And in his 'Autobiographies' he speaks about the sense of 'absence': "But we shall never become conscious of the absent as such, only conscious that what we seek for is not present."

This silent, intangible, unseen God is very different from the God that appears to be experienced by many believers and that we read of in much of the Bible. Such a God is the 'talking God', frequently communicating with people. Take, for example, Isaiah 6:8: "And I heard the voice of the Lord saying, 'Whom shall I send, and who will go for us?' Then I said, 'Here am I! Send me.'"

My article 'Pain and Integrity: reform from within' (Appendix A) indicates that I have serious doubts about revelation and the reality of people's so-called experience of this 'talking God'. To my mind, though others would strenuously disagree, such people are interpreting various voices in their heads to be the voice of God, when they give such voices a religious meaning. The power of our imaginations is not to be underestimated; religious experience is partly a product of our imaginations. Even to look at a beautiful sunset and to say it reveals the beauty and glory of God is to draw on the creativity of our imaginations as exercised in the service of our faith.

When I think of God I think of mystery. In this life nobody sees God. In this life we use images and metaphors, analogies and symbols drawn from ordinary human experience to help speak about this mystery we call God. Words such as 'king', 'father', 'shepherd', 'rock', and 'light' have been commonly used. "God is king," "Our Father who art in heaven," "The Lord is my Shepherd," "God is my rock," and "The Lord is my Light," are examples. Many of us as human beings seem unable to restrain ourselves from speaking with each other of this God and, as some of us believe, to this mysterious God as well.

One of the symbols that I use to help me imagine and speak about the relationship between God and the 'human family' is the ring. To use the analogy of marriage for this relationship, or of some other committed relationship for which a ring might be worn, is not new or original. It goes back many centuries to much earlier times. For example, the prophet Hosea used the analogy of God as husband and the nation of Israel as wife. The ring can speak of a commitment 'for better and for worse', of 'a faithfulness no matter what', of 'a love that will not let us go'. Neither the sense of the absence of God nor the awareness of the silence of God need imply that God is reneging on his or her commitment to the world and its people. Could it not be said that we need this absence, mystery, and silence so that we can become fully adult ourselves? Could it not be held that our freedom and responsibility require that terrifying aloneness that is an essential constituent of human maturity, responsibility, and living?

To my mind, when we examine the liturgies of the Churches we find that there is a great deal of fantasy and escapism within them. The liturgies present us with a God who is near at hand to help, who is our protector, our guide, and our support. Is that really how things are? Why so many disasters and tragedies? There is strength to be gained from meeting together with people who share common values with us. We may feel that both our values, and we ourselves too, have been affirmed by the experience of our worshiping together. However, the theology that the liturgies express leads to a false atmosphere, characterized as they are by the presentation in Scripture, prayers, hymns, and frequently in sermons or homilies too, of the interventionist God, the talking God, the God who is alleged to have literally become a human being.

The mystics used the analogy of the ocean and the waves to express their sense of the incredible closeness of God (the 'ocean') to her Creation (the 'waves'). By their growth as human beings, by their striving to reach the heights of their humanity, by their time spent in contemplation, meditation, and prayer, did they reach insights that the rest of us have not had? "My me is God, and I do not know myself save in Him," wrote St Catherine of Genoa. What experiences did these people have which led them, in faith, to make such amazing statements? Could an agnostic or an atheist have had a similar experience, even though he or she would not have interpreted the experience in a religious sense?

Supposing someone says that in the context of great beauty, perhaps through listening to music or being surrounded by a beautiful landscape, she had a deep sense within her of joy and exhilaration, of appreciation and gratitude, a sense of love and of being most truly herself and that all of this was mysteriously combined with a sense of being united with all that is: what are we expected to make of such a statement? Does it tell us something fundamentally true about our lives and the universe in which we live? If given a religious interpretation, does it tell us something that it is credible to believe about the relationship of all life to its Creator? Have not some mystics spoken not only of occasionally having such unifying experiences, but also of being afflicted by a profound emptiness in their lives and by a sense of the absence of God? I like this poem, which I found in Mark Oakley's *The Collage of God* p.73; it captures something of the silence, the mystery, and the absence of God.

First forgive the silence
That answers prayer,
Then forgive the prayer
That stains the silence

Excuse the absence
That feels like presence,
Then excuse the feeling
That insists on presence

Pardon the delay
Of revelation,
Then ask pardon for revealing
Your impatience

Forgive God
For being only a word

Then ask God to forgive
The betrayal of language.
Mark Jarman, 'Psalm: First Forgive the Silence'

My hunch is that, as we go on learning more about the precious planet which we inhabit, often so irresponsibly, and the universe of which it is a tiny little part, we will discover more and more about how all life is interconnected and interdependent. We may well discover new types of energy that will help explain much that remains unexplained and mysterious today. I think of such things as the relation of mind to matter, the effect of thoughts and prayers of love and compassion or of hatred and anger as they are 'directed' towards others. Such phenomena as telepathy and clairvoyance may become properly understood. So too the migration of birds or the way water divining works may both become part of a larger web of understanding. As knowledge advances so we may have a pool of new images, metaphors, symbols, and analogies to help us talk about the unresolvable mystery some of us call God. Scientific knowledge may be available to anyone with the appropriate talents and training, and it offers its own profound beauty and satisfaction. The artistically gifted live in a world with amazing richness to enjoy. The spiritually holy look out at their world and ours through eyes of deep compassion, forgiveness, and authentic love and see beauty, courage, and achievement where we would not notice it. They also see the darkness more clearly and recognize its damaging power and its potential for transformation. The humble see that they are accepted as they are, no matter what they have been or done, by a love more deeply caring than words can express. In all their different ways such people are being touched, metaphorically speaking I would contend, by the mystery behind and within all life. We have begun our development if we are led to wonder. In his book, *Celebrating Life*, Jonathan Sacks, the chief rabbi in the UK, writes, "Faith is not a complex set of theological propositions. It is simpler and deeper than that. It is about not taking things for granted. It is a sustained discipline of meditation on the miracle of being. 'Not how the world is, but that it is, is the mystical,' said Wittgenstein. Not how we are, but that we are, is cause for wonder, and faith is the symphony on that theme."

Chapter 19

Celebrating the Eucharist with integrity?

I look on the Eucharist as a sacrament of solidarity. It is a great symbolic rite full of rich diversity for a Church without walls. I heard about some refugees who were being cared for at a church. Although not Christians, they came to the Eucharist on Sundays and received communion. I found this a profound and moving story. I wanted to tell it to you, but when I checked the details of this eucharistic hospitality – offered and received – I discovered that it was not quite clear after all whether they had received communion or what the other details were. On account of this, I have decided to leave to one side this story. Perhaps it is true or perhaps it is not. So, instead, I will create my own fictional story.

I ask you to imagine that there had been some refugees who were cared for by the members of a Christian community. For the first few days there had been no interpreter, and there had been confusion at times about the meaning of various hand signals and facial expressions, which had been used as the only means of communication. Laughter and friendliness had helped mitigate the effect of some of the inevitable misunderstandings. In the first few days of their care a bond began to grow between these traumatized people and the carers they were daily encountering in an alien land and culture. The building in which they stayed was beside the church and on the first Sunday morning they entered it, and were warmly welcomed. These refugees were members of another of the world's great faith traditions and had never been in a church before. They seemed to want to sit as a group together; you could see them watching the regular congregation among whom were some of their carers. When they stood up or sat down the refugees did the same. The previous day an interpreter had arrived and was staying the weekend. She explained that the celebrant had invited them, if they wished to do so, to share in the bread and wine with the others. The refugees watched for a while as people went forward to receive communion. Then to many people's surprise, and to their pleasure, the refugees came forward, and with some of their carers coming alongside them, received communion.

It had been a difficult week as these two groups of people, strangers to each other, had gradually adjusted to life in the church hall. People watched the refugees and their carers returning to where they had been seated. They noticed something different in their bearing and in their faces too. They seemed more relaxed, and both carer and refugee radiated a quiet, but nevertheless genuine, joy. I would be putting words into the mouths of the refugees if I said what it had meant to them to share with others in receiving this bread and wine; no doubt it meant slightly different things to each of them. Perhaps you will permit me to surmise. Let us assume that they were aware that what was going on in this strange building had some connection with their own places of worship at home. Maybe their interpreter had said something to them about the church and the Christian faith over breakfast that Sunday. I feel that some of them at least might have had a sense, as they joined their carers and the other Christian communicants, of a belonging together that transcended the boundaries of language, ethnicity, religion, and culture. They may have connected the feeling of being cared for and of friendliness that they had experienced during the week with the welcome they received on entering the church and the atmosphere of love and friendship in which the worship was being expressed. Maybe the receiving and eating of the bread and the drinking of the wine spoke to them symbolically of human dependence for life on the tangible and the intangible.

If I had been the celebrant that day, what would have been in my mind? I would have been aware, as I invited everyone to share in the hospitality of the Christian community, of breaking my church's red tape. My reasoning for doing so would have been that, at its heart, the Eucharist is a rich symbolic rite in which, in each other's presence, we live out a faith in a God of all-embracing and inclusive love. It would not have mattered to me that these people, whom we had welcomed so recently to the care of our community, did not understand the Christian faith. They were aliens in a foreign land. I would not have wanted to make them feel excluded as we celebrated our rite of solidarity and inter-dependence. I would also have rejoiced as the young children of Christian families came to receive. They would sense too that they had been included. Human life is not just lived as the enterprise of individuals, it is essentially a corporate adventure. People bring different levels of understanding as they ponder the rich diversity of this sacrament of solidarity and love. Perhaps in the congregation that day were a husband and wife whose love had died, yet they battled on, carrying all their pain and unresolved conflicts. For them to communicate made a difference. In fact, years later when love and joy had come slowly seeping back into their relationship, they would tell others of that barren, desperate time. They had no longer been held together by each other's love, but had only survived through a trust in the mysterious unseen love believed to hold all life in being.

At its deepest and most profound level, this ancient sacrament addresses us in the midst of our becoming, in the contexts of our conflicts, in the togetherness and in the fragmentation of our lives, in the cultural and social diversity in which our churches are rooted. When we speak of offering Eucharistic hospitality to others, should we not mean that as we are received, welcomed, and accepted unconditionally to the table, so are they? All are equal there and of sacred worth, found loveable, forgivable, and reconcilable by God. Creation, metaphorically speaking, is an extension of God's home; it is where we now find hospitality. By implication, this is a way of saying that the values of hospitality should shape our relationships with each other. The hostess/host has the freedom to invite whom she/he wants – our lives come to us as gifts from God. As guests we are expected to behave well towards each other, to befriend and respect each other, and to accept that while there may be differences between us, it is because of the love of the hostess/host that we are gathered together, and that is a love which transcends whatever boundaries or borders there may be between us.

I view the Eucharist as a profoundly important symbolic rite. It exists as a central part of the Christian liturgy because it is a symbol relating modern Christians to Jesus, his teaching and vision of God, and the way in which he lived and died. It expresses the Christian hope and belief that death is not the end, and that Jesus now lives in the eternity of God. He taught of loving one's enemies, of endless forgiveness, of a father welcoming home the prodigal son, of a shepherd going out to search for and to find a lost sheep. At its deepest level, the Eucharist, as a religious symbolic rite, is affirming a faith that love is the ultimate reality in life and behind and beyond life. It is love alone that can deal with evil, but in a way that is neither easy nor speedily accomplished. The Eucharist is a celebration of a profound human hope and faith claim – that ultimately love will prove victorious and life will be healed and fulfilled. It is the great Christian symbol of love in the midst of evil doing its redeeming work.

As I have described in other chapters, as the story of the historical Jesus was told, so that story became a faith story. In a sense, of course, even the story of the historical Jesus had the potential to be told as a faith story for both he and his story-tellers constructed their sense of what reality was and what it included through wearing the lenses of faith. The story of the historical Jesus became the story of the Christ of faith. This is the figure who symbolizes the love, forgiveness, and reconciliation of God. As I celebrated the Eucharist, I did so conscious that it is a symbolic rite pointing us to a God both hidden and ineffable. In saying, "take this in memory that Christ died for you," I was affirming the faith that the cross of Jesus and the death of Jesus are metaphors for the endless forgiveness and infinite love of God.

I was interviewed on one of the Irish TV channels, on 2nd January 2002, by Pat Kenny, in the presence of a large audience including some of my former parishioners. The program was called *The Late Late Show.* My parishioners were saying that because I did not literally believe that Jesus was the Son of God, I could not say with integrity "This is the body of Christ which was given for you." I responded by saying that in my view the Eucharist was at its heart about a costly, invincible, divine love. I further stated that in his life and dying Jesus expressed a love that was both costly and invincible. To say "Christ had died for you" was a symbolical way of making a significant faith claim that because of the love of God towards us we are loved, forgiven, and reconciled. I was suggesting that if you delved down deep enough, you would discover that my parishioners and I were in agreement about the profound reality underlying the Eucharist. I do not accept that you have to believe that God became a human being in some literal, historical sense to be able to celebrate the Eucharist with integrity. Nor do I accept that to celebrate the Eucharist with integrity you have to believe that in some literal way Jesus died for everyone's sins; such a faith claim does not seem credible to me, as I have argued in Chapter 14. I never managed to understand why my bishop questioned my integrity in celebrating this great symbolic rite.

Rules surround the Eucharist. Before you receive do you have to have been baptized first; do you also need to have been confirmed? Must you be over a certain age? Must you have done a course of instruction? I did not like one rule, concerning women, which I encountered when working in Zimbabwe. A girl might have been baptized and confirmed when she was young, and become a regular communicant. However, if she became a wife and mother, and for cultural reasons had not married in church, a rule prohibited her from receiving communion.

The Eucharist is a deeply meaningful, symbolical religious rite that is full of a rich diversity. It is a sacrament of solidarity, of reconciliation, of self-sacrificing praise, and of a profound remembering of the story of its roots and origins. It is pointing us to the mystery of a love that transcends all borders and boundaries and it is claiming that life is inter-dependent. We belong together no matter who we are. In my view, we have no right to exclude anyone who wants to share with us in receiving communion. We need to be a Church without walls. How dare we prohibit someone from reaching out towards the all-embracing, inclusive love of God?

Yes, it is true that I put forward some radical thoughts about liturgy for the future in the next chapter. However, so long as the celebrant sees the Christ figure as a symbol of this all-embracing, inclusive love, then to my mind, she/he is able to celebrate this profound rite with integrity and joy, as I have believed I used to do when I was the bearer of a bishop's license to work and worship as a priest.

In Appendix F, John Baker refers to Don Cupitt, whom he claims "has written off Christianity altogether, and certainly no longer believes in God." Cupitt regards himself still, despite such views, as a priest of the Church and is a communicant. I would not set myself up to judge the level of understanding or the nature of understanding of any person – young or old, able or disabled, sinner or saint. If she/he feels drawn to receive communion that is, to my mind, their right, and I for one would not stand in their way.

I am happy to think of a three-year-old enjoying communion. I think she/he senses that she/he has been included rather than excluded. She/he will not be able to articulate this. The very fact that she/he does receive communion is a tangible witness to others who are older. Is it not saying, in faith, that whether young or old, we are all caught up into the one bundle of life and embraced by the same mystery that holds all life together in an awesome, faithful, committed, wounded, and victorious love? We are created in love, for love, and by a God of love.

Chapter 20

Has the time come for new liturgies?

The current liturgies of the Churches presuppose that God is an interventionist God; they also assume belief in the Incarnation in a literal sense. I have been arguing that these are not credible beliefs for the twenty-first century, although many people will no doubt continue to believe that they are still credible. The Eucharist and the Mass are dominated by the so-called literal salvific death of Jesus. The bread and wine are related, it is held, in one way or another (depending on the theology of a particular Church) to the crucified and risen Lord. "He died for the sins of the world" is the way in which, in Christian circles, his death has been interpreted. In other chapters I have argued that it does not make sense to see Jesus' death as having this salvific role in a literal sense, yet it is still the belief of a majority of Christians. Although they can be used as extended metaphors for a belief in a God who finds us loveable and forgivable, I believe that the Eucharist and the Mass need to be replaced by new liturgies, despite what I have just written in the previous chapter about this sacrament as a symbolical religious rite full of rich diversity.

In most Churches, the 'Christian year' is described through the lenses of a traditional Christian framework. There is a liturgical year made up of different seasons: the traditional ones are Advent, Christmas, Epiphany, Lent, Holy Week and Easter, Ascension, Pentecost, and Trinity. The liturgical year centers on the birth, life, and ministry of Jesus, his passion and death, his resurrection and ascension, and the coming of the Holy Spirit and the beginning of the Church. Throughout the year the liturgical calendars of some of the Churches include Saints' days and other special occasions such as a Harvest Thanksgiving Festival, Christian Unity Week, and Mothering Sunday.

If more and more people are not going to find it credible to believe, in a literal sense, that God entered our environment to live as a human being in the person of Jesus of Nazareth, and if they no longer see his death as being in some objective way for the salvation of the world, then radical change in the liturgy is essential. Up until now the worship of the Church through the year has been dominated by the life of Jesus. All the time we have to look back to events that took place nearly 2000 years ago, as we go on and on remembering the stories (whether we treat them literally or not) of his birth, his boyhood, his baptism, his temptation in the wilderness, his ministry, his death, resurrection, and ascension. If the time has come to leave Jesus to his place in history and to move on then we need a completely fresh liturgy, no longer dominated by that outstanding member of the community of Israel, who, if he could return and join us in one of our churches one Sunday, would be amazed and affronted to see the way we have been worshiping for the last 2000 years.

For years I and many others have been doing a considerable amount of mental theological gymnastics, as we joined in and maybe led acts of Christian worship. At the deepest level of our sense of worship is a fundamental conviction that love lies at the heart of the universe, love is how the mystery of God is best characterized. The Eucharist or the Mass can be seen as a symbolic way of expressing this belief. At the heart of the Eucharist or the Mass is a belief that eventually love will prove itself invincible and triumphant. When we communicate and receive the bread (or both the bread and the wine) in memory that Christ died for us, this is a symbolic way of saying that we believe ourselves (and the rest of humanity) to be loveable, forgivable, and reconcilable in the sight of God. In the context of worship we seek to rededicate ourselves to the demanding ways of love, and to the overcoming of evil by doing good.

We can make the liturgy work for us, but it is hard work and there is a constant sense of being alienated as we share in it. We do not believe that Jesus is God incarnate or that he is savior in some literal sense. Many of the hymns composed for use during a Eucharist or Mass are addressed to Jesus in a very literal way; however symbolically we may try to treat these words, sometimes it is simpler just not to sing them at all.

Christianity was born, and Christian worship was shaped, in an era when animal sacrifice was in common use for worship in Judaism and in some of the other religions practiced in the Mediterranean world of the first century CE. It is understandable, given those circumstances, that Jesus should have been symbolized as the Lamb of God who takes away the sins of the world. However, in the twenty-first century it is hard to connect with these thought forms of animal sacrifice and the link between this and the need for forgiveness. Inevitably, there is an air in Christian worship today of unreality, because we are being presented with symbols and metaphors that belong to a world long since gone. In addition to this, the theology by which these symbols were interpreted in the liturgy is also, in my view, outdated and redundant. We need something fresh and new. Can ancient institutions, steeped in history as part of their very self-definition, allow for radical change? Are the institutions even sufficiently democratic to allow for minority rights? Could they make provision for those who see the need for change in the liturgy to be given space for experimentation and innovative attempts at new liturgy?

In such new forms of worship there will be a place for readings from the Bible, but such readings will not have any special authority per se (simply because they come from the Bible), rather they will be received as the thinking and believing of people from a very different social reality to our own, and we may or may not engage with them in a meaningful way. The real search will be to find contemporary material from poetry and drama, from literature, film, and professional theological writing that speaks with relevance and challenge in areas such as justice, personal growth and healing, ethical exploration, wisdom, and worship. Good liturgy will seek to deepen the mystery of life, but not to resolve it.

There will be questions about whether to have a liturgical calendar or not, whether to simply have a framework for worship allowing much freedom within it, what new feasts, festivals, or symbols might there be, will there be a new story of Creation, including much that the Genesis myths do not have? It will take time to become used to not having such occasions as Christmas and Easter as highlights in the year, but it will also be a great relief not to have to go through with them. Rowan Williams' words point in the right direction: "Where we find a developing and imaginative liturgical idiom operating in a community that is itself constantly re-imaging itself and its past we may recognize that worship is at some level doing its job," (*On Christian Theology* p.7). The Internet, and the networking it makes possible, should prove a most valuable vehicle for people seeking to create new liturgies. What new liturgies might be composed for the rites of passage, for example? The liturgies for baptism, marriage, and funerals all contain, at present, the Incarnational and Christological theology that I am arguing needs to be replaced. There is clearly here a huge challenge for the mainstream institutionalized traditions of Christianity. Will they hold onto their radical thinkers or will they chase them away?

A new study of worship and liturgy is called for. Using insights from sociology, anthropology, psychology, psychiatry, ethics, drama, poetry, visual arts, communication technologies, architecture, music, and theology we will need to ask what it is we are seeking to do in our liturgies, what do we expect from them and how can they feed into a religion that may be symbolized as both 'wound' and 'womb' (see Chapter 21)?

The purpose of vehicles is transport and the function of signposts is to give direction. I see Christian worship as something that can provide the person seeking to worship with a means to convey her/his worship in the 'direction' of God as she/he reaches out to God in praise and gratitude, penitence and remorse, bewilderment and pain, trust and rage, dependence and responsibility.

Vehicles carry goods. Liturgical vehicles carry a range of diverse goods, such as those 'contents of the heart and mind' mentioned in the previous paragraph, and they carry people too. People are constantly being 'lifted up' in the prayer, pain, and praises conveyed to God. The roads on which liturgical vehicles travel are constructed out of materials that are contained in the ethical code and spiritual vision of the person reaching out to his or her

God. I think of such ethical and spiritual values as: peace, forgiveness, justice, compassion, hope, accountability, freedom, dignity, worth, love, and co-operation. These values are all found in Christian worship.

The God who is worshiped is a hidden and mysterious God who does not leave herself/himself open to observation. Such a God, during this earthly stage of our human journey, is strictly speaking unknowable. We have beliefs about what such a God might be like, but no knowledge of God, nor proof that our beliefs are correct. Likewise such a God's existence is unproven.

For many people, religion is primarily about how to live out and shape a human life; to them the theoretical side of religion is far less important. The history of many of humanity's religions is in part a record of an endless series of debates and disputes between people with conflicting ideas and beliefs. Sometimes such discussion can lead to new and creative insights and the development of a deeper religious vision. On the other hand, it can sometimes reasonably be seen to have been a waste of precious time and energy and an escape from the real issues of the day that needed to be engaged in and acted upon.

If in some highly mysterious way, in our current liturgies, our 'acts of continuing to remember' Jesus of Nazareth serve as liturgical vehicles and sacramental signposts, it may well be because of that self-effacing quality which characterized his life. He sought to encourage others to explore the depths of life and to reach out to that infinite mystery we call 'God'. Our 'acts of remembering him' need to be understood in a metaphorical rather than a literal sense if they are to form acts of worship. For to remember the stories of faith relating to Jesus Christ is to use them as extended metaphors that point us to a God who finds us loveable and forgivable, a God faithfully committed to our world for better and for worse. Jesus taught about his belief in a God of love, and in his acts of compassion and care he sought to express his own love. In the Christian tradition he has become the metaphor for the love of God. That does not mean he is literally divine himself or that he is God.

Chapter 21

Symbolizing religion as wound and womb

Religions use symbols; many are drawn from nature, such as fire, light, and water. Symbols have life-enhancing qualities as well as death-dealing, destructive ones. For example, fire can warm, but it can also burn and destroy; light can illuminate, but it can also blind; water can satisfy thirst, but it can also drown. I consider religion under the heading of two symbols, wound and womb, and look at how they may be life-enhancing or death-dealing.

RELIGION AS WOUND

Heresy may be a wound, as I will be suggesting later on in this chapter, but first I want to refer to a remark of the English playwright, Denis Potter. In his book, *Doubts and Loves*, Richard Holloway quotes from something that Denis Potter said to the interviewer Melvin Bragg on British television shortly before he died: "For me, religion has always been the wound, never the bandage." In this chapter, I want to develop my own understanding of religion as wound, first in its life-enhancing sense.

I had the immense privilege of living and working in Zimbabwe for 11 years (1983-94) and am grateful that I received such wonderful encouragement when I was learning the Shona language. In a greeting commonly used the first person will say, "Muri wadi here?" which translates as, "Are you well?" The other person will reply, "Ndiri wadi, kana muri wadiwo" meaning, "I am well, if you are well."

My well-being is dependent on your well-being. If you are seriously ill or have just suffered a tragedy, how can I be other than concerned, distressed, and anxious if I care about you? Here, built into the consciousness of a people, is the sense of sharing in corporate life, living as a caring community. Compare how a greeting in English might be: "How are you?", "I'm fine and how are you?", "Oh, I'm OK, thanks." In this greeting, our individualism is expressed.

Another example of the difference between cultures can be seen in the way in which a child in a Shona culture is taught the importance of sharing. For example, if you give a child some sweets she is expected to share them with others. She belongs in community and lives a life shared with others. On the other hand, in a Western culture, we commonly hear of children unwilling to share their toys with other children. "That's my toy, you can't play with it."

Religion as wound is living with a strong awareness that our lives are interdependent within the human family. It is a moral and spiritual awareness. We share in a wider interdependence in an ecological sense as part of the universe that we inhabit, often so irresponsibly.

It is hard to keep the wound open; it is much easier to let it close over, so that we shield ourselves from the world's pain and injustices. How can I be well, when so many in the world are desperately poor, victims of torture and other human rights abuses, living without the opportunity to use their talents in appropriate work, dying of sicknesses such as AIDS which they may have innocently contracted? How can I be well, when others are caught up in the world's wars, living in the midst of the most troubled parts of the world, suffering from fear, grief, injury, powerlessness, and insecurity? Religion as wound means renewing the depleted resources of compassion, fury, hope, responsibility, resolve, generosity, self-sacrificing love, thirst for knowledge and understanding, penitence, courage, and the sense of our mutual interdependence. This is not a kill-joy religion, but it is a religion that calls for sacrifice, awareness and sensitivity, vulnerability, and action.

Religion as wound holds out hope to the people of the world for, by being practiced well, it can restore faith in the goodness of human beings and in our capacity to live moral lives of depth, passion, and integrity which lead to change and improvement in the life of the world. The wound we carry daily within us speaks of an empathy and a solidarity with others, although none of us can feel all the world's pain and be affected by it. The pain of the wound cleanses the dirty, despairing vision we may sometimes have of human nature in its apathy, selfishness, and corruption.

Religion as wound is an acknowledgement, though, of more than not being well because we are constantly being affected by the suffering of the world. There is another sense of 'wound'. There is our own individual sickness as human beings. You may know this quotation from Jung: "One does not become enlightened by imagining figures of light, but by making the darkness conscious." None of us is either psychologically or spiritually fully well. To think of religion as wound is to imply that religion has a particular perception on human life: it sees it as always wounded and in need of further healing; nobody is cured, we all bear afflictions, carry damage within, and have the capacity to spread our diseases and influence others for the worse. So part of the truth of who we are is that we are wounded people, living in a wounded world. To recognize this truth is better than to deny it. Religion as wound reminds us of our need for the 'doctor'; nobody is so wise that they always know how best to treat themselves, and most of us find that the best medicine comes to us from others. Each religion too has a vast treasury of wisdom about human life. Delve within and something may well be found for your healing.

The search for truth, or what one believes to be truth, is often a costly one. In the long history of the Church, and in the experience too of other religious traditions, the search for truth has often involved serious conflicts, intellectual battles and charges of heresy. On the Dean's page on the parish website I had presented the Cathedral as a focus of unity, but I also said that I envisaged it as a forum for conflict. We may be united in a search for truth, but there needs to be room for conflict and an acceptance that finding there are conflicting views is quite normal. It has often been in times of open debating of contested issues that the Church has been most alive. Religion as wound, in so far as the search for truth is concerned, may be a reminder that the search may be painful and divisive and needs to be conducted in a spirit of tolerance and awareness; the wounds are part of the price of our development – the price of life. Today's heresy may often prove to be tomorrow's orthodoxy: a statement that does not only apply in religion, but in many other fields too.

Just before I left Trim, after my 'skirmish' with the Church, I attended the Cathedral for Sunday worship. The priest on duty knew that I would be coming. Whether it was by chance or not I do not know, but the first hymn we were invited to sing was, 'The church's one foundation is Jesus Christ her Lord'. As you may know, this hymn has these lines about the life of the Church: 'By schisms rent asunder, by heresies distressed'. I had to smile to myself and wondered if anyone else in the Cathedral that morning noticed that on this Sunday, when I was attending Sunday worship in the Cathedral for the first time since my imposed leave of absence, such a hymn had been chosen. However, I was not just smiling to myself; I was reminded by the words of the pain I had been enduring and of the pain experienced by the members of the parish. The Church lives a wounded life.

If religion as wound has its life-enhancing qualities, it also has its destructive, death-dealing ones. At their worst, religions spread and promulgate prejudice, hatred, arrogance, intolerance, elitism, resistance to change, escapism, damaging theologies, narrowness, meanness of spirit, abuse, jealousy, dishonesty, and denial of the rights of people, in particular of women. The religions are sick. Religion as wound can remind us of this festering sore that exists alongside so much that is healthy and good. Religion as wound may be death-dealing in the context of the search for truth, when there is an authoritarian controlling attitude taken by the religious tradition's leaders; when a person may be called on to resign from a post when they hold a legitimate position within a debate being pursued by the Church worldwide; when the Church stifles or makes it too dangerous for the search for truth to be pursued within it. I do not value a unity sought after, achieved, and celebrated, if it is at the cost of an authentic diversity being rejected and despised. I am not the first, and will not be the last, to have suffered in this way.

RELIGION AS WOMB

The symbol of the womb has its life-enhancing as well as its death-dealing qualities. The womb is a place of nurture, a place for growth, and a safe place in which to be. It may also be an escape, a regression, a confining place in which to be.

In its life-enhancing sense, religion as womb suggests the need for a community of people whom it is safe to be with, a group who will try to accept me as I am. It is a community that provides me with nurture and care, support and appreciation. It is a community that challenges me to grow and to grow up. Through its listening and its love, its understanding and its acceptance, its wisdom and its hilarity, its insights and its illumination, it can provide balm for my wounds and healing for some of my sicknesses of soul, of mind, and of spirit. It might conceivably be a house group but is more likely to be made up of a range of different people to whom one relates on an individual basis; or it might consist of a group of people within a larger community, with whom one can be oneself with transparency and depth. "It is in the shelter of each other that people live" were words on a greeting card I once received.

Religion as womb does not necessarily mean that one is restricted to those who share the same religious beliefs and vision. However, it is likely that a concern for values such as truth and justice, tolerance and respect, will be common ground between oneself and those with whom one relates at depth, in both joy and in pain, in confusion and in bewilderment, and in times characterized by clarity and conviction.

In the context of religion as womb, if it is sometimes appropriate to ask oneself the question: "What healing do I need before the next stage of my journey?', it may also be necessary to ask oneself the question: "What may I be escaping from by doing my theological thinking or religious reflection?" Religion may function as a womb into which we escape from our responsibilities. Religion can lead us away from the world we are called upon to suffer within. Religion as womb may represent regression towards immaturity, towards the womb we were meant to have left and left behind. Perhaps we engage in and indulge ourselves in misleading beliefs. We begin to allow ourselves to picture God in ways that are no longer appropriate. We pray to God as an interventionist and protector God. We allow ourselves to expect that it is reasonable to believe that God will respond in this way or in that. We diminish ourselves for a while by hiding away from our true responsibilities and placing them onto God's shoulders. We want to escape the fear, the pain, and the uncertainties of life. We want to rewrite our past, as if parts of it had never happened. We want to delude ourselves that to be forgiven is somehow to rewrite our history and destroy the record books.

I recall the time when I arrived to work in Zimbabwe in 1983. Independence had come three years previously. Both before and after independence a great many 'white-skinned' people had emigrated. Among those 'whites' who stayed, there were many who were grieving over the loss of their identity as Rhodesians. Emotionally they were finding it very painful to think of themselves now as Zimbabweans. I remember being amazed at the new charismatic and fundamentalist churches populated by these people. Within these churches there was great emphasis put on being citizens of the kingdom or disciples of Jesus; there was an emphasis, too, on the next life: your true citizenship is in heaven. It seemed to me that these churches were offering people an escapist womb from the real world that they were having such difficulty in embracing. The churches were not helping people work through their grief over the past that had now gone, taking with it their old identity. Neither were they enabling people to move on to live and serve in the real world of the new Zimbabwe that they now belonged to.

Religious authorities and leaders will often treat their fellow believers as if they are only fit for a life of the womb. They will feed them with safe, certain, and uncontroversial sermons. They will hide from them the results of academic research and the internal controversies and conflicts within theological thinking. They will not expose them to the bracing winds of change felt in the continuous interpretation of the faith in each generation. These attitudes partly stem from fear: how will the laity react? They also stem from a false paternalistic concern: they don't want to rock the boat or upset people's cherished understanding of their faith. Yet does not history show that eventually hot topics do reach the person in the pew? It was impossible to prevent people forever from hearing about Darwinism, and from thinking about what implications it might have for their beliefs. It has always been impossible to prevent people from asking themselves profound questions about the mystery of God. Is God a protector God; is God an interventionist God? Is it credible to believe that God, in some literal sense, became a human being? Is the 'talking God' of the Scriptures, who plans and acts, and communicates his thoughts, attitudes and decisions to his people, the real God or a figment of human imagination or a metaphorical way of people expressing their deepest beliefs and ultimate concerns?

To treat people as if they may best be served with this sort of religion of the womb is to confine them; it is to prevent them from stretching their minds; it is to restrict their spiritual and moral growth. Too much of it is still happening throughout the world. The questioner, the doubter, and the radical thinker are quietly excluded and made to feel unwelcome. They are presented as people who are failures: they do not have enough faith; they are unable to trust and be grateful for the certainties of belief; they deny that God has truly made his promises to his people and entered into covenant relationships with them. Networks and organizations, such as The Center for Progressive Christianity and The Sea of Faith Network, now exist in many countries and across continents to offer support to people whose experiences of this particular faith have been alienating, abusive, confining, restrictive, and demeaning.

Chapter 22

Religion as creed, code, cult, and community

The Church always exists within a particular social reality and the worldwide Church exists in a diverse range of social realities. The Church's thinking, organization, and world-view are profoundly influenced by the social reality in which it is embedded. It is a dynamic relationship, and not just one way. For the Church helps to construct social reality, to influence it and critique it. In traditional Christian thinking, the Church proclaims its belief that this social reality is a part of a greater reality that includes both time and eternity, the life of God, the life of heaven, and the life of Creation. To say that religion may be considered under the four headings of creed, code, cult, and community is just one model by which to analyze and describe its contents. I came across this model some years ago. It is a model that I find helpful. I am conscious that I am doing so in a Western European Christian cultural context, and not, for example, out of a Buddhist, Hindu, or Islamic cultural context.

I do not regard any religion as unchanging; to my mind they all are developed over time, and relate to our fundamental needs as human beings, and for some of us a profound need is to proclaim the glory of God. Each generation and each person brings their own assumptions and presuppositions, their own world-view to the interpretation of their religious tradition, as well as their own religious experience. Tradition and experience interact in complex and subtle ways. Within each generation there is diversity of interpretation; religions are constantly being divided into new strands or denominations. There is a living, dynamic creativity being brought to bear on the various religious traditions and a tension exists between the conservative members and the more radical or liberal ones over many issues to do with the tradition and its current expression. But get behind the interpretations and you will find the same human needs, and within many Christian interpretations essentially the same faith claims.

RELIGION AS CREED

In his book *The Great Disruption*, Francis Fukuyama examines how we have created the information age and he speculates on the shape of religion in such an age. With an ever-expanding amount of information available to more and more people, he thinks that the centralized authority and powerful hierarchies of many religious denominations will be greatly eroded. Instead of great weight being placed on creeds as the official beliefs of a group of people (maybe numbering millions), there will be a much greater acceptance of diversity of belief and interpretation. Clearly a religion is partly constituted by what its members in the past and in the present have believed and do believe. Who are we? Have we and our universe been created? If so, by whom? Is there anything beyond death? Can suffering be justified? Is the universe part of a great 'scheme of things'? Is God knowable? What claims are made about the founder(s) of the religion?

As religions are studied in their historical development, it becomes clearer how 'historic creeds' emerged. The influences brought to bear on the shaping of a creed, such as the Nicene Creed, were varied and complex, and were far from simply theological. Political, philosophical, personal, socio-economic, cultural, historical, and ecclesiastical factors were some of those involved. There was a real element of contingency. For example, if there had been a different emperor at the time, different personalities, different rivalries; if some theological viewpoints had been stronger or had had more capable proponents; if some bishops had not traveled to the Council, and if some who did not go had attended, and so on. In the future, religious institutions (if they are still in existence) and religious organizations, movements, and networks will need to allow for greater diversity if the members are going to feel a sense of democratic involvement and ownership. There will be much less emphasis on orthodoxy. The Church will be a real place where truth can be explored and there will be an acknowledgment that the religious quest is a life-long commitment. A healthy Church will place more emphasis on the asking of questions, on living with uncertainty and diversity, and much less emphasis on having answers. Theology is a speculative undertaking and, inevitably, if people are going to be honest about this, it would be surprising if there were not a whole range of differing interpretations and understandings.

However, the question is understandably being asked about boundaries and identities of religions. Does not a religion, or a denomination within it, have the right to try to define its boundaries and to construct and define its identity? And if that is agreed to be the case, who has the power to do such work? In the case of the older religious traditions, who has the power to interpret the faith for a new age? I do not have all the answers to these questions and anyway there are likely to be a number of conflicting answers. In more general terms, I believe that churches need to encourage more democratic participation in decision-making. I believe there is need for a general open invitation to those who might like to come and explore. Perhaps they have seen a particular religion expressed in action, or they have been impressed by the way a vision is made concrete in practical ways. The invitation indicates that people are free to come and go. They are encouraged to ask their questions; they may request suggestions as to how their present journeying in life, with the provisional vision of faith that they find drawn to, might relate to elements in the religious tradition they are exploring in a contemporary setting. A young couple, reflecting on what it means to build a loving relationship, might ask how does this building connect with the tradition within Christianity of building loving relationships in contexts where love has been sorely tested or where it has failed, as well as where it has triumphed? In what way might human experience of love reflect divine love?

The current climate of thinking in post-modernism puts an emphasis on each individual's perspective and unique vision and interpretation. This has the implication, in some people's minds, that religious reflection as a human endeavor cannot be prescriptive. Theology cannot escape from its roots in conjecture, however rich and brilliant its results may appear to be. The faith claims of a God whose being and character help to make sense of our experiences and those of others are inevitably speculative, for God remains hidden and unknowable, and people ask these profound questions from the context of differing social realities. The faith of other generations will be interpreted against each individual's own experience and each person's journeying to date. There cannot be a uniform response; there cannot be total agreement. Wittgenstein wrote of family resemblances between different games, they resembled each other in a variety of ways, but how one game resembled another one was likely to be dissimilar to how it resembled a different one. It could be argued that there are such family resemblances between members of a faith tradition, where the member's life experience, social reality, journeying to date, and interpretation of the tradition are what count as a 'game' in this analogy. One can talk about generalities, and be vague about specifics as one compares and contrasts the membership. Ultimately it comes down to an attitude of mind and a wisdom built upon the history of what has happened when creedal orthodoxy has been given supreme value. Does not the wisdom of the ages suggest "that the peculiarly Christian desire for doctrinal uniformity can only make for division and enmity"? (a quotation from the section entitled 'Worldwide responses').

Values of tolerance, of openness to change and to revising one's thinking, together with respectful dialogue and debate, will all be important. In societies that are becoming more and more multiracial, and more and more multi-faith, the need to understand other people's faiths, as well as one's own, has the potential to lead to greater harmony and mutual understanding, and hopefully to much less prejudice and discrimination. There is scope for much mutual enrichment by people of differing faiths and cultures as they talk to each other about their faith. A person can learn how their faith is understood by a member of a different faith. This means, for example, hearing from someone looking through Buddhist lenses how Christianity is perceived and understood. If the majority of Christians, who still interpret much of their faith in a literal way, were to move away from seeing themselves as having a faith that is inherently superior to other faiths, because their God has, as they have claimed, entered our environment and become a human being in a literal sense in the person of Jesus of Nazareth, and if they were to move away from looking on him, in a literal sense, as the world's Savior, then there is the real possibility for much better dialogue between people of all faiths. To see religion as a human creation is a starting point that has enormous potential for better understanding and peace between people of faith.

RELIGION AS CODE

Religions are there to be lived out in practice. They are meant to shape lifestyles. They are intended to be a source of wisdom for the making of moral choices. By religion as code is meant the code of values that members of the religion believe is important and that ought to be expressed where applicable in human life. It is not always realized that logically, at least, if not in historical sequence, the ethical commitment a person makes is prior to her theological commitment. A person must first regard goodness and compassion, for instance, as universal values she ought to seek to express in her own life and which others ought to express too, before she can value a God believed to manifest the same values of goodness and compassion. A commitment to ethical values is independent of a commitment to a God. A society and its members' values are in constant need of being critiqued; the hypocrisy that so often masks a people's true values and motives needs continuously to be exposed. As a society changes and evolves differing values will take precedence and a greater self-awareness in relation to these factors will be helpful to people, as they seek to adjust and adapt to new ways of living.

Religions have traditionally been one important vehicle for the passing on to the next generation of the values of their parents and perhaps of their society and culture too. This will probably remain one of the reasons why people will join a religion and bring their children to a mosque, a synagogue, a church, or a temple. The stories of a particular religion are preserved within it, interpreted anew by each generation and passed on to the next one. For members of a religion to do this in a healthy way, the stories that contain many of the ethical values of the religion concerned will need to be critiqued, for not every story contains values that are still respected today. Understandably there will be a measure of conflict between members about values and their practical expression.

RELIGION AS CULT

Will societies in the future place a different value on the traditional rites of passage? Will they look to their religions to make provision for them? In Chapter 20, I made the point that a radically transformed Christianity would need to rewrite its liturgies for the rites of passage. Birth and death, and the formal entering into committed relationships through a public act, will need such new liturgies I contended. In the future, will societies and members of religions want to mark the process of moving from childhood to adulthood?

The cult also includes the public provisions for worship and its leadership. In what way will a non-interventionist God be worshiped and prayed to? How will the cult help to maintain the role of religion as 'wound' in people's lives and how will it provide for religion as 'womb'? As psychological insights and sociological ones are brought to bear on the creative work of refashioning liturgies, there will need to be greater recognition of differing personality types and the different ways in which such personalities engage in worship. What makes a satisfying experience of worship for one person may not do so for another. Peoples of different cultures will bring a desire to worship in ways distinctive to themselves. Today one can travel to many parts of the world and enter a Catholic church or an Anglican one, for example, and expect to find a liturgy recognizable as being similar to what one experiences at home. Could it be that this will be much less so in the future, as greater emphasis is placed on local communities creating their own forms of liturgy? How will the challenge be met when the criticism is made that a community's liturgy has become boring, irrelevant, alienating, escapist? Will the local community have the power to be able to do something about the criticism, or will the community feel largely powerless, because authority for change and decision-making is still centralized and slow to act?

RELIGION AS COMMUNITY

Human beings are social beings. We live in multi-layered social realities. In a globalized world there are many theories to try to explain this multi-dimensional experience. While religion has its personal, private, and individual aspects, it is also about belonging, sharing with others in a common vision, meeting with others to worship, joining in social events and in actions of varying kinds together. A good religion will have a vision (though not necessarily an uncontested one) for what sort of community its members are trying to create, for what sort of world they seek to shape. To what extent will gender-mainstreaming and equality be a priority? The values of the religion will help members in the building up of their community as well as in the critiquing of it. Democracy and communication, power sharing and leadership will often need to be under review, as will the ways in which and the extent to which the community genuinely expresses care and compassion to its members and those beyond, and how it empowers them to live out their faith. How well does it allow for the growth spiritually of its members, for learning theology and studying the world and its continuing needs for justice, peace, stability, and sustainable lifestyles? Is the community good at innovative practices and permitting experimentation in a variety of ways? How will communities network with each other in the future? Will globalization, better methods of communication, and perhaps a shorter working week for many people mean that more time can be devoted to all sorts of activities that help to build a better quality of life for more people? What difficulties might there be in what could come to be perceived as too much diversity and fragmentation: pluralism run to extremes in things religious?

At their best, religious communities will reinforce people's sense of being of value, having an inherent and inalienable dignity, and of being of sacred worth. They will strengthen people's hold on their values by the mutual affirmation of each other as holders of the community's values. They will be a place for transparency, trust, openness, love, laughter, and tears.

Chapter 23

The ring – getting close to the heart of my theology

I availed myself of an opportunity to lead experimental worship when I was training at Westcott House, Cambridge from 1970-1972. I decided to try to lead a group meditation on the theme of trust and wanted a visual image to offer to people as a focus. I asked Claude Riches, who was a fellow ordinand and an artist, if he would paint a picture of a ring for me, which he kindly did. I was thinking of the ring as a symbol of trust. I had in mind God's trust in us and ours in God. Claude painted the picture on a piece of hardboard that he painted black; it measured about one and a half feet wide by two and a half feet long. In the middle he painted a gold ring that has a diameter of about a foot. I still have it and treasure it. This ring was photographed to help make up the picture on my website. If you go to my website, http://myhome.iolfree.ie/ ~ andrewfurlong, you will find on the front page an interesting picture. This is what I wrote about it.

> Different people will see and interpret the home page picture on my website in various ways, and it will be very interesting to receive some of these interpretations and to learn from them. For me, the dominant symbol in the picture is the ring; within the context of marriage it is rich in symbolism, and I draw on that symbolism and place it within a spiritual and religious vision and understanding of life.
>
> Incidentally, I believe that the ring can transcend its traditional setting within the context of heterosexual marriage and so is able to speak, symbolically, to people of varying sexual orientations and differing sexual lifestyles at the profoundest levels of their being. It may also speak to people in religious orders of their commitment.
>
> This is how the picture came together in my mind and imagination, during a sleepless night: the idea for the seven faces inside the wedding ring was suggested to me by the seven ages of man in Shakespeare's play *As You Like It*. They are the faces of seven members of the human family from around the world. They represent human life from birth into old age. The sun, in the bottom left-hand corner, represents God. If there were no sun, there could be no life here on our planet earth. The sun, as a religious symbol, stands for God, without whom, I believe, there would be no life or universe. However, the sun is obscured by

cloud which is a symbolic way of pointing to the fact that God (if there is a God) remains hidden and mysterious and not open to observation (though that does not mean, for me, that God is inactive or uninvolved, only that we do not see the whole picture of what is going on all the time and we cannot understand its complete meaning).

The seven faces are arranged inside the ring and have together a circular shape as does the sun. Symbolically, I see this as alluding to a belief that there is some affinity between the human family and our Maker. This might be expressed in terms of values such as love, freedom, responsibility, accountability, vulnerability, tenderness, and goodness or in terms of abilities such as being inventive, innovative, artistic, intelligent, and purposeful.

The ring itself, in its setting within close and intimate human relationships, speaks of trust. The picture is saying, in effect, that God trusts in the belief that she/he has in us that eventually we will all ascend to the heights of our humanity and fulfill our destiny and, on the other hand, the ring is saying that, in the Christian vision of life, we put our trust in the faithfulness and ability of God to help us reach our goals.

The sun is in the background of the picture, which suggests to me the sense of the absence of God; God is at a distance, hidden and mysterious. However, that is not the whole truth. For the ring, encircling the human family, I see next as a symbol of love, a love that encompasses the human family, cradles it, and holds it. If a God exists, then this love can only credibly be believed to be a divine love, committed faithfully, for better and for worse, to the world and to the human family within it. Such a God holds, as it were, her/his family in her/his arms in all their brokenness, confusion, vulnerability, vitality, and versatility. As the ring is a symbol of love, so are God's arms the arms of a deep and tender love.

Finally (though I probably should not use the word finally because I go on discovering fresh meanings in the picture), the ring given and received in the context of a marriage service resonates with themes of honoring, joy, respect, dignity, and sharing. These too speak of the richness of a divine-human relationship. There is the possibility of our honoring and respecting our God, of our acknowledging the significance and dignity of our God, and of our seeing our lives as a sharing in one great life into which we are all caught up: a life which embraces both the human and the divine and everything else too. There is also the wonder of being before a God who honors us, respects us, gladly acknowledges our eternal worth, inalienable dignity and loveableness, and shares with us in the hazardous adventure whose destiny lies far over the horizon.

The horizon is where the ocean and the sky meet. Both have been powerful religious symbols in the past; can they still speak to us today and for tomorrow and how do such interpretations fit into an overall interpretation of the picture? What difference does it make if you view the sun on the horizon as a sunrise rather than as a sunset or vice versa? Do you see elements of a contemporary Celtic spirituality in the interpretation I have shared? It is over to you for your ideas and responses.

Symbols, as I have written in the chapter about symbolizing religion as wound and womb, may have both life-enhancing as well as death-dealing qualities. In the case of the ring, its life-enhancing quality is to represent freely offered commitment and faithfulness; on the other hand, its death-dealing quality is to represent compulsion. For example, a bull will be led by an attendant holding a rope fixed to a ring that goes through the bull's nose. The symbol of the ring in its spiritual and religious context represents, at its best, a commitment on both sides freely offered. For me, it is a great symbol of hope.

Chapter 24

Credo: mine and other people's

I have written in several chapters that I think there is a need for churches to put much less emphasis on creedal orthodoxy. If you are going to have a thinking membership in a church, then you must expect that there will be diversity of insights and ways of expressing people's deepest convictions about life and about the vision at the heart of the religious tradition. Through both the media and my website I invited people to send me their credo.

One of the Church's early and defining creeds is the Apostles' Creed. In preparation for the BBC Radio program, *Sunday*, on 30 December 2001, people of all faiths and none were invited to submit their own personal credo: who or what is the origin of your universe, how would you express the essentials of what you believe about God (if you believe in God), about the purpose of life, and spiritual reality? I said, in my invitation to people to send me their credo, that their thinking, believing, doubting, and searching would probably make me want to modify my present credo. This is it:

A CREDO FOR THE TWENTY-FIRST CENTURY

As individual and social beings, we are challenged to ascend to the heights of our humanity, and avoid sinking to the depths of our depravity.

In beliefs expect diversity, mine evolve. Religions are motorways needing widening. All life is gift; human life is of eternal worth, found loveable by God, who is hidden, active, committed to us for better, for worse.

Religious symbols: wedding ring, journey, fire, light, darkness, horizon, sun, cloud, ocean, wave. The destiny of this risky adventure of life lies over the horizon, in eternity; the meaning of life continues to grow.

Let life be developed and used, be open-minded, courageous, and humorous, seek to adore.

Here is a selection of credos that people sent me from around the world. While I find that it is very interesting to read these credos, I lack an awareness of what social reality each person belongs to, nor do I know what their journey in life has meant for them so far.

Credo: I believe in an Originator of all that is created, both physical and of the mind and spirit, and which is the source of all that we know of Love and Goodness in humanity.

I believe that this Originator is beyond our knowing or understanding, but that in speaking of God we attempt to define that source of our being.

I believe that in the Bible we have glimpses of the sublime beyond our mortal existence, within the limits of language, imagery and human understanding.

I believe that in Jesus we see the one who was closest to comprehending the creative spirit which is both beyond and within us, and who was able to show us how to be conscious of and aspire to live in accordance with that spirit.

I believe that in trusting the encompassing benevolence of that Originating spirit we have nothing to fear in facing death, because in some way we shall continue to exist and will have understanding that we lack in this material world.

Credo: I have formulated what I think represents my present beliefs. Present – because I do not think belief is static, but must be subject to change in a positive dynamic manner.

I BELIEVE in God who is the very depth of my being, and of Everyman. I only know that he is there and is physically evidenced by and in the world around me and beyond. I appreciate him in the wonders of each day. The starry sky, the views from a mountaintop, the prickly spinal response to music, and the manner in which healing takes place. He also is present at times of grief, war, misery, poverty, innocent suffering – if only to induce a feeling of man's lack of concern for his fellow men.

I BELIEVE in Jesus Christ – The Man – whose recorded life, teaching and thought provide a meaningful way to try to live – summed up in love for one's neighbour – "to do to him as you would he should do to you". His reported Resurrection provides a powerful symbol of renewal of life, of starting again after failure, and induces thoughts of spring and all that it represents.

I BELIEVE in a Universal Church encompassing many varied multi-coloured strands making an ever-expanding web committed to extending the boundaries of peace and the common good.

I BELIEVE in a life perpetuated after death by the memories in others of my ideas and actions during life, and if I have been blessed with children by the continued physical presence of me in them.

Credo: (developing upon the Christian Church's Nicene Creed) I believe in one God, an almighty entity, which is everything; all that is believed and all that is real, Heaven and Earth. I believe that I am within God and all my actions, thoughts, great or small must help God grow and flourish.

I believe that through the ages God has given us great teachers to help us in this task. Confucius, Jesus, and Mohammed – and others known or not at all – have all helped spread this message of loving God and respect for others. They have guided us from evil ways and challenged us to face our weaknesses.

I believe in the universal power of this love, the Hidden Spirit, to move people, to challenge ideas, to build on wisdom. All of these give more life to God.

And when I die I will be judged by those in God who, by my words and deeds, I have touched in whatever way during my time on earth.

Credo: I believe in one God, who is the life energy of being, in all things. All matter is formed of particles of energy, and God is the soul and source of all energy. In Heaven, which is our spiritual realm, our souls are sparks of the life energy of God. On Earth, which is our physical realm, we are spiritual beings having a physical life experience. Our purpose is to evolve in spirit. Through living our life on Earth, and growing in Love, which is of God, we will grow and evolve in spirit. The Commandments and Teaching of Jesus are my Inspiration and my Way. He is my Guide.

Credo: I believe in one God, Source of creation, of essence one, of manifestations infinite, Expanding ever to elude, in love embracing all that is. I honour his Prophets, whose teachings brought Faith to the world.

(The following section is adaptable for other faiths): I honour especially the prophets of the kindred faiths of the People of the Book, Moses, Jesus the Christ, and Mohammed. I hold sacred above all the memory of Jesus, By whose life and witness God's love was made manifest, By whose death Love's victory was made certain, By the triumph of whose spirit redeemed humanity received the hope of life eternal. I believe in the loving spirit of God, Working for good in the world.

Credo: For me, god cannot be personified and doing so creates difficulty in contacting the divine, throws the mind into a concrete place and out of a formless state where there is knowledge in the silence beyond words. God is such as cannot be described, but I feel closer to description with ideas like 'energy', or 'atmosphere', a permeating-ness. Maybe an attempt to break the cliché comes near it, as in: love is god. But that's not possible to say, freshly, now. To live by, I believe the key words to be integrity, service, non-judgemental, kindness in thought as much as in action.

My ideas and responses to them from others

INTRODUCTION

This part of the book contains some of my own writing as well as that of my consultants and of the editors of *The Irish Times* and of *The Church of Ireland Gazette*. Appendices A, B, and C were cited by my bishop, Richard Clarke, in the Petition in which I was charged by him. Although extracts from these three articles may be found in Part Two, I include them here in full for historical reasons, in that this book is in part a record of my alleged heresy story. Earlier in the book I have drawn on other people's views – both in the section on 'Worldwide responses' and in Chapter 24. Appendices D, E, F, and G contain further examples of how people responded to my views and how they criticized them. I agree with some, but not all of their views, as I have indicated in Part 2. Appendix H is an interview that Bill Bowder of *The Church Times* had with me. I wrote Appendix I 25 years ago. The liberal voice in the dialogues is mine. Here is the theology – expressed by Susan in the dialogues – that I found attractive, credible, and appealing while I studied in Cambridge from 1969-1972.

Appendix A

Pain and Integrity: reform from within (2001)

This article has been slightly modified for inclusion here.

INTRODUCTION

William Butterfield, the great Victorian church architect, designed three churches in Ireland. One of these distinctive Butterfield buildings is my old school chapel at St Columba's College, Dublin. On one of the walls is a tablet commemorating my former housemaster, Sandham Willis, who taught in the school for over 40 years. In addition to his name and the dates of his teaching at the school, there is this brief inscription, which reads: "he was a good teacher who loved learning". While I was studying theology at Cambridge, I used to visit him when back in Dublin on holidays. He was retired at this stage. Evidence of his desire to go on learning was all around him in his flat, with books on a range of different subjects. He would have made a list of questions and topics that he wanted to ask me about. Much of our conversations I can hardly remember now. However, I do recall him saying something that seemed to me surprising at the time, which was this: "the older I become, the more conscious I get of how little I really know." I believe that one subject, to which he would have applied this remark was theology, in which he was interested and which we discussed.

Donald Nicholl in a sermon called 'the beatitude of truth' speaks of the life of the intellectual, the person who in one way or another seeks to serve the truth. He mentions that in his commentary on the beatitude "blessed are those who mourn", St Thomas Aquinas says that this is the special beatitude of those whose calling it is to be intellectuals, extending the boundaries of knowledge where possible. They will mourn, says St Thomas, because their serving of the truth will be a costly exercise which will involve giving up, at times, beliefs and ideas that held great significance for them. They will come to realize that these beliefs and ideas are no longer plausible or credible, and so must be given up, no matter how hard it is to do so. My former housemaster would have agreed with what St Thomas wrote, I am sure.

Those who think about what is written in this paper will all have journeyed, I imagine, in differing ways in the course of a life in which the serving of truth is an important value and challenge. All, I suspect, will have made some significant changes to the beliefs that they have held; and for some such changes will have raised for them questions of integrity, because of the work that they do or the role that they uphold.

In the main part of this paper I want to look at three areas that have engaged my thinking, and in which my ideas and beliefs have changed or developed. These areas are: the action of God, who Jesus was, and some thoughts about worship.

PART ONE

I have always been puzzled by people who seem to talk easily and with conviction about the action of God in our world. My sense of God is of God's hiddenness and mysteriousness. Strictly speaking, I would say that I know nothing about God, either in the sense of what God is like, or in the sense of what God does, or how God acts. At best, I have a range of speculative ideas of how I imagine God to be, but much is mystery. So, let me turn first to the subject of Revelation: does it happen?

An old man opened his mouth to laugh, and in doing so, revealed one solitary tooth. It was said of the same old man that, through his love and compassion, he revealed to people the face of God. The word "revealed" is being used differently in these two sentences. In the first, the tooth, which would not normally be visible, is seen when the man laughs. In the second, the face of God does not become visible; so what do we mean by "revealed" in this use? It is a paradoxical use of the word, for God always remains hidden, unseen, and mysterious and, strictly speaking, unknowable by us in this life. As Hegel said: "God does not offer himself" (/herself) "for observation." The old man's love made people think, "that's what God's love is like too." This result depended on two factors: that some people who knew him had a faith in God; and that they believed that human love and compassion helped people imagine what the love of God might be like.

On the other hand, it could have been said that God had revealed himself/herself through the old man's love and compassion. This is often the sense in which the word is used in religious discourse and points to a God who, though unseen, is believed to act and communicate in his/her world and with his/her people. The difficulty in speaking like this is that people need to find grounds for believing that God is taking the initiative and finding a way to reveal himself/herself, or his/her will, or his/her plans or purposes. One use of "reveal" stressed the human side, where people themselves came to believe that the old man's love spoke to them of divine love; another stressed that it is the unseen and hidden God who chose to reveal herself/himself through this man's love for others.

Can believers in God really have good grounds for their beliefs (not knowledge or certainty) about what such an unseen God is doing? Some people use a simple interpretative framework of belief: if something good happens, it is God rewarding them; if something bad happens, it is God punishing them, if they have to do something difficult, it is God testing them. Such an interpretative framework, however, will often not work.

For myself, I think of God as ceaselessly active and involved. However, we cannot observe his/her work. What we know about our world is an incomplete picture of all that is going on; and consequently we do not fully understand the meaning of all that is happening.

In religions such as Judaism, Islam, and Christianity the emphasis has been on divine initiative when speaking of revelation. Over the centuries the content of what has been claimed to have been revealed has been very diverse: some of it has presented a moral God, some an immoral God; Jews had "Jewish revelations", Muslims had "Islamic ones", and Christians had "Christian ones"; in many cases what the God, supposedly, said she/he was about to do never in fact took place. Revelations were claimed to have been received by both the psychologically stable and by others suffering from psychiatric illnesses. They came through dreams and visions, through thoughts entering the mind or voices heard in the head, through events or people in which a divine message was discerned, through meditation on the Scriptures and through worship. Incidentally, if a God allegedly revealed herself/himself by becoming a human being (and nothing but that), what reasons could there be for thinking such a person was anything more than a human being?

In the situations where the emphasis was on divine initiative, such revelations can never be proved to have taken place, and are always open to doubt. They might have been created by the person's own imagination, come out of their religious fantasizing, or have come from their subconscious or the outer limits of some other part of their mind.

Revelation is conditioned in its character by the person's beliefs (Christian, Jewish, Islamic, etc.), culture, and socio-economic position. It is influenced by the person's mental state and by their convictions of what it would be appropriate for their God to do or not to do (such as calling for a child to be sacrificed or helping to destroy a people's enemies).

All this tends to push the argument towards thinking that in fact 'revelation' is a product of human religious experience. Carl Jung held that the sacred depths of the psyche provided the origin of all religious and mystical experience. Even if it is a matter of both/and yet still the activity of God, whatever it may be, remains hidden, inaccessible to human investigation, and mysterious. This does not mean that having faith is not a valid activity; rather it means that the mystery in life deepens.

PART TWO

The second area that has engaged my thinking over the last 30 years is who Jesus was. Growing up as a boy and as a teenager, I held the traditional orthodox views of Jesus as both human and divine. I was very happy to sing hymns such as 'O Jesus I have promised' and 'Jesu, thou joy of loving hearts', and much of my private prayer would have been addressed to Jesus. As I studied theology, I found all of this had to change. It was both a painful and a liberating time. I had to ask myself "Is Christianity a faith that is fundamentally flawed?"

There are many books today about Jesus which demonstrate that there are conflicting understandings and interpretations of him among Christian believers. In studying Jesus, a starting-point is to observe (though some dispute this) that John the Baptist, Jesus, and his disciples all believed that the world was about to end; they expected a major intervention by their God (e.g. Matthew 10.23: "When they persecute you in one town, flee to the next; for truly I tell you, you will not have gone through all the towns of Israel, before the Son of Man comes" or Luke 3:2-9; Matt.19:28; Mark 9:1); it did not happen, the world is still here, they were mistaken. The cast for this 'end-time drama' and its varied ideas came from the speculative thinking of previous generations who had endured conquest, exile, and rule by foreign powers, and who had longed for independence again and peace. There might be a time of tribulation, the arrival of a Messiah and/or a Son of Man, a judgment of the living and the dead, and then the inauguration by their God of an everlasting kingdom of peace (e.g. Daniel 12.1-2,4: "At that time shall arise Michael, the great prince who has charge of your people. And there shall be a time of trouble, such as never has been since there was a nation till that time; but at that time your people shall be delivered, every one whose name shall be found written in the book. And many of those who sleep in the dust of the earth shall awake, some to everlasting life, and some to shame and everlasting contempt ... But you, Daniel, shut up the words, and seal the book, until the time of the end"; or Matthew 19.28: "Jesus said to them, 'Truly, I say to you, in the new world, when the Son of man shall sit on his glorious throne, you who have followed me will also sit on twelve thrones, judging the twelve tribes of Israel'"; or Daniel 7:9-10, 13-14; Isaiah 9:6-7; 11:1-9; 53:1-12; Luke 3:15; Mark 8:27-31; 9:11-13; ch.13).

Possibly, Jesus came to believe that he would have to endure some of this supposed end-time tribulation resulting in his death, after which the new kingdom would come (e.g. Luke 12:49-50: "I came to cast fire upon the earth; and would that it were already kindled! I have a baptism to be baptized with; and how I am constrained until it is accomplished!"; or Mark 9:30-32; 10:45; 14:25). In fact, the most likely reason he died was because some of the pilgrims in Jerusalem for Passover hailed him as the Messiah and Pilate saw that by removing him, the excitable crowds would be quelled.

The disciples' belief in his resurrection is probably best explained as arising from a combination of several factors: primarily, their understanding that his death was a part of this supposed 'end-time drama', which they imagined would be followed by the coming of the new kingdom in which they would meet him again (e.g. 1 Thess. 4:15-17: "For this we declare to you by the word of the Lord, that we who are alive, who are left until the coming of the Lord, shall not precede those who have fallen asleep. For the Lord himself will descend from heaven with a cry of command, with the archangel's call, and with the sound of the trumpet of God. And the dead in Christ will rise first; then we who are alive, who are left, shall be caught up together with them in the clouds to meet the Lord in the air; and so we shall always be with the Lord"; or 1 Thess.1:9-10), and some visions of him induced by their bereavement (e.g. Mark 16:9-13). In fact, no new kingdom ever arrived, nor did Jesus return as judge and savior, and the world has continued on its way. Indeed, what reasons, if any, would God have had to resurrect him? In today's world would we not question the mental stability and judgment of people who live daily convinced that their God is about to end the world and who try to persuade others of their amazing beliefs?

So, was Jesus a savior and mediator between God and his people? It depends on how you interpret the meaning of his death and whether you think a savior or mediator is required, which in itself will depend on your understanding of what a supremely loving God is like. There are three main objections to the traditional beliefs that Jesus was a mediator and that by his death he saved humankind: from science, death is a natural process and not (as traditionally believed) a punishment for sin and a power needing to be defeated (e.g. Romans 5.12: "Therefore as sin came into the world through one man and death through sin, and so death spread to all because all men sinned"); from ethics, an innocent person (claimed to be Jesus) should not bear the punishment of the guilty (e.g. Romans 5; 6); from theology, to require for the forgiveness/salvation process a human death and sacrifice suggests divine sadism (e.g. Hebrews 9.11-14: "But when Christ appeared as a high priest of the good things to come, then through the greater and more perfect tent (not made with hands, that is, not of this creation) he entered once for all into the Holy Place, taking not the blood of goats and calves but his own blood, thus securing an eternal redemption. For if the sprinkling of defiled persons with the blood of goats and bulls and with ashes of a heifer sanctifies for the purification of the flesh, how much more shall the blood of Christ, who through the eternal spirit offered himself without blemish to God, purify your conscience from dead works to serve the living God").

With the deepest respect for others and their beliefs, to my mind, Jesus, and John the Baptist also, were mistaken and misguided 'end-time' prophets; Jesus was neither a mediator nor a savior, neither super-human nor divine. The time has come to leave Jesus to his place in history, and to move on. As Kahlil Gibran observed: "For life goes not backward, nor tarries with yesterday."

The deeply attractive vision of a God of infinite love is, for me, (with all the problems and paradoxes it raises) part of the great and challenging mystery of the life we are caught up in. It is this vision that I reach out towards in a search to transform traditional forms of Christianity. Joan D. Chittister wrote in her book, *Heart of Flesh* p.172, "The revolutions that count come silently, come first in the heart ... Revolutions of this magnitude do not overturn a system and then shape it. They reshape thought, and then the system overturns without the firing of a single cannon. Revolutions such as this dismantle walls people thought would never fall because no wall, whatever its size, can contain a people whose minds have long ago scaled and vaulted and surmounted it."

PART THREE

The third area that I come to now is thought about worship. You will have realized that the theological positions which have been described above are not the positions of the majority of members of the Christian Churches; many of whom would question the right of people with views like mine to be in positions of leadership, let alone quite simply to remain as members of the Church. How do you preach or worship through the Christian year and remain true to your own vision, for example, at Christmas, Good Friday, or Easter?

The Church's worship, with much of it focused on and through Jesus, whether in prayers, hymns, canticles, or sacraments, became a world in which there was for me loneliness and alienation, disappointment and anger, and the constant tension between what I could believe to be true and the Church's official position, to much of which I could not subscribe. Could I stay the course without succumbing to the madness of the situation? And so for nearly 30 years, I have teetered on the edge of membership, wondering whether to stay or go. Speaking for myself, I find the two most stressful periods of the year to be Christmas and Holy Week/Easter. As the Christmas carols are sung at carol services, on Christmas Day, and on other occasions, and in other places in addition to churches, words or others like them such as: "O come let us adore him, Christ the Lord" appear idolatrous and painful. There is an awful sense of loneliness and alienation, a sense of belonging to a minority outlook within the Church as a whole that is swamped by the majority's singing and convictions.

"God so loved the world that He gave His only Son": at the very least, I can focus on my idea or vision of the love of God and of how much we and the whole world mean to her/him. I will speak of a world with all its sin and trouble cradled in the love of God, but not of God coming into the world as a little baby to be cradled in a stall in Bethlehem. "You matter infinitely and eternally to God" will be my message, and if you could but see the hidden Creator at her/his unseen work you would find her/him in the midst of all the muck and mess of the world as well as in its beauty, for such is the commitment and faithfulness of the Creator to the immensity of her/his task.

"God so loved the world that He sent His only Son": the Christ figure is a symbol of the relationship of God to her/his world, a relationship of love. (God the Father symbolizes the God who is before us, beyond us and in front of us. God the Holy Spirit symbolizes the ever-present unseen reality in which we live, the love, however mysterious and paradoxical, that will never let us go.)

Holy Week and Easter focus enormously on Jesus as Savior and Lord, crucified and risen. As with Christmas, no matter what the preacher says or fails to say, the whole liturgy speaks powerfully of the convictions of the majority in the Church. Hymns, prayers, and readings, drama or film, whatever is included in the liturgy tells the story. Once again inevitably there is silent suffering, alienation, loneliness, as the days for Holy Week and the Easter season go by, for anyone unable to subscribe to the central beliefs about Jesus.

I would not find myself able to say "Jesus died for you" or "Jesus died for your sins". I would speak about the costliness of God's suffering love and forgiveness; of the challenge to repentance and to offer forgiveness and to receive it; of the call to look with compassion on a broken world and to act to help to mend and restore it; of the human hoping which is centered in God, both for our own future and the world's, both here and in eternity.

In the Eucharist, I find myself detaching the bread and the wine, in my mind, from a link with Jesus. The bread becomes a symbol for dependence on God the Creator and Sustainer of all life, and a symbol of our interdependent, corporate life; the wine becomes a symbol both of suffering and of joy. Anyone who commits themselves to a moral vision of life will come inevitably to suffer for what they believe in. The wine symbolizes the costliness of such a commitment and its continuing challenge; but it also symbolizes the joy we will one day have of celebrating the fulfillment of the created order. The moment of receiving communion, and the way I would speak to God at the time, will often be significant and deep; but where is my integrity, as I have stood and said beforehand the words of the eucharistic prayer of thanksgiving?

Could I survive the tensions between Christian worship and belief, with so much focusing on Jesus, and my own theocentric leanings? And, if I could survive, at what cost to my psyche and my soul? More importantly, what about those among whom I ministered? Were they not being deprived of essential teaching? My lack of Christocentric spirituality was surely going to make a difference; were there not whole areas of deception, lack of transparency, and integrity that were not being addressed? In what sort of way could some of these issues be resolved?

As I have struggled with these matters over the years, I have found a number of things helpful. First, I looked at the entirety of life, taking a holistic view. Yes, in any human being's life there is the search for truth, the spectrum in which thinking and believing takes place, the searching is never finished, never complete. With further wisdom, experience, and thought it is possible that views, ideas, attitudes, and positions might well be revised, modified, or given up. What seemed true before might no longer seem true now. But isn't every area of life imperfect and incomplete: work, relationships, commitments to issues of justice and compassion, a relationship with God?

In a holistic view, every area of life, including thinking and believing, has its incompleteness and imperfection. I might have weaknesses in some areas of ministry, strengths in other areas; nobody offers the complete and perfect ministry, though other's weaknesses and strengths in their work and ministries might well be different to mine. Second there is the need for balance: it was easy, I found, for issues of thought and believing to get out of perspective; it was tempting for me to become over-concerned and obsessive about them. A good afternoon's pastoral visiting combined with a good deal of self-forgetfulness often proved to have beneficial effects.

When laypeople come out with their own difficulties of belief (some similar to mine, some not), for example not believing in an afterlife or not believing in the divinity of Jesus, then some of the loneliness of feeling different and in a minority is mitigated in this way.

I think, now, I try to ask more questions than I would have done before in sermons, encouraging people to think for themselves. I present them with some of the conflicts within Christianity where there are different attitudes to and interpretations of the Bible, differing views on some of the moral dilemmas of our day, different interpretations of the Easter stories. In the case of my present position in the Athboy and Trim Group of Parishes, I have been trying to become more and more transparent in relation to my beliefs, and a growing number of people in the parish know my thinking. In previous parishes I was much more reticent about sharing my beliefs. Is it the fear of upsetting the faithful, is it the recognition that most laity are not equipped with the same amount of theological learning as clergy, is it the fear of rejection, of people feeling that they could no longer find my ministry acceptable to them?

In the Trim and Athboy Group of Parishes, we launched this year, in July, a parish website: www.cathedral.meath.anglican.org. On the page that introduces our parish, I wrote the following:

> WELCOME: We are always glad to welcome visitors to our services, as well as new members; and people who are exploring, or seeking a spiritual home, are welcome to come and see if either of our churches and our congregations provide them with the sense that here is a place in which they could come to feel at home, ask their questions, go on growing in their spiritual journey; and through belonging to a caring,

compassionate, supportive community find courage, vision, commitment, and love to seek to go on trying to change both themselves and their world. As a group of people here, we see ourselves as called to try to make a difference in the world, for good and for God. People in this group of parishes find themselves in different places on the theological map of believing: some are evangelical, some are conservative and traditional, some are radical and liberal, some are still processing the faith they received in childhood and working on it in order to achieve a more credible and mature faith. There is a sense that different people have journeyed in different ways, as well as a spirit of respect and tolerance for others' beliefs. There are conflicting viewpoints but there is the shared unity found in seeking to serve the truth of God within the one vision of Love as the ultimate reality in life, its source, its central and deepest mystery, its hardest, harshest, and most crushing paradox, and its eternal hope.

Christian worship has presumed that Jesus is divine. If he is no longer to be thought to be divine, then the whole pattern of such worship needs to be changed; a revolution is required. No more Eucharist or Mass (or priesthood), no more prayers, hymns, or devotions addressed to/ through Jesus; Christmas, Good Friday, and Easter lose their traditional significance. There's something to discuss.

An enormous challenge lies ahead for those who do not want to give up on the Christian tradition, but who recognize the need to radically reform it. This twenty-first century may well see a great burst of creativity as new forms of worship are developed to reflect the new understanding, and as new festivals are created. Poets and dramatists, novelists and painters, potters and sculptors, musicians and songwriters, film-makers and liturgists can share in this new spiritual searching for appropriate ways to respond to the mystery in life together with the 'ordinary person' (young and not so young: people "unafraid to reason and unashamed to adore" Mark Oakley, *The Collage of God*, p. 56). Rowan Williams' words point in the right direction (though he would not agree with the general tenor of this paper): "where we find a developing and imaginative liturgical idiom operating in a community that is itself constantly re-imaging itself and its past we may recognize that worship is at some level doing its job" (*On Christian Theology*, p. 7). Great art, and theology too, begin in the unconscious; sometimes artists and theologians have to wait until, in Bergman's words "the gods throw down their fire". A new 'vision' is awaited of God to emerge and enthuse, to deepen the mystery of life and love, though not to resolve it.

What such radical changes will mean for the mainline institutional Churches remains to be seen. However, if Francis Fukuyama in his book *The Great Disruption* is correct, then this new Information age will see a decline in the "centralized religious orthodoxies". I believe that a new spirit of freedom will be sensed. People, nurtured in the Christian tradition, will no longer constantly be looking back over their shoulders to some allegedly complete and full revelation of divine love and human perfection, because they will not find such old beliefs credible any more.

Ethical values for a global community will be discussed and prioritized. The challenge to join with others in ascending to the heights of our humanity will remain, as well as the temptation to descend to its ugly and wicked depths.

Spiritual searching for meaning in life, for identity, dignity, self-esteem, and worth, for an awareness of the sacredness of the precious gift of human life entrusted to each of us, and for credible images of God, will lead into a search for new symbols; and for new rituals, which resonate to mark the significant stages of our inter-dependent life: both of sorrow and of joy, of failure and achievement, of belonging and believing.

A symbol worth exploring further is the symbol of the ring. In human relationships it is used as a sign of commitment, of trust, and love. It could also be extended to have another meaning, which would speak of the relationship between human beings and the divine sacred mystery of life. The ring could symbolize that we are invited to put our trust in this mysterious hidden God (unknowable by us in this present life) and to believe that she/he ultimately trusts us to respond to her/him and her/his belief in us. On the home page of our parish website, already referred to, there is an unusual picture. It is a seaside landscape with a difference. Let me try to describe it to you. There is the shoreline and a calm sea. On the horizon, in the left-hand corner, partially covered by cloud, is the sun and around it the sky is a lovely mixture of red and golden colors; the rest of the sky is partly clear and partly filled with light clouds. The unusual feature in the landscape is found in the top right-hand corner where there is a large gold wedding ring balanced on its side. Filling the middle of this ring are seven human faces, which seem to smile out at you as you look at them. The youngest face is that of a baby and the oldest that of a lady in her nineties. What is it all about? Under this strange surreal picture is an invitation: if you want to read an interpretation of this picture, then click on it with your mouse. This is part of what I tried to say:

> Different people will see and interpret our home page picture in various ways, and it will be very interesting to receive some of these interpretations and to learn from them. For me, the dominant symbol in the picture is the ring; within the context of marriage it is rich in symbolism and I draw on that symbolism and place it within a spiritual and religious vision and understanding of life.

Incidentally, I believe that the ring can transcend its traditional setting within the context of heterosexual marriage and so is able to speak, symbolically, to people of varying sexual orientations and differing sexual lifestyles at the profoundest levels of their being.

This is how the picture came together in my mind and imagination: the idea for the seven faces inside the wedding ring was suggested to me by the seven ages of man in Shakespeare's play *As you like it..* They are the faces of seven members of our parish and will be changed periodically. They represent human life from birth into old age. The sun, in the bottom left-hand corner, represents God. If there were no sun, there could be no life here on our planet earth. The sun, as a religious symbol, stands for God without whom there would be no life or universe. However, the sun is obscured by cloud which is a symbolical way of pointing to the fact that God (if there is a God) remains hidden and mysterious and not open to observation (though that does not mean, for me, that God is inactive or uninvolved, only that we do not see the whole picture of what is going on all the time nor can we understand its complete meaning).

The seven faces are arranged inside the ring and have together a circular shape as does the sun. Symbolically, I see this as alluding to a belief that there is some affinity between the human family and our Maker. This might be expressed in terms of values such as love, freedom, responsibility, accountability, vulnerability, tenderness, and goodness or in terms of abilities such as being inventive, innovative, artistic, intelligent, and purposeful.

The ring itself, in its setting within close and intimate human relationships, speaks of trust. The picture is saying, in effect, that God trusts in the belief that she/he has in us that eventually we will all ascend to the heights of our humanity and fulfill our destiny; and, on the other hand, the ring is saying that, in the Christian vision of life, we put our trust in the faithfulness and ability of God to help us reach our goals.

The sun is in the background of the picture, which suggests to me the sense of the absence of God; God is at a distance, hidden, and mysterious. However, that is not the whole truth. For the ring, encircling the human family, I see next as a symbol of love, a love that encompasses the human family, cradles it, and holds it. If a God exists, then this love can only credibly be believed to be a divine love committed faithfully, for better and for worse, to the world and the human family within it. Such a God holds, as it were, her/his family in her/his arms in all their brokenness, confusion, vulnerability, vitality, and versatility. As the ring is a symbol of love, so are God's arms the arms of a deep and tender love.

Finally, though I probably should not use that word, because I go on discovering fresh meanings in the picture, the ring given and received in the context of a marriage service resonates with themes of honoring, joy, respect, dignity, and sharing. These too speak of the richness of a divine-human relationship. There is the possibility of our honoring and respecting our God, of our acknowledging the significance and dignity of our God, and of our seeing our lives as a sharing in one great life into which we are all caught up: a life which embraces both the human and the divine, and everything else too. There is also the wonder of being before a God who honors us, respects us, gladly acknowledges our eternal worth, inalienable dignity and loveableness, and shares with us in the hazardous adventure whose destiny lies far over the horizon.

The horizon is where the ocean and the sky meet. Both of these have been powerful religious symbols in the past, can they still speak to us today and for tomorrow and how do such interpretations fit into an overall interpretation of the picture? What difference does it make, do you think, if you view the sun on the horizon as a sunrise rather than as a sunset or vice versa? Do you see elements of a contemporary Celtic spirituality in the interpretation I have shared? It is over to you for your ideas and responses.

It must be obvious that I have meditated on the symbolic meaning of the ring. A large part of my private prayer consists of sitting in silence in a little prayer room, which I am fortunate to have in my present house. I wish I had a group with whom to join in corporate acts of meditation, as I have found this very helpful in the past. I think of God in both personal terms as well as non-personal terms, such as God as an ocean and human beings as waves on the ocean. Probably the personal conceptions for God feature more in my quiet times. I am looking to reach down deeper into myself, to see the world more clearly, to create inner space within myself and to draw in more stillness. But there are conversations going on as well, within myself and directed towards God. I seek to reach out to God in both bewilderment and praise, in pain and trust, in penitence and remorse, in gratitude and horror. The challenges to grow more mature, to reform myself, to take freedom and responsibility more seriously, and the world's injustices too, are all part of this time of quietness. If the central reality and mystery in life is really love, then there are times when I am moved to reach out in love, tenderness, and compassion to God and God's world. I can be myself in these times of meditation, unimpeded and unconstrained by the normal liturgy and its Trinitarian doctrines. I am free to be as open as I can be and as true to myself and my beliefs as possible. I value these times very much.

In the epilogue to his book, *Why Christianity must change or die*, J. S. Spong wrote:

Is my reformulation of Christianity adequate for our new world? I would be surprised if it is judged to be so. It is at least the best I know how to offer at this moment, given when I live and how far into the future I can see. But if I were asked to bet on what will happen tomorrow, my best guess would be that my approach will prove to be not too radical, as my critics will claim, but rather not nearly radical enough. I suspect that the next generation might even dismiss me as an old-fashioned religious man who could not quite cut the umbilicus to the past in order to enter the future. (p. 227)

There is a clear sense that Spong feels it important to go on holding onto Jesus; he remains the 'God-bearer'. By contrast, people like myself see a need now "to leave Jesus to his place in history and to move on" and want to take the scissors and cut the "umbilical cord" between ourselves and Jesus. Or, to put it in another way, Jesus no longer functions as an archetype for us. Monica Furlong wrote: "One of the symbols Jung cited was that of Jesus as the 'archetype of the self' that is to say the symbol which helped us as individuals or as groups to become what is in us to become." (*C of E: The State It's In*, p. 96)

Harry Williams quoted from Steinbeck: "Or as the preacher puts it in John Steinbeck's novel, *The Grapes of Wrath*: 'Don't you love Jesus?' Well, I thought and thought, and finally I says, 'No, I don't know nobody name' Jesus. I know a bunch of stories, but I only love people.'" (*Poverty, Chastity and Obedience*, p.118)

A radical implication of my position is that the cross as a symbol may be jettisoned, and the symbol of the ring become the prime one – speaking of our trust in God, of God's faithfulness to us, and so of our destiny and glory. This is not, however, to deny the costliness of loving or forgiving; these must always be taken seriously, there can be no meaningful insight into the character of God if this costliness is not emphasized clearly and forcefully. To adapt words of Gabriel Marcel: if we treat God superficially, we will end up treating ourselves superficially too. For those who have "cut the umbilical cord between themselves and Jesus", Kierkegaard's words make sense (he imagined this question being addressed to us at the gates to heaven): "I will be asked not why I am not more like Christ, but why I am not more like myself."

If some or all of the Provinces of the Anglican Communion ever were to make room for what would, at present, be new forms of non-Trinitarian worship for minority groupings, then all sorts of difficult practical problems would have to be sorted out. If the minority grouping did not practice baptism, what provision might there be for new members and how would the majority accommodate themselves to another initiatory rite other than baptism? Would an ordained minister be required for these new and constantly updated contemporary forms of worship? What about marriage, for example? By dispensing with traditional Christology many reappraisals are required: in relation to the authority of the Bible, the three-fold ordained ministry, forms of democracy within the Churches, and in Christian art, poetry, drama, and music. An attempt to answer some or all of these questions will have to wait till another paper.

CONCLUSION

Any person working on his/her faith and doing some theology needs to take cognizance of the warning of Merold Westphal; this quotation comes from a reference to him in Garrett Green's book *Theology, Hermeneutics and Imagination:* "Merold Westphal characterizes the common hermeneutic of suspicion in Marx, Nietzsche, and Freud as follows: 'the deliberate attempt to expose the self-deceptions involved in hiding our actual operative motives from ourselves, individually or collectively, in order not to notice how and how much our behavior and our beliefs are shaped by values we profess to disown'" pp. 12-13. In their seeking to serve the truth, people can easily be deceived and this is why belonging to a Church of unlike-minded people may help challenge them to constantly test the authenticity of their beliefs, values, and lives. But they need to listen to others outside the Church too, as the quotation from Merold Westphal reminds them.

In one of her interviews for her book, *C of E: The State It's In*, Monica Furlong talked with Archbishop George Carey, whom she quotes as having said:

> I'd like to argue, you know, that the broad Church that we are now is probably a foretaste of what is to come. If we want to think about the coming great Church, then it is going to be one in which we have to accept huge differences within the family, and we are not going to have final answers this side of eternity. Living with differences, I think, is actually the genius of Anglicanism. (p. 162)

This quotation from George Carey's interview with Monica Furlong speaks of a basic trust in Anglicanism, in its soft edges, in its ability to live not just with diversity, but also with the conflicts that surround it. Time will tell how hard its members will fight to preserve this genius and whether or not they will be successful if they so fight. It would be surprising indeed if the future did not hold many unexpected challenges and revolutions. This present paper is itself making a challenge and calling for a revolution. Let me remind you again of that powerful quotation from Joan Chittister: "The revolutions that count come silently, come first in the heart, come with the force of steel, because they come with no force at all. Revolutions of this magnitude do not overturn a system and then shape it. They reshape thought, and then the system overturns without the firing of a single cannon. Revolutions such as this dismantle walls people thought would never fall because no wall, whatever its size, can contain a people whose minds have long ago scaled and vaulted and surmounted it."

There have been those within Anglicanism who have replied to the position within this paper by saying that if people do not believe in a Trinitarian conception of God and in an Incarnational God, then they need to look elsewhere for a different spiritual home, such as the Unitarian Universalist Church. This works for some people, but for others who feel the "reforming fire" in their hearts and minds, it does not appear to be a viable alternative. There is a cost to being in a minority camp, as there is a cost to tolerating minorities within the main grouping.

The Anglican Provinces have never been strangers to tension and conflict within their membership. Out of such tension and conflict growth has come. The reformer may be thought of as a heretic and a traitor, but history has confirmed his loyalty and his role on many occasions. Furthermore, within Anglicanism, while there have been some believers who have claimed to have seen, in faith, the actions and hand of God in many ways, there have been others who have felt much more a sense of unknowing and of mystery as they have thought about their faith and the activity of God. Anglicanism is bigger than the beliefs of any one individual with his or her own limited perspective, and is enriched by the diversity of experience of its members.

A Church of unlike-minded people is a guard against any one group within it becoming convinced that it has all the answers, and is not in need of the different perspectives of other groups. The one who sees himself or herself as a reformer needs to remember that they could well be mistaken about what they are most convinced about as true; history has its lessons to teach in this regard. However, at the risk of error, the reformer obeys the instinct to study and to think, to discuss and write, to work for change, and to bear with the slowness with which change may come about, if it ever does.

Neolithic man living in County Meath 5000 years ago thought, no doubt, that in the generations to come people would be much the same as him: wear the same type of clothes, eat the same sort of food, travel the same way, communicate the same way, build more of those amazing burial chambers, and have the same world outlook, culture, and beliefs. The Normans built their castles 500 years ago in County Meath to last for centuries and also no doubt did not expect radical change in future generations. Both Neolithic man and the Normans were mistaken; the world did change radically in ways they could not have imagined.

It may well be that in the future the Christian man and woman, with their own distinctive outlook, will cease to populate the world. The Christian religion will have run its course and come to its end or it will continue, radically different, and under a new name. What are needed now are people who will venture forth crossing over from Christianity by a bridge, still being constructed, and journey in a wilderness with no familiar landmarks. This does not mean that values such as truth, love, justice, goodness, beauty, forgiveness, and outrage will be abandoned, but the Christian vision of an Incarnate God being revealed through Christ nearly 2000 years ago will cease to be found credible. Neither the Neolithics nor the Normans saw the writing on the wall, and very few Christians do today. "We do not need a new landscape, but new eyes to see it with," said Marcel Proust. If you can imagine yourself for a moment standing on the banks of a river and watching the water flowing past, then remember the message of the river, which says that life brings change.

The days of the "faith once delivered to the saints" have gone. Each generation is free to construct their own faith in response to their world. As Kahlil Gibran wrote of children: "You may give them your love but not your thoughts, for they have their own thoughts. You may house their bodies but not their souls, for their souls dwell in the house of tomorrow, which you cannot visit, not even in your dreams."

Appendix B

Treasure in Earthen Vessels: reflections of a reformer (1999)

This paper was written for a meeting of fellow clergy in the Diocese of Meath and Kildare where we all worked, and read to them in June 1999. It has been slightly modified for inclusion here.

The story I would share with you today is a story of loneliness and guilt, of fear and uncertainty, it's a story of questing and questioning, of grief and betrayal, of anger and conflict, it is a part of the story of my own life over the last 25 years or so, but it would also find echoes (parallels, resonances) in the experiences of others.

It's a story that some may listen to gladly, they will be able to share in it, with relief they may sense common ground and a shared suffering. However, others will hear this story with a growing sense of alienation, with bewilderment, anger, and pain. I am sensitive to that and to them in this regard. Do I then perceive a risk in telling this story, and if so, why take that risk? I will try to answer those two questions later on in this paper. Ideally I would hope that both the story and the storyteller might be received with both understanding and compassion, whatever other thoughts, emotions, and reactions may arise.

At the heart of this story is the matter of believing and thinking, but the story is more complex than that. When I was a theological student and ordinand I was asked to read about and explore the central doctrines of Christianity. It was a perplexing task, sometimes exhilarating, sometimes tedious, sometimes surprising. My study continued on after ordination, and perhaps two years or so after being ordained I emerged, clearly and painfully aware, that I had been stripped of many of my previous beliefs. IN A NUTSHELL I FOUND I WAS STILL BELIEVING IN GOD, BUT NO LONGER BELIEVING IN JESUS. None of the atonement doctrines appeared credible to me, arguments for Jesus' divinity or for his resurrection held no weight for me; and that God had come into our environment to live as a human being no longer seemed plausible to me. All of this was a great shock to me, I felt betrayed by my religion and let down, I was torn by guilt as I wondered what right had I, if any, to remain either as a priest or as a member of the Church. Much of my devotional life had centered on Jesus, it seemed to me that he could no longer be a focus or channel for my worship, it would be idolatry. I grieved that I could no longer sing, "Jesu, thou joy of loving hearts" or "Jesu, thou joy of man's desiring" or "O Jesus I have promised". The Church's worship, with much of it focused on and through Jesus, whether in prayers, hymns, canticles, or sacraments, became a world in which there was for me loneliness and alienation, disappointment and anger, and the constant tension between what I could believe to be true and the Church's official position, to much of which I could not subscribe. Could I stay the course without succumbing to the madness of the situation? And so for 25 years or so I have teetered on the edge of membership, wondering whether to stay or go.

Jesus was for me a Jewish believer. I like, for example, the parables of the Good Samaritan and of the Prodigal Son ascribed to him. When I am in an uncharitable mood (and I don't mean to be offensive to others) I think of him as a "crackpot", a term I would feel inclined to apply to anyone who came to my front-door to tell me that it was their religious belief that the world was about to end. Rightly or wrongly I take a passage such as Matthew 10:23 to, at least, reflect the outlook of Jesus at some stage of his life: "When they persecute you in one town, flee to the next; for truly I say to you, you will not have gone through all the towns of Israel, before the Son of Man comes."

There does not appear to be evidence suggesting that every Jew living at this time was caught up in eschatological or apocalyptic fervor. But there were the Jews living in the Essene community, John the Baptist and his disciples, as well as Jesus and his disciples; the disciples also being part of the first generation of Christians who also believed themselves to be living in the end-time. We usually look on sects like these as made up of a pretty queer or strange bunch of people, out of touch with reality.

It is said that beliefs in a general judgment and in resurrection were imported into Jewish thinking and believing at a comparatively late stage from Iranian philosophy and religion. The whole basket of ideas which include a Son of Man, a Messiah, end-time suffering and tribulation, an end-time collective judgment of the living and the dead, Christ as the first-fruits of those who have fallen asleep – is a whole complex of ideas I find implausible and mistaken.

I do believe in an afterlife for the following reasons, which don't prove, of course, that there is one, there might not be. I believe that at death God receives people into the afterlife. The New Testament position that Christ is the first-fruits from the dead, and by implication that no one had entered the afterlife before, I do not agree with. My reasons for believing in an afterlife would include that, if there is a God, then she/he has made at least some people to have a deep yearning and longing for another life beyond this present one. Second, it could be argued on the grounds of justice and fairness that some people's lives are so short, or so full of suffering, that they deserve a better life after this one. Third, I believe that such is the love of any

God who might credibly exist, that each person would be so precious to her/him that she/he would want to enjoy their friendship not just for the years given to them here on earth, but also for eternity.

Furthermore, I find myself convinced that the goodness of a Creator God is greater than any evil that may have arisen in her/his creation; and ultimately I find myself drawn to believe that God in her/his patience, compassion, goodness, and suffering love will find a way, with our help, to absorb and remove all evil from all that exists, so that eventually all people will be drawn gladly and gratefully into the joy of her/his friendship and love. In other words, the afterlife I envisage, with all its mystery and hiddenness to us now, is a place where there will need to be much personal change and growth; the healing of many relationships; much deep penitence and forgiveness both between God and her/his people, as well as between peoples themselves. It inevitably will be costly, so I think.

There will be no final joy till all have freely entered into friendship with God and all human relationships have been healed and restored. The relationship between Creator and creation, between what happens in time and eternity, defy our attempts at full or complete understanding. Human believing for me is shaped by a moral vision and a spiritual aspiration expressed in worship and awe. Theology, as Karl Barth said, is rational wrestling with mystery.

If you believe in God and you do not believe in Jesus, how do you get through the Christian year? And if, in addition, you are an ordained person with responsibilities for preaching and teaching, how do you fulfil them, or can you fulfil them? Speaking for myself, I find the two most stressful periods of the year to be Christmas and Holy Week/Easter. As the Christmas carols are sung at carol services, on Christmas Day and on other occasions, and in other places in addition to churches, words or others like them such as: "O come let us adore him, Christ the Lord" appear idolatrous and painful. There is an awful sense of loneliness and alienation, a sense of belonging to a minority outlook within the Church as a whole that is swamped by the majority's singing and convictions.

"God so loved the world that He gave His only Son": at the very least, I can focus on my idea or vision of the love of God and of how much we and the whole world mean to her/him. I will speak of a world with all its sin and trouble cradled in the love of God, but not of God coming into the world as a little baby to be cradled in a stall in Bethlehem. You matter infinitely and eternally to God will be my message, and if you could but see the hidden Creator at her/his unseen work you would find her/him in the midst of all the muck and mess of the world as well as in its beauty, for such is the commitment and faithfulness of the Creator to the immensity of her/his task.

"God so loved the world that He sent His only Son": the Christ figure is a symbol of the relationship of God to her/his world, a relationship of love.

(God the Father symbolizes the God who is before us, beyond us and in front of us. God the Holy Spirit symbolizes the ever-present unseen reality in which we live, the love that will never let us go.)

Holy Week and Easter focus enormously on Jesus as Savior and Lord, crucified and risen. As with Christmas, no matter what the preacher says or fails to say, the whole liturgy speaks powerfully of the convictions of the majority in the Church. Hymns, prayers, and readings, drama or film, whatever is included in the liturgy tells the story. Once again inevitably there is silent suffering, alienation, loneliness, as the days for Holy Week and the Easter season go by, for anyone unable to subscribe to the centrals beliefs about Jesus.

I would not find myself able to say, "Jesus died for you" or, "Jesus died for your sins." I would speak about the costliness of God's suffering love and forgiveness; of the challenge to repentance and to offer forgiveness and to receive it; of the call to look with compassion on a broken world and to act to help to mend and restore it; of the human hoping which is centered in God, both for our own future and the world's, both here and in eternity.

With the sacraments of baptism and the Eucharist I continuously look for ways in which I can connect with them, what can I affirm that they speak about? In baptism, I find I cannot subscribe to the theology of being baptized into Christ's death, or being born again in Christ, or becoming a member of the body of Christ, or of turning to Christ, or of obeying and serving Christ. But I can affirm the theology of a Creator God, the child to be baptized is the child of the same heavenly Mother/Father; I can affirm that the child's destiny spans time and eternity, and that to be brought up by Christian parents includes being shaped by a religious outlook on life which includes both a moral vision of life and a spiritual aspiration to worship and awe. The child, like us too, has been entrusted with the sacred, precious gift of a human life and, like us too, the child is a sacred person. If I were to vote on whether to continue the practice of baptism or not, and if not whether to replace it by some other rite, I would be inclined toward another rite. In the case of children it would acknowledge their birth and arrival in the world, their membership of an immediate family circle as well as their membership of the whole family of God, and their welcoming into the fellowship of a believing community. Such a community is part of an interdependent world, which is seen in faith as a part of the mystery of creation that spans time and eternity; everything and everyone is held together within the one love of God.

In the Eucharist, I find myself detaching the bread and the wine, in my mind, from a link with Jesus. The bread becomes a symbol for dependence on God the Creator and Sustainer of all life, and a symbol of our interdependent, corporate life; the wine becomes a symbol both of suffering and of joy. Anyone who commits themselves to a moral vision of life will come inevitably to suffer for what they believe in. The wine symbolizes the costliness of such a commitment and its continuing challenge; but it also symbolizes the joy we will one day have of celebrating the fulfillment of the created order. The moment of receiving communion, and the way I would speak to God at the time, will often be significant and deep; but where is my integrity, as I have stood and said beforehand the words of the eucharistic prayer of thanksgiving?

As we approach a new millennium those who hold to the central doctrines which relate to Jesus will celebrate 2000 years since his birth and much else too. What about that minority within the Church as a whole, of which I would count myself a part, who do not hold to those central doctrines? As I look into the next millennium I would hope, from my point of view, that as theological education expands, more people might find themselves questioning the traditional presentation of the faith, and that they would have the courage to continue on an inevitably painful quest and journey, but it may not be so.

As I look back, and I belong to a post-Holocaust generation, I can ponder on how history might have been, if the central doctrines relating to Jesus had not been formulated. Probably there would have been no Church and some of the atrocities caused directly or indirectly because of Christian belief might not have taken place; but on the other hand how much good might never have been done, which its agents did because they drew their inspiration and courage from the life of Jesus and from their religious experience (as experience interpreted through Christian lenses)?

How you are reacting to this story and what it is meaning for you, I may hear from you in the discussion after this paper. There are a number of other matters I would share with you, however, before I end, if I can still count on your patience, tolerance and attention?

First there is the question of biblical authority. Do the Scriptures have any authority for me or for others of a similar outlook? In so far as the Scriptures present a vision of God as holy and just, loving and merciful, compassionate and understanding, then, if such a God exists (and that is a matter of faith and trust), how does that connect with notions of authority? One could say that the Scriptures in themselves do not contain authority, but in so far as they point to a Creator God, they point to her/his authority over all life because she/he is the Creator and the most powerful component in the relationship between Creator and creation.

On the other hand one could ask how authoritative are the Scriptures over issues of life, faith, morals, God, or Jesus. My conscience, my thinking, and my reasoning faculties are my authority; in so far as I find truth in the Scriptures, whether truths of fact or truths of faith, or moral truth, then in that respect I affirm those parts of the Scriptures (to my mind) to be speaking authoritatively, which is another way of saying I think what they say is true or correct (when interpreted in a specific way).

The different people whose thoughts, words, actions, lives, or writings find expression in the Scriptures have presented us with a very mixed bag. I decide for myself, as best I can, whether I think something to be true or false, or I withhold a decision on its truth or falsity if I am not sure. Yes, the Scriptures contain much that helps my thinking and feeds my inner life and spirit; the words I read and reflect upon come from fellow human beings over several millennia who have sought and strived and struggled to make sense of life, and to find a credible vision of the unseen power they believed to be life's Creator.

I am not an 'organizations-man'; I think less in terms of organizations, institutions, hierarchies of leadership, levels of management, groups, or corporate life and more in terms of individual people in themselves. I am interested in individuals, their stories and inner lives and worlds, relationships, and lives. I accept that any movement, such as a religious movement, will need organization and various forms of leadership. But I sit lightly to that side of life. It does not seem very important to me whether there are bishops, priests, deacons, deans, canons, or whatever or whether there is some other form of leadership. It does not matter to me whether you can trace historical successions or not. People in themselves interest me more than their status or office, and our equality before God means more to me, I hope, than our human differences in Church or society.

Let me, if you will, come back to the point I made about teetering on the edge of membership. Should I stay or should I go? I am conscious that many other people have had and continue to have all sorts of difficulties in relationship to their membership of the Church; and many of you, I imagine, have your own areas of difficulty and suffering in this regard and also ask yourselves, will I stay or will I go? You may have felt for one reason or another you have had enough, and you may have wanted to throw in the towel. Should I stay or should I go?

Could I survive the tensions between Christian worship and belief, with so much focusing on Jesus, and my own theocentric leanings? And if I could survive, at what cost to my psyche and my soul? More importantly, what about those among whom I ministered? Were they not being deprived of essential teaching, my lack of Christocentric spirituality was surely going to make a difference; were there not whole areas of deception, lack of transparency, and integrity that were not being addressed? In what sort of way could some of these issues be resolved?

As I have struggled with these matters over the years, I have found a number of things helpful. First, I looked at the entirety of life, taking a holistic view. Yes, in any human being's life there is the search for truth, the spectrum in which thinking and believing takes place, the searching is never finished, never complete. With further wisdom, experience, and thought it is possible that views, ideas, attitudes, and positions might well be revised, modified, or given up. What seemed true before might no longer seem true now. But isn't every area of life imperfect and incomplete: work, relationships, commitments to issues of justice and compassion, a relationship with God? In a holistic view, every area of life, including thinking and believing, has its incompleteness and imperfection. I might have weaknesses in some areas of ministry, strengths in other areas; nobody offers the complete and perfect ministry, though other's weaknesses and strengths in their work and ministries might well be different to mine.

Second, there is the need for balance; it was easy I found for issues of thought and believing to get out of perspective; it was tempting for me to become over-concerned and obsessive about them. A good afternoon's pastoral visiting combined with a good deal of self-forgetfulness often proved to have beneficial effects. When lay people come out with their own difficulties of belief (some similar to mine, some not), for example, not believing in an afterlife or not believing in the divinity of Jesus, then some of the loneliness of feeling different and in a minority is mitigated in this way.

I think, now, I try to ask more questions than I would have done before in sermons, encouraging people to think for themselves. I present them with some of the conflicts within Christianity where there are different attitudes and interpretations of the Bible, differing views on some of the moral dilemmas of our day, different interpretations of the Easter stories. In the case of my present position in the Athboy and Trim Group of Parishes, I have been trying to become more and more transparent in relation to my beliefs, and a growing number of people in the parish know my thinking. In previous parishes I was much more reticent about sharing my beliefs. Is it the fear of upsetting the faithful; is it the recognition that most laity are not equipped with the same amount of theological learning as clergy; is it the fear of rejection, of people feeling that they could no longer find my ministry acceptable to them?

There is no doubt that in a multiplicity of areas of life we are all very used to experts or so-called experts coming out with conflicting viewpoints. In the world of politics, divergence of outlook and variety of policy are part of a multi-party state or democracy. Christians, too, for many centuries have been aware of conflicting views over many issues; and the Scriptures themselves record much disagreement. Does this mean then that many Christians today could handle, with tolerance, quite open and real differences and conflicts between their own thinking and believing and that, for instance, that of their ministers? I wonder what you would think yourselves. I can think of some people for whom it would be no great problem and others for whom it would be quite intolerable, a very genuine barrier and obstacle.

Is not the thinking and believing of finite minds, when they attempt to concern themselves with the Infinite, always a case of "treasure in earthen vessels"? I do believe I have a positive faith and spirituality. I am drawn towards a treasure beyond my understanding; what I can imagine of it I express in earthen vessels: finite, imperfect forms.

If there is a risk in telling others that my earthen vessels appear to some extent to be different to theirs, and the risk is misunderstanding, or rejection, or inability to communicate, is the risk not worth taking in the hope that at least some others might recognize the treasure more clearly through my earthen vessels and find it more credible to believe, to trust, to worship, serve, and adore? I apologize to those whose blood-pressure I have made to boil, while they have been reading this article; we may have deep differences in our thinking and believing, I hope we can continue to see ourselves as held together within the all-embracing friendship of God and open to the mystery of her/his leading and guiding.

And a final question to leave you with, as I think how God must have watched countless generations within her/his human family, of all sorts of different faiths, discuss, argue, agree, and disagree (Christians are not alone in this by any means). This is the question: They are connected, of course, but to the mind of God would it perhaps be true that being and becoming are more important than believing?

Appendix C

Why the Church must be willing to alter the path it follows (2002)

This article has been slightly modified for inclusion here. It was published first in *The Irish Times* on 8 January 2002.

The Church can be likened to a great motorway – a route for people to follow if they so choose – but it is always in need of an extra lane.

For some people, it is alright to stay in the Church. For others, it is alright to leave the Church; they are free to take the next exit, to travel and explore another route. They are, of course, welcome to rejoin the motorway, if they want to, at a later stage. Other people will have traveled in a number of lanes during their lifetime to date. Perhaps they started in a conservative lane, then moved into a charismatic one and then moved on again outward into a radical one. Others began in an evangelistic lane or in a fundamentalist lane and moved over to a lane where social justice and human rights were central concerns. However, there is also another group of believers who want to stay, but need the Church to broaden its boundaries – the motorway needs another lane.

"The time has come to leave Jesus" (this remarkable and unforgettable person) "to his place in history and to move on." If you agree with this statement of personal conviction, then you and I can only begin from where we are now, as we continue our journeying into 2002.

To some of those who agree with me, that "Jesus was neither a mediator nor a savior, neither super-human nor divine," I say, "It's alright to leave the Church"; to others I say, "Try and stay on if you can." The world has seen religions come and go; to my mind, no religion is guaranteed permanence, only the searching human spirit, mind, and heart are perennial.

One of the Church's early and defining creeds is the Apostles' Creed. In preparation for a program on BBC's *Sunday* on 30 December 2001, people of all faiths and none were invited to submit their own personal credo: who or what is the origin of your universe, how would you express the essentials of what you believe about God (if you believe in God), about the purpose of life, and spiritual reality? Your thinking, believing, doubting, and searching would probably make me want to modify my present credo. This is it:

As individual and social beings, we are challenged to ascend to the heights of our humanity, and avoid sinking to the depths of our depravity.

In beliefs expect diversity, mine evolve. Religions are motorways needing widening. All life is gift; human life is of eternal worth, found loveable by God, who is hidden, active, committed to us for better, for worse.

Religious symbols: wedding ring, journey, fire, light, darkness, horizon, sun, cloud, ocean, wave. The destiny of this risky adventure of life lies over the horizon, in eternity; the meaning of life continues to grow.

Let life be developed and used, be open-minded, courageous, and humorous, seek to adore.

My main questions at the beginning of 2002 are these: in a liberal, pluralistic, modern democracy, how can a centuries-old institution, like the Church, catch up? Is it realistic for members of any church to expect that their leaders' thinking, over a working lifetime of 40 years, will always be in agreement with the current orthodoxy of the day? Is this not too much to expect? What place for reformers? Is it an illusion to dream of a doctrinally pure Church? My main concern is that we remember religions should be 70 per cent or more action, however necessary and healthy debate might be.

My ancillary concern is that the situation that we have now should not be repeated in the future. There have been 250 years of honorable academic study, using the latest and best research tools, into the significance of Jesus, Christianity's founder. However, the leadership of our churches, myself included, has largely failed, probably out of fear and/or a misguided protective love, to inform its membership that the results of such research have produced a rich diversity of interpretations of Jesus. Like it or not, orthodoxy has been challenged and questioned.

Appendix D

Letters written by Andrew Mayes (2002)

(the Erasmus Smith Professor of Hebrew in Trinity College, Dublin to the editors of *The Irish Times* and *The Church of Ireland Gazette*)

The first of Andrew Mayes' letters, below, to *The Irish Times* will be understood better if read in context. So I include a quotation from my Press statement, issued on 15 December 2001, which appeared in the 'This Week they Said' column of *The Irish Times* on 24 December 2001; I also include the editorial in *The Irish Times* of the same day, and my letter to the editor in response to that editorial, published on 29 December 2001:

The Irish Times (24 December 2001)

This Week they Said

Jesus was neither a mediator nor a saviour, neither super-human nor divine ... the time has come to leave Jesus to his place in history and move on.
– The Church of Ireland Dean of Clonmacnoise and Rector of Trim, Very Revd Andrew Furlong

The Irish Times editorial (24 December 2001)

THE MEANING OF CHRISTMAS

A cathedral dean has brought his own doubts about faith and the relevance of Christian belief today into the public forum, first on his own website, and, in more recent days, with lengthy and candid interviews in all sections of the media. When a priest publicly questions the traditional beliefs that have been central to the celebrations of the great Christian festivals – particularly Christmas and Easter – it may appear his bishop has little choice but to suspend him from exercising his priestly offices in the Church.

The incarnation is not just an old folk story that provides a good excuse for shopping and merriment, or eating and drinking to excess. It also challenges our values and priorities in a world that would, if needed, find plenty of other excuses for those excesses.

The story of the God who gives up everything to share in the sufferings of humanity, to enter into the squalor of poverty, to identify with the blind, the deaf, the dumb, the diseased, the prisoners, the broken, the lonely and the oppressed, remains deeply disturbing and challenging in an age that may think it has matured beyond the messages of faith and belief but values only success and riches.

The events of September 11th are a warning of the dangers of religious fundamentalism of every variety. But even when superstition is outgrown and fundamentalism abandoned, we need to be challenged about our priorities. And the priorities of the Child born in Bethlehem are in stark contrast to many of the priorities, public and private, political and social, that have gripped Ireland in recent years. Now that our future prosperity is shrouded in doubts, the priorities at the heart of the Christmas message take on added value.

But it is not just the Christmas story that makes shocking demands on us: there are challenges in all the stories that have become part of the Christmas tradition. The story of the three kings is one of free giving and a powerful image of political leaders getting their priorities right. The story of the flight into Egypt begs many questions in today's Ireland: would the Child Jesus and his family have found shelter as a homeless family? Would they be welcome here as refugees or asylum seekers, or would they be turned back at the point of arrival? Even the story of Santa Claus, with its origins in the generosity of an early Byzantine bishop, is a reminder of the priority children should have all the time and of the value of giving freely without expecting anything in return.

The central stories of Christmas are best told in poetry and drama. To reduce them to debates about historicity, literalism and modernity is to lose their poetic truth and dramatic impact, and to deprive them of their relevance. The Dean of Clonmacnoise may think Jesus was mistaken and misguided. He may say he does not believe in Christmas. But the incarnation – the story of the God who bothers to give up everything and who declares his priorities are with the poor, the suffering and the marginalised – remains relevant and challenging, not just at Christmas, but throughout all time.

My letter to the editor of *The Irish Times* (29 December 2001) in response to the editorial (24 December 2001)

DEAN AND THE INCARNATION

Sir,

Reading your editorial "The meaning of Christmas" (December 24th) left me with a sense that I had been diminished as a human being. However, first let me applaud you for focusing on ethics.

A religion, to my mind, should be 70 per cent the working out in practice of its ethical and theological vision, 10 per cent liturgy, 10 per cent escapism (can anyone consistently face the hard challenges of her/his faith?), and 10 per cent speculation, insight, debate, doubt and belief.

There is a Shona greeting (which I used every day for 11 years in Zimbabwe): "Are you well?" "I am well if you are well," comes the answer. It highlights that corporate awareness that we are all caught up in the one bundle of life, which is far from well. We are all disabled, wounded and sick; a mixture of health and disease. The ethical vision and challenge of life calls on us to mend, restore and heal where we can.

Now, to my main point: my reaction was due to both what was said and what was not said, but needs to be said in a Christmas message. The sound of the drums of Christmas beats in the depths of the wounded psyches of the Jewish and Islamic communities. If the life of that remarkable and unforgettable person, Jesus of Nazareth, has inspired many within the evolving tradition of Christianity to aspire to the heights of their humanity, have we not also seen that many, too, in his name, have reached the depths of their depravity?

I write as one who lives currently, still, in Trim, "inward with all the tensions of our age" (R. S. Thomas). I belong to the post-Holocaust era and to the post-September world. We cannot ignore the demonic suffering and the innumerable human deaths, which the followers of Jesus of Nazareth have inflicted over the centuries on their brothers and sisters of other religious traditions, especially Judaism and Islam.

Every Christmas message should include an apology and re-commitment to reconciliation. This year it was not made in an editorial which purported to be giving the Christian viewpoint, and I feel diminished.

The message of the Incarnation has always sounded painfully in Jewish and Islamic ears (because they could not conceive of their God becoming human) and has reverberated with the drumbeat of a triumphalist and superior religion which considered itself unable to enter into inter-faith dialogue with them on a level platform.

I question this position, as is now clear; and believe that the Christian tradition is in fact on a level platform. Over the past 250 years human knowledge has progressed in every subject, including theology. I want to honour theological research into the significance of Jesus and affirm the diverse interpretations (both orthodox and alternative) that have resulted from this study. Like it or not, the orthodox interpretation of Jesus has been challenged. I am not the first to do so; many others have.

It may seem, to quote from your editorial, that "the central stories of Christmas are best told in poetry and drama. To reduce them to debates about historicity, literalism and modernity is to lose their poetic truth and dramatic impact, and to deprive them of their relevance". However, I believe it is of incalculable importance that every follower of Jesus studies the claims made about him, becomes properly informed, and makes their own mind up for themselves.

At the very least, we owe it to all those who have suffered and died within Islam and Judaism to revisit the question of Jesus' significance for ourselves (see, e.g., *The Shape of Living*, by David Ford and *Reason to Believe*, by Maurice Wiles). I do not fully subscribe to this saying of Voltaire, but in this case it has its point: "To the living we owe respect, to the dead only truth."

I think in the future, whether the Christian tradition survives or not, we can find a way to put across a strong ethical and theological challenge to each generation without invoking, as per your editorial, the story of the Incarnation. I share two things with the (to my mind) real Jesus: a belief in his God and a disbelief in the Incarnation of his God (he would not even have considered it a possibility as a member of the ancient community of Israel). – *Yours, etc.,*

Very Revd Andrew Furlong, Dean of Clonmacnoise, Trim, Co Meath.

Andrew Mayes' letter to the editor of *The Irish Times* (9 January 2002)

DEAN AND THE INCARNATION

Sir, It is to be hoped that recent reports and letters relating to the view of the Dean of Clonmacnoise will lead to fruitful debate, rather than to sniping from entrenched positions or the stifling imposition of ecclesiastical authority. For what is at issue here is a matter of fundamental concern to anyone who gives more than a moment's thought to the implications of their membership (or, indeed, their rejection of membership) in any religious community.

Mr Furlong's reported view that Jesus was a mistaken and misguided end-time prophet may or may not be compatible with his position in the Church of Ireland, but it would seem to me that a decision on that is a matter of whether or not he is happy to remain in dialogue with those with whom he may find considerable disagreement, rather than of any attempt to silence or exclude him on the basis of a perceived failure to adhere to a given set of beliefs.

Full Church membership must always be a matter of extending the boundaries rather than of retreat into the false security of a narrow sectarianism. For my own part I very much hope that he will not be excluded, that he will remain in dialogue, and that in doing so he will contribute to a fresh understanding of what being a member of the Church of Ireland means.

Mr Furlong has posed the issue in a particularly stark form, but in doing so he is at once too radical and yet not radical enough. He is too radical in that he suggests that because Jesus was a mistaken and misguided end-time prophet (if that is indeed what he was) it is time to leave him in the past and move on. Such a view of the past and of our relationship to the past is somewhat simplistic: it assumes that we have access to the historical event in itself and to the historical person in himself, about which judgements may be made free of all interpretations; and it rejects the possibility that the significance of that event or person may become apparent only over time and within the context of our relationship in the here and now to that event and that person. That is the type of simplistic approach typical of many fundamentalists and atheists (between which categories there are notable parallels).

But Mr Furlong is not radical enough. He apparently finds difficulty with the claims made about Jesus particularly in relation to the Incarnation. In this, however, there is an assumption that language, including religious language, must be literal and referential, and that its truth value lies precisely in its being just that. Surely it is clear that religious language (but, I would hold, all language) is metaphorical. To say "I believe in God" and that "Jesus is the son of God" can only be metaphorical – the means by which we try to say, on the one hand, that life is not exhausted by its physical and material limitations, and, on the other, that (to use other metaphorical language) "God was in Christ reconciling the world to himself". The biblical stories of the birth, death, and resurrection of Jesus can only be extended metaphors through which realities that transcend the literal are expressed.

To take these stories in other terms, to say that they are either historical or false, is a reductionist approach which misses the meaning and transformative significance that the stories have had in contexts far removed from those that gave rise to them. These stories have established themselves as classic expressions of faith, not because they report historical events, but because they have responded to the hopes and fears of countless generations by giving expression to fundamental convictions in relation to what is ultimately true.

That "the followers of Jesus of Nazareth have inflicted (suffering and death) over the centuries on their brothers and sisters of other religious traditions" cannot be denied. These actions, however, reflected (among other things) the intolerant, fundamentalist claim to full possession of the truth, and have little to do with the truth that the stories of the Incarnation convey, a truth that is inclusive rather than exclusive, world-embracing rather than world-dividing.

Mr Furlong's views, or at least the public expression of them, require further clarification and debate. His statements that he affirms the diverse interpretations (both orthodox and alternative) that have resulted from theological research into the significance of Jesus, sit awkwardly with his disbelief in the Incarnation, unless some metaphorical kind of understanding is present.

In any case, the discussion should continue, and continue especially within the Church – and that despite (or perhaps indeed because of) the appalling views on false teaching expressed in the 'Thinking Anew' column, printed (surely through some diabolical mischief) in close proximity to the Dean's letter in your issue of Saturday December 29th.

Andrew Mayes, Dublin

Andrew Mayes' letter to the editor of *The Church of Ireland Gazette* (1 March 2002)

FURLONG CONTROVERSY

Only recently have I had the opportunity to view (a tape of) *The Late, Late Show* in which Dean Furlong and a number of his parishioners participated. Anyone who saw that programme will undoubtedly have experienced a variety of reactions. First, it was indeed sad to see a breakdown in the relationship between a rector and his parishioners become the subject of such a programme. Pat Kenny handled the situation with some delicacy, but by their nature such programmes depend on the sensational for their appeal. Moreover, opinions expressed in such public contexts tend to become fixed, making the task of reconciliation more difficult.

Secondly, however, despite the setting, it was remarkable that the Dean was so mild and unconfrontational in the expression of his views. He is clearly a person of great sensitivity, and one who (and it was good to see this expressed clearly in the programme) has been a very effective pastoral clergyman.

Thirdly, at the end it was still not very clear where exactly the issues lay. The Dean defined God as 'unconditional love' and sees this love as exemplified in Jesus. He has difficulty with the labels which are used of Jesus, particularly Son of God and Saviour, and would regard these, together with the language of sacrifice, as more appropriate to a first-century Mediterranean world than to a twenty-first-century European one. But is not this indeed the case? We all, whether consciously or unconsciously, give meanings to these labels, which we can now understand, so that the labels become shorthand for the meanings which we attach to them, meanings which, moreover, are not necessarily those in the minds of the original users of this language. We are constantly updating our religious practice and expression, in the use of new liturgies, fresh translations of the Bible and revisions of hymnbooks. To pretend that there are some elements of this language which are somehow fixed for all time with a single and stable meaning, so that faith can be adequately expressed in the simple repetition of phrases like 'Jesus is Lord', is effectively to abrogate the responsibility which lies on all of us to understand and make sense of what we are doing and saying.

Fourthly, the crux of the matter is probably more to do with the fact that the Dean is perceived to have deceived his parishioners and others, on the occasion of his institution, by pretending to believe what he did not believe; indeed, the Dean has himself apparently admitted to this. I think, however, that the Dean does himself a disservice, and does so in the interests of a rigorous honesty and a deep sensitivity, of which not many are capable. The deception to which he admits apparently consists in that he gave his assent to the Thirty-nine Articles of religion and to the Book of Common Prayer, and agreed that he believed the doctrine of the Church of Ireland as therein set forth to be agreeable to the Word of God, at the same time knowing that his interpretation of the significance of these documents and of what they mean may well have differed from the understanding of others.

It is here that the most important issue seems to lie, the fundamental importance of these documents for the faith of the Church of Ireland is not to be denied. Through them has been achieved a depth of wisdom and understanding that justifies their place as classic expressions of faith.

It must be said, however, that the role of these documents is that of defining the tradition of the Church, and that assent to them means that one recognizes in them the touchstone of the definition of faith. To take them in other terms, as statements which in themselves are the inscripted truth demanding our submission, is a form of idolatry which the Church of Ireland has always rightly resisted. These statements are interpretations of the faith, rather than the faith in itself. If this is so, then it seems to me that the Dean's 'deception' must be taken for exactly what it was, viz. an undeclared rejection of any literalistic approach to that to which he gave his assent. How many other clergy in the Church of Ireland have practised the same 'deception'?

It is to be hoped that the Church of Ireland can accommodate someone with the courage, integrity and thoughtfulness which Dean Furlong has shown. What we cannot afford to lose are people of deep faith who are yet open to ever new understanding and sensitive to the changing needs of the times in which we live.

Andrew Mayes, Dublin

Appendix E

Article written by David FitzPatrick, a member of the Church of Ireland (2002)

THE DEAN IN CONTEXT

"The old sacred and pre-scientific universe passed away long ago. It was given up by degrees, very slowly and reluctantly, between about 1500 and 1900 – Erasmus to Nietzsche. Today it is irrecoverable, and nobody seriously thinks of returning to the view that earthquakes are acts of God, that sickness is a divine visitation, or that a human being may wield supernatural powers.

Since about 1880 the old world-view has been finally dead. But still we cling to it – in fact, more determinedly than ever. The carol service, a classic example of popular supernaturalism, may pretend to be medieval but it dates in fact from 1918 – after the birth of modern physics! ...

The clergy spend most of their energies in staging re-enactments of the old sacred world-view, and devote their sermons to explaining its symbolism and commending it. In fact we are so busy trying to market our heritage religion that nobody has time to think what kind of religion we'd come up with if we threw out all the nostalgia and sentimentality, and tried to keep strictly within the parameters of today's world.

It's time to throw off the nostalgia and the illusions and make a fresh start. Fantasies of wielding supernatural power are not of much help to children and the belief that unseen powers will look after us and make sure that nothing very bad ever happens to us doesn't do adults very much good either. If we could see the old pre-scientific culture more clearly we wouldn't really want to go back to it. If we were not so weighed down by false nostalgia we might be able to create something very much better, and more suited to our own time."

No – Not the thoughts of the Dean of Clonmacnoise but of Don Cupitt – Anglican priest and Fellow of Emmanuel College, Cambridge. For most of the twentieth century debate has taken place about the relevance of Christianity in the modern world. Dietrich Bonhoeffer writing from prison in the early 1940s addressed the questions raised from the development of a society without religion; how do we speak of God without religion? How do we speak in secular fashion of God? What is the significance of a Church in a religionless world? Paul Tillich, in *Shaking of the foundations*, in 1949 published a sermon 'The depth of existence' in which he brought God down to earth describing Him as the Ground of our very Being. Rudolf Bultmann in 1941 developed his theme of demythologisation published in English as *New Testament and Mythology* (1953) These writers and others pursuing similar lines of thought gave rise to the publication of *Honest to God* in 1963 by John Robinson. This of course, as many will remember, was followed by enormous controversy. One of the areas of discussion in *Honest to God* was that "the centre of today's debate is concerned not with the relation of particular myths to history, but with how far Christianity is committed to a mythological, or supranaturalist, picture of the universe at all." Is it necessary for the biblical faith to be expressed in terms of this world-view, which in its way is as primitive philosophically as the Genesis stories are primitive scientifically?

Dr Robinson followed *Honest to God* with other books: *The New Reformation* (1965) and *The Human Face of God* (1973) The debate continued but less in the public eye and the Church at large settled back into its comfortable pew. In the late 1980s the Bishop of Durham caused a further disturbance when he said that he did not believe in the Virgin Birth or the Resurrection. In 1999 the Church of England introduced a code of practice and said that clergy who profess atheism or who deny the doctrine of the Trinity or the Incarnation should be disciplined. This was regarded as a return to heresy trials, the last of which was held in 1847. It is not clear if the proposal was passed or implemented but it itself gave rise to controversy. A BBC poll asking the question, "Would the Church be right to expel 'Godless Vicars'?" was given an 84 per cent NO response.

Later, Don Cupitt wrote in a *Guardian* article (July 2001): "The Church is understandably terrified of ideas. In the past when the common people have become interested in theology it has led to bishops being burnt, exiled to Paris and having their palaces burnt down. We can't have that. The correct response to any flare-up of ideas in the Church is always to deplore it, and to look for the best way to calm it down. This is best done by kicking the question upstairs to the doctrine commission. After that the years will pass and no more will ever be heard of it. When an issue has been buried by referral to the commission it stays buried. The commission really exists not to promote the discussion of Christian doctrine but as a safety valve which is used to ensure that the Church never gets carried away by dangerous and unsettling ideas."

In view of these attitudes it is not surprising that over the past twenty years or so a number of groups has developed worldwide who would seem to be concerned primarily with promoting the relevance of the Church and Christianity to the world today. These include: The Sea of Faith Network, The Center for Progressive Christianity and the Jesus Seminar. These vary in their orthodoxy but would have in common the objective of bringing modern critical theology to the general public.

This then is the context in which the writings and ideas expressed by the present Dean of Clonmacnoise should be considered. When *Honest to God* was published Andrew Furlong was 16 and, having studied Philosophy in Trinity College, Dublin, went to Cambridge where he obtained an honours degree in Theology and before being ordained in 1972 studied at Westcott House Theological College in Cambridge. It is probably not irrelevant that Dr John Robinson was in Cambridge at that time having been a Fellow of Trinity College, Cambridge from 1969. It is also obvious from his writings that the Dean has spent many hours in the last thirty years reading widely and agonising within himself about his ideas and beliefs. It is a criticism of our Church that this has had to be done almost alone and that he has felt inhibited from being transparent about these. With regard to his present position in Trim he says that a growing number of his parishioners have come to know his thinking whereas previously he had been much more reticent about sharing his beliefs.

In his paper 'Pain and Integrity: reform from within' Dean Furlong has detailed his present beliefs. There is no doubt that many of these are controversial and one would have to differ from his attitude towards Christ whom he seems to abandon. However, has Christ not been abandoned before and did not those by whom he was denied return as faithful followers? However, he does look on the "Christ figure as a symbol of the relationship of God to her/his world, a relationship of love. (God the Father symbolises the God who is ever before us, beyond us and in front of us. God the Holy Spirit symbolises the ever present reality in which we live, the love, however mysterious and paradoxical, that will never let us go)."

The themes which pervade Dean Furlong's writing are those of compassion, integrity and understanding. He also, by placing Christ in the politico-religious context of His time, suggests that the Church today must concentrate on how the message of Christianity as it has been delivered over the centuries can be made relevant to those living in a secular world. He would speak of "the costliness of God's suffering love and forgiveness ... of the call to look with compassion on a broken world ... and of the human hoping centred in God, both for our own future and the world's both here and in eternity." To this end – that of increasing the relevance of the Church – Furlong has suggested that revision of our creeds would be timely, and indeed invites his readers to consider their beliefs and write what they consider to be contemporary creeds.

Dr Richard Clarke in his book *And is it True?* (2000) points out that the creeds developed over centuries amid controversy and hostility on all sides. He also comments that the language of the creeds is that of Greek philosophy and not a mode of thought or expression which is fully understood today. He continues "If we were to write creeds today, they would be vastly different, both in language and the concerns addressed. The creeds should, nevertheless, be taken both seriously and intelligently. But we should hold, in some form of tension, the function of the historical creeds in opposing distortions, with their settings in cultures and thought patterns totally different to ours."

One of the concerns many people would have regarding Dean Furlong's thoughts would relate to his attitude towards the Eucharist. He "finds himself detaching the bread and the wine in his mind, from a link with Jesus. The bread becomes a symbol for dependence on God ... and a symbol of our interdependent corporate life; the wine becomes a symbol of suffering and of joy. Anyone who commits himself/herself to a moral vision of life will come inevitably to suffer for what they believe in. The wine symbolises the costliness of such a commitment ... it also symbolises the joy we will have one day of celebrating the fulfilment of the created order."

It is possible to regard these ideas as being extensions of the traditional view of the Eucharist. There are similarities – viz. the bread a symbol "of interdependent corporate life" and "We being many are one body for we all share in the one bread"; the concept of the wine as a symbol "of suffering and joy" (presumably of the world as well as individuals) and the conventional view of the wine representing the suffering of Christ and the Resurrection.

Whether the Dean would agree or not his view of the Eucharist would seem to have developed from the usual interpretation of its significance. His interpretation provides a meaning for it, which those lacking in faith or who are sceptical about the reality of the Incarnation and the Resurrection can accept. Such acceptance should only lead to an increased awareness of the problems which beset the world and it might be hoped a furtherance of Christian values which would be generally welcomed.

Dean Furlong would 'jettison' the cross as a symbol – "a radical implication of my position". He would replace it with the ring and he defines its symbolism. "In human relationships it is used as a sign of commitment, of trust and love. It could also have another meaning, which would speak of the relationship between human beings and the divine mystery of life. The ring could symbolise that we are invited to put our trust in this mysterious hidden God."

Tradition suggests that the symbol used by early Christians was a fish. This obviously changed but just when the Cross became the universal symbol is debatable. It is worth remembering the problems that the use of the Cross as a symbol caused in the Church of Ireland as recently as the last century. The controversy in St Bartholomew's Church comes to mind, as does the debate in the 1960s before the placing of a Cross on the altar was accepted. Even then this was allowed only with the express consent of the Vestry of the Parish concerned. The practice of making the sign of the Cross is still an illegal practice. Is it not odd that making the sign of one's faith is forbidden? It is difficult, however, to envisage a situation in which the Cross would be replaced. Dean Furlong might find it possible to compromise by using the ring in conjunction with the Cross symbolising both the conventional tradition and the innovation suggested by him.

At the present time the controversy caused by Dean Furlong's expression of his ideas both on paper and verbally to his parishioners has died down. This is probably a temporary lull and when the Dean has completed the period of reflection he was asked to observe by Bishop Clarke one cannot but think that further publicity and controversy will follow.

What has he done? He would appear to have thought deeply about his faith consistently over a period of some thirty years. He has formulated and expressed views which at best are controversial and to some disturbing. To others these ideas verge on the heretical and have caused many to sit less comfortably in the pews where they have listened happily to sermons which for a great part may be platitudinous or boring. At the same time he has stimulated discussion although much of this has been muted. Because the Church of Ireland is one of the more conservative members of the Anglican Communion the initial official reaction has been to ask the Dean to go away quietly for a time, presumably to let the dust settle. The official reaction as typified by that of the Archbishop of Dublin has been to dismiss the Dean's position as unacceptable but no attempt appears to have been made to consider his views with any attempt at understanding them.

This attitude seems to confirm the thoughts expressed in Don Cupitt's *Guardian* article quoted earlier. It also answers the rhetorical question asked by John Robinson in *The New Reformation* – "Is the Church [of England] not an archaic and well-protected institution for the preservation of something that is irrelevant and incredible?"

So what is to be done or what will happen now? The simplistic answer would be that Dean Furlong should resign and go away or else be asked to do so. But perhaps this is to dodge the issue in the hope that it will go away.

John Robinson wrote in *The New Reformation* – "There are many who would sympathise with the German theological student quoted by Dr A. Vidler in *20th Century Defenders of the Faith* 'we must try to be at one and the same time for the Church and against the Church. They alone can serve her faithfully whose consciences are continually exercised as to whether for Christ's sake, to leave her.' As one who knows in his bones that he could not put himself outside I want to plead for those who feel they must."

Monica Furlong in *C of E: The State It's In* is quoted by Dean Furlong. She quotes Dr George Carey as having said, "I'd like to argue you know that the broad Church that we are now is probably a foretaste of what is to come. If we want to think about the coming great Church, then it is going to be one in which we have to accept huge differences within the family, and we are not going to final answers this side of eternity. Living with differences I think is actually the genius of Anglicanism."

Finally, Dr Clarke (op. cit.): "The Church must therefore always be in the process of risking its survival, and thus living outside the walls of the ghetto. Any community functions best as a real community when it works for a focus beyond itself and its own continuance. The Christian community is at its most effective when it is not feverishly plotting its own survival, but is functioning unselfconsciously for an end beyond itself and its survival. That is by any calculation, what the overused word mission actually means."

Andrew Furlong is within the Church and struggling to stay there. He has undoubtedly ruffled some feathers, but he has also caused some people to reflect and reassess their own beliefs. He has not insisted that others should believe as he does. At the same time the Church of Ireland might be stimulated were it as a community to consider his writings and their relevance to the Church and the wider community to which it belongs. Instead of pushing him away from the ghetto perhaps the Church should encourage him to remain within and join in the process of looking beyond the walls.

Appendix F

Responses from Maurice Wiles, a former Regius Professor of Divinity at Oxford University and John Baker, a former Bishop of Salisbury, UK (2002)

MAURICE WILES' RESPONSE

I strongly endorse the plea, very well expressed in the opening of 'Pain and Integrity', that a more open, questioning, searching and agnostic style of faith should be treated as a fully recognized ingredient in the Anglican Church. It is not something that can properly be ruled out by a simple appeal to the historic creeds or the Book of Common Prayer. But there are limits to approaches that can be regarded as acceptable in the case of those who serve as leaders in the Church, even though there is no way limits can be spelled out in advance.

In your March 17th broadcast you spoke of the Church as a "community which preserved the stories of Christianity, re-interpreted them and passed them on to the next generation," and again I applaud that definition. The aspect of 'Pain and Integrity' that worries me is how little it has to say about that process of re-interpretation. The attitude of that paper to the past (with its references to leaving "Jesus to his place in history" (p. 4) and cutting "the umbilical cord" between us and Jesus (p. 10)) seems much more negative than the language of re-interpretation suggests.

Valuing past tradition does not necessarily involve "looking over one's shoulder to some allegedly complete and full revelation" (p. 7). My own view is that the sense of a surrounding mystery of love that we call God, strong enough to shape and inspire our attitudes to the world and to one another, needs particular images that are rooted in the past, have grown over time and thus have deep resonance in the tradition to which a person belongs. (Rahner has been a significant influence here.) So for me the stories of Jesus and 'the myth of God incarnate' are not, despite all the problems they raise, alienating in the way you describe; rather they have the potential, appropriately understood, to serve as powerful symbols of the spiritual realities that you want to affirm.

I am not sure how far you feel able to go in that direction. The positive aspects of your 'Treasure in Earthen Vessels', which I also read off the Internet, are more extensive than those in 'Pain and Integrity', but, as you point out, they are very broadly theistic in character and not related to Jesus at all. So perhaps you don't want to adopt that sort of line I take at this point. But there are two hints in what I have read, which suggest a possible move in that direction. On page 5 of 'Pain and Integrity' you speak of the Christ figure as "a symbol of the relationship of God to her/his world, a relationship of love", and go on to give a symbolic interpretation of traditional Trinitarian language. And in the Press release you balance your remark about leaving Jesus to his place in history with a concern "to re-discover his place in the totality of the Christian community as we understand it now". How far do you feel you could extend those hints? That seems to me the crucial question if you are to stay in a leadership role within the Anglican Church. If symbolic language is as central to religious faith, as I think we both believe it to be, is it not possible for more of the traditional imagery to serve the spiritual quest to which you want to contribute? Many of the poets and dramatists, to whom you look as fellow-contributors to that quest, still use that imagery in bold and striking ways. Taken in that poetic way direct talk of, for example, 'the body of Christ' in a eucharistic context seems to me both an acceptable and a valuable form of speech – however much one may want to disassociate oneself from some of the ways in which it has been, and sometimes still is, understood.

I am open to your suggestion that we can have no idea what humankind's religious future may be in the long-run, including whether it will always remain explicitly Christian. But for the present I see it as the task of the Church to carry forward the specific Christian tradition in the open spirit you commend. And that does seem to me to require a more positive interpretation of Jesus and the Christ tradition than you appear to allow. If there is more of this in your thinking than I have sensed from the small amount of your writings that I have read, I would think that would be something to stress in the tribunal. But if it is not (and, if that is your position, I fully respect it), it does seem to me very difficult to pursue it in an Anglican setting. A Unitarian or Quaker setting would seem more appropriate – and it would still be contributing to humankind's spiritual development in our ecumenical and inter-religious world.

JOHN AUSTIN BAKER'S RESPONSE

Thank you for your latest packet. As the Court is to sit on 8 April, I had better get this off to you as soon as possible, even though that means going into less detail and reflecting less than I would like. The many questions that arise being so complex, I am sure you should do as you have been advised, and apply for more time to prepare.

I shall marshal my thoughts under three heads.

1) The common ground between you and the Christian Tradition.

Plainly your belief in a Creator God of patience, goodness, compassion and suffering love, to whom all his children matter eternally, is and has always been at the heart of Christianity. So is your teaching that this God will eventually succeed in overcoming and eliminating evil; and that he will draw all people (and presumably any 'people-like' other creatures in the immensity of the universe) into the joy of her/his friendship and love. (The use of he/she to refer to God is, of course, entirely orthodox.) Your belief in an afterlife in which there will be personal change and growth, with the healing of relationships, penitence and forgiveness, whatever the cost, is certainly Catholic (Dante would have called it Purgatory) but hardly new or unorthodox! You say: "if you could but see the hidden Creator at her/his unseen work you would find her/him in the midst of all the muck and mess of the world as well as in its beauty, for such is the commitment and faithfulness of the Creator to the immensity of her/his task." That has been at the heart of Christian belief and spirituality for centuries. Your insistence that, at the same time as holding such beliefs, we have to recognize that God and his activity remain hidden and mysterious, and that in one sense we can know nothing about God, is simply what is known as 'apophatic' theology, and something theologians and mystics have always taught.

2) The areas where you and orthodoxy diverge.

It is clear from the papers you have sent me that these areas are almost all related to the person and work of Jesus. What you have to say here is hardly startlingly new. Even your sentence in capitals – "IN A NUT-SHELL I FOUND I WAS STILL BELIEVING IN GOD, BUT NO LONGER BELIEVING IN JESUS" – is not so far from some words of Denis Nineham near the end of that book which caused such a furor in 1977, *The Myth of God Incarnate*. What Nineham wrote was this: "... one of the things we shall surely have to take seriously is the question ... shall the Christian myth or story of the future be a story primarily about God, or shall it, if I may put it so without irreverence, be a story which co-stars Jesus and God? Shall it be a story in which Jesus shares the leading role and has a unique or perfect status of some sort assigned to him? Or shall it be a story in which the protagonist's role belongs undividedly to God, though of course the story would tell how once he worked in a vitally important way – though not in a way necessarily unique – through the man Jesus to bring the Christian people into a relationship of reconciliation and oneness with himself?" Nineham seems to be putting the matter diplomatically by framing it as though what he is talking about is topics for discussion. But his 'God only' alternative is quite clearly the thrust of the book as a whole, and no one was in any doubt about that.

Another of the collaborators in that book, John Hick, once remarked to me, "I know you think the Incarnation vitally important but quite a few of us see no need for it." And such opinions are not confined to academic circles. A significant proportion of church members or fringe members in the C of E accept Jesus as a good man but not as God. Then in ECUSA there is a considerable following for the views of Bishop Spong. In England the Sea of Faith movement, disciples of Don Cupitt, have gone even further in some respects than yourself, while Cupitt of course has written off Christianity altogether, and certainly no longer believes in God.

All that said, however, both the official and majority standpoints in the C of E are that Jesus was divine, a position usually expressed in sermons by saying that in him God lived an authentic human life, or shared our human experience, or lived as one of us. This is non-negotiable in mainstream Anglicanism, not least because it is for many people the only way they feel they can call God good or loving in face of the evil and suffering in the world. Moreover this belief is not metaphorical. It is seen as crucial that it should be a fact, not a symbolic way of saying something about God's character. Clearly in this area you are radically at odds with most Anglican thinking.

You mention the Atonement, but, so far as I can see, it is the substitutionary theory that you cannot accept, and in that you would probably be with the majority. Atonement as such simply means 'reconciliation', and in modern times Anglicanism has declined to back any one view of how this is brought about. Despite the language of the BCP and the 39 Articles, in the C of E (which, I agree, may not be regarded as an exemplar, but is the only province to which I can testify) penal substitution is widely rejected. For many Evangelicals it is indeed the core of their faith, but even in that tradition there are quite a number of preachers and teachers who try to express in a more acceptable way what they feel it is trying to get at. My own belief (to put it in a very small nutshell) is that we cannot talk about atonement except in terms of both the Cross and the Resurrection. It is the return of Jesus at the first Easter with the greeting of "Peace!", after he had been abandoned, denied, and rejected, and tortured and crucified in a travesty of justice, which made it clear beyond a peradventure that the God who had raised him from the dead was one who will always reach out to us with the offer of reconciliation, whatever we have done. Moreover this was not just a matter of words but of an event, a fact, the renewing of a personal relationship. It is this demonstration which opens up the way to communion with God for all people in all generations. I can see, however, that if you do not believe in Jesus as divine, or in the resurrection, the whole question of atonement/reconciliation is off the map for you – and that certainly would put you at odds with the Church.

For the Resurrection, too, is ruled out in your papers. But I have to say that the reasons you give for this position are rather thin. At a time when even a Jewish scholar like Pinhas Lapide can accept it one might ask whether thought on this topic has not moved on a good deal since you formed your own position. But the most powerful reason for believing in the reality of the resurrection is the unshakable conviction of the earliest Church that God's end-time was about to arrive. In the Jewish mind the general resurrection was inseparably linked with the Last Day and the coming of the Reign of God. Jesus' resurrection, therefore, was seen as absolute proof that this Day was near. This is why St Paul talks of Jesus as "firstborn from the dead" or the "first fruits of the harvest of the dead". There is no need for me to point out that the Resurrection as an objective fact, even allowing for legitimate argument about details, is also non-negotiable for the Anglican Church. In England this was made clear in the 80s, when the House of Bishops issued its statement, *The Nature of Christian Belief*, in response to disquiet about the utterances of Hugh Montefiore and David Jenkins.

Which brings us to a subject which clearly has exercised you greatly: Jesus' belief that the end-time was imminent. Any honest reading of the Synoptics must accept that this is a fact. Equally we know that the end did not come, and has not yet come; and this clearly bothered people like those for whom 2 Peter was written, or poor Hymenaeus and Philetus, who are said in 2 Timothy to have taught that the resurrection had already happened, a somewhat desperate expedient! But while we might feel justified in applying terms like 'crackpot' to those in our own day who have set a date when God will end the world, there was nothing in the least absurd in believing within the religious culture of first-century Judaism that the end was near, as the evidence you cite abundantly illustrates. The real issue here is actually the Incarnation again, and what we believe this might entail. I shall come back to this in a moment.

Turning to the sacraments, I am quite sure that some of the NT language you quote about baptism affords much puzzlement to our congregations, but that does not mean that we cannot give legitimate interpretation to at least some of it. If, e.g., the Church is regarded as a body of people taking their inspiration from Jesus' life and teaching, and trying to carry on his work in the world of today, that is a perfectly reasonable and acceptable way of explaining the phrase "the Body of Christ", and one which I am sure is widely used, and one with which I would not have thought, from what you write, that you could have any problems. If a child or adult is admitted to membership of the Church, then becoming a member of the Body of Christ is surely a colourful and uncontentious image for that. "Baptism into the death of Christ" is, I agree, more obscure, as is "being born again" – but the real difficulty, I imagine, for you is again what such phrases imply about the person and role of Jesus rather than the imagery itself.

So far as the Eucharist is concerned, I would have thought that any practising Christian would happily go along with all the positive things you say on your website 'Treasure in earthen vessels' p. 3. The queries arise when you talk of "detaching the bread and wine, in your mind, from a link with Jesus." If the rite is in any sense a Christian Eucharist, it would seem to be very difficult to do that. As to your problems with the words "This is my body" and "This is my blood", I am certain that many Anglicans, if not Roman Catholics or Orthodox, share your unease, and, I would say, very understandably in the light of what has been made of these words in Christian history. It is tragic that all the quarrels and divisions and indeed murders that have resulted from theological argument over these words have been totally unnecessary, because in the light of biblical scholarship it is now perfectly clear that Jesus himself cannot have held the ideas that have been attributed to him. (I am sorry that it would take too long to justify that statement here, but if you have access to my book, *The Faith of a Christian*, you can find the evidence set out there in Appendix B, pp. 201-211). Definitions, therefore, like those in the BCP which attempt to steer a middle way between conflicting sixteenth-century dogmatic positions, however praiseworthy they may have been at the time, are really quite irrelevant. I am not, however, clear exactly what is meant by the phrase in the Petition, "the efficacy of the sacraments". Does this refer to the belief that, when these rites are properly conducted by an authorised minister, certain results follow, i.e. membership of Christ for the baptised and or the presence of Christ in the soul of the communicant? I must have overlooked the passages where you discuss these matters.

3) Is this confrontation really necessary?
As I have said already, and as you yourself recognize, the heart of the matter is your understanding of the person and role of Christ. Everything else relates back to this by some route or other. What seems to me so very sad is that when you came across certain problems during your theological training, you surrendered to the conclusion that these invalidated the core beliefs of Christianity, and – perhaps because your teachers paid little attention to these things, or even had no positive suggestions to make – you were confirmed in this conviction and, in your own words, "I felt betrayed by my religion and let down." You assumed that the objections and difficulties which you recognized reasonably enough to be serious were in fact the last word on the matter; and so, as you say, "for 25 years or so I have teetered on the edge of membership, wondering whether to stay or go", using up your mental and spiritual energy in "loneliness and alienation, disappointment and anger", instead of in constructive wrestling with the challenge. Many in your position, like friends of my own, would have given up the idea of ordination altogether, as, I gather, your bishop and others do indeed feel you should have done. It would be impertinent of me to express a view on that, not being in your confidence about what were no doubt complex feelings, and perhaps hopes that somehow things would become clearer as time went on. My concern is simply with your theological position.

Why I said that your story is sad, is not just because of the cost to yourself, others and the Church, but because in rejecting Jesus as God incarnate you seem to me to reject the only good reason there has ever been for believing, as you do, in a God of love and compassion, a God who is on our side. The Creation does not justify such a belief; it is at best ambiguous on the point. For myself, as I have often argued, a God who was not incarnate would be less good than we are, at least at our best, for we have to stand for love and goodness in what you yourself have called "the muck and mess". How you would argue for a God in the muck and the mess without faith in the Incarnation I find perplexing. The joy of the gospel, its transforming power in one's life, comes precisely from its message of God alongside us, God in it all with us. This is the seed of hope. If I did not believe in the Incarnation, I could not believe in God at all, and millions hold to the same faith for the same reason. This is what other faiths cannot offer, much good though they may have in them in other ways. I am afraid I simply cannot see how one can be a Christian minister if one does not hold this belief. It is the defining contribution of Christian faith to humanity's religious understanding of the world.

I accept that you, like quite a few Christians today, find difficulty in accepting this belief. But I do wonder whether this is not in part because the Church has not sufficiently rigorously thought through what it ought to entail. People seem to think that if he were God Christ ought to have been right about everything. But why? Even today our understanding of the universe changes in fundamental ways every few years. If he did think the end time was coming, what matter? We all ought to live with that uncertain imminence, which after all only reflects the uncertain imminence of our own deaths. What is essential is that the terms on which he lived his life must have been the same as ours. Traditional teaching has assumed that Jesus was conscious of being divine; but if he was, then his life could not have been an authentic human life, nor could his death have been a genuine human death; and the interesting thing is that on careful examination the Gospels, except for one or two passages in John, afford no grounds for believing that he did think of himself as divine. It is this genuineness of his human experience which supports the core message, "God is Love." That is what the Incarnation is about, not having a brain like a monster computer, or working miracles, or whatever.

Other exciting conclusions follow from belief in the Incarnation. For instance, though the Church has never developed this, it means that God unilaterally took the whole human race as his own family. This is not a pious metaphor but a literal fact. All members of the species *Homo sapiens* share the same distinctive DNA. We are all cousins, however many times removed, so God himself is our cousin. It is therefore not that by believing we qualify for adoption by God into his family, but that faith is the point where we accept that he has already adopted us. (This fits in splendidly with some of your positive remarks about baptism; but drop the Incarnation and you have no basis for these at all.) This resolves very happily, too, the puzzles about justification, i.e. is justification the one work needful for salvation. The point about Jesus is that he is the place where God joined the human race, not the Church. This also deals with the question of those born before Christ, those who have never heard of him, and those of other faiths. Of course, it is better if everyone realises what God is like and what he has done; but whether they do or not, even indeed if they reject the faith, they are still inside, by God's own act, not out. Which surely backs up nicely your God of universal love?

Why do I myself believe all this? Because, as I see it, in the Resurrection God put his tick in the Jesus box. This, he says, is where the key to human living, now and in eternity, is to be found. I have already noted that you cannot accept the Resurrection either, but, as I said earlier, your reasons seem to me insufficient, though I have not time to go into the details of that here. You will find the basic argument for linking the Resurrection with the Incarnation in *The Faith of a Christian*, p.108.

4) Conclusion.

I have no doubt that my comments will be very different from those you get from Maurice Wiles, but then that is to be expected! What I have been trying to say is this. The Church today does need people who are prepared, as you are, to think radically, and to challenge a lot of the things that have traditionally been taught. In that general principle I support you, though, as I have tried to explain briefly, I cannot accept your central theological positions with regard to Jesus. What I would add is simply this. It is in fact the traditional core doctrine about the Person of Christ which is the real source for radical and exciting theological development, and I have tried to give briefly one or two examples of this out of many possible ones. What is more, I have found that when we put things on this basis our congregations are ready to listen and be persuaded, because we are being positive, cleaning the picture of the faith, not wiping it off.

One topic I see that I have not touched on is that of the authority of Scripture. I myself believe that Scripture has unique authority, because it is an archive from the historical process by which a people was prepared by God to be the one in which the Incarnation could happen. (It could hardly have been a success, for example, in the society of the Book of Joshua!) Without the Bible we cannot put Jesus in his faith context, or understand and interpret his significance. But if we truly take the authority of Scripture seriously, one thing we cannot do is precisely what too many Christians do do, and that is to treat it as a fixed and static repository of infallible statements. We cannot do this, for the simple reason that the Scripture itself does not do this. In its pages the picture of God and the understanding of his nature and purposes is continually changing. Yes, there is also continuity, and certain themes and features, once built in, are kept as part of the pattern, though their significance deepens and modifies as other things change around them. The right use of Scripture is achieved when a just balance is kept between change and continuity. It is an organic process. What is more, it has always gone on in the teaching of the Church. Where did the Reformation come from if not from those twin approaches? Where, for that matter, did my chief love, the doctrine of the Incarnation, come from, except from development of insights into Jesus in Scripture, for there are certainly no unambiguous proof texts of that doctrine in its pages. All of which could, I suppose, lead you to say, "Ah, there you are, I'm simply ahead of my time, and the Church will eventually catch up." (Don Cupitt thought much the same.) But hard though it may be to define, there is a difference between transformation and abolition, and my own feeling is that you at present are on the far side of that line. My argument in this letter has simply been that to secure the beliefs about God which rightly mean so much to you, you do not need to cross that line. They are already there or potentially there in Christianity itself.

What I wish could happen in your case is that you could be granted a sabbatical in which you could review and research some of these theological questions, to see whether you still want to hold to your present positions. In a case in the diocese of Chichester some time back that is what the bishop did. Of course there can be no guarantee that you would change your mind; and it could be emotionally difficult to do so, after you have invested so much in your current courageous stand. But having wrestled with these issues myself over many years, and so having sympathy for your concerns, I think for your own sake and for that of those who value your pastoral ministry this would be the right way forward. As for the question of discipline, I remember that in England Michael Goulder resigned his orders for reasons similar to yours, and this was counted to him for righteousness; but he did have an academic post to live on, and I find myself wishing that the same were true in your case. You would then be free of the promises you made at various stages, and in breach of which you now find yourself, which cannot be happy for someone of your integrity.

I am afraid this is all I have to offer. It comes with my warmest good wishes, and my continuing prayers for you and your Bishop and the Court in all the difficult issues with which you will all have to engage, and for yourself in the problematic days ahead.

Appendix G

Editorials from *The Church of Ireland Gazette and The Irish Times* (2002)

The Church of Ireland Gazette **editorial (25 January 2002)**

WE LOVE YOU MR DEAN

Jesus, of course, is renowned for his use of parable. He used, for example, contemporary life situations in farming to illustrate his radical teaching. The Dean of Clonmacnoise also uses contemporary imagery to illustrate his radical teaching: motorways, vehicles, the change of currency, bureaux de change. What is more, the Dean is taking on the religious establishment, like Jesus – only different.

If there are elements of some kind of Jesus-style drama in the whole Furlong controversy (radical teaching, a spiritual emphasis, inventive use of imagery, conflict with ecclesiastical authorities), it is perhaps not surprising that Dean Furlong, while on the one hand describing Jesus as 'mistaken and misguided' as an end-time prophet, on the other has actually set himself alongside Jesus as a man. He told the BBC: 'I see myself, like Jesus, as a person who is God-focused ... I think if Jesus was here he would agree with what I say ...'

However, Dean Furlong's rather off-beat, unorthodox teaching does not excuse the Church from loving Andrew Furlong. The Bishop of Meath and Kildare has rightly given him time for quiet reflection and, while Dr Clarke is more than capable of entering the public debate, he has steered clear of the media blitz out of pastoral concern for both the Dean and his parishioners. Contrary to Dean Furlong's stated view, it surely is not really possible to engage in reflection while taking part in a public debate for, no doubt, the media are constantly ringing up in search of comment. The response of the select vestries of Trim and Athboy in calling for Dean Furlong to go was an understandable expression of deep hurt, but as well as the select vestry resolutions there have been quite moving tributes to the Dean's pastoral ministry.

Despite the discomfort he has caused, and even though, if necessary, the law of the Church must take its course, the Church must continue to engage with Andrew Furlong on his search and not cease to love him; indeed, despite his actions, he seems to love the Church. A fundamental question with which he must grapple, however, is whether or not, while allowing for differences in teaching, he thinks there is ultimately no real difference between Jesus and himself as human beings. A basic difference between being Church and not Church, between being Christian and non-Christian, is the belief that Jesus was not simply another one of us reaching, or even pointing, to God, but the living God actually, mysteriously and wonderfully reaching to us. That makes Jesus different from the rest of us, and spells divine incarnation.

The Church of Ireland Gazette editorial (17 May 2002)

THE IMPORTANCE OF BEING POSITIVE

The resignation of Andrew Furlong marks a sad end of what has come to be known as the Furlong controversy. While the debate will go on and while Andrew Furlong no doubt will continue to publish controversial articles, the controversy – at least in its present form – is over. It is over because what made Andrew Furlong's views particularly controversial was the fact that he held them while also holding ministerial office in the Church of Ireland. Thus, with his resignation comes the end of the controversy as it was.

The Bishop of Meath and Kildare had little option but to proceed to the Court of the General Synod, because Andrew Furlong had denied the divinity and saviourhood of Christ. It is not possible to deny these things and continue to preach and celebrate the sacraments in the Church of Ireland. The only way in which the Court could have been avoided would have been if Andrew Furlong had withdrawn his statements. That, it would appear, he was unwilling to do; certainly, those statements, written by him, are still to be found on his personal website.

Without doubt, it is important that the theology of the incarnation should be discussed, but to deny the incarnation is, in effect, to end the discussion. What Christian theologians have to do is to expound ways in which the incarnation can be understood today and to help people to understand what the Church means in confessing that Jesus Christ is indeed the Son of the living God. To say that he wasn't, or isn't, just does not help.

If Andrew Furlong had been able to say that he understood the incarnation as God, in a sacred, unique and humanly incomprehensible way entering our world in the person of Jesus of Nazareth for our salvation, he would very probably still be Dean of Clonmacnoise and rector of Trim and Athboy. But, instead, he chose to deny the incarnation. He chose to discuss from a negative rather than a positive perspective.

It is a pity that Andrew Furlong was unable to adopt a more positive perspective. Nonetheless, despite all the heartache that the controversy has caused, there is still within the Church of Ireland a deep affection for him personally.

Have we all learned anything as a result of the Furlong controversy? One thing, surely, that we have learned is that while understanding the faith is not a precise science, the interpretation of the faith really does have limits.

The Irish Times **editorial (10 May 2002)**

THE DEAN RESIGNS

After months of prolonged crisis, the Very Revd Andrew Furlong has eased the pain of his parishioners, his bishop and his Church by resigning as Dean of Clonmacnoise and as Rector of Trim and Athboy. His resignation avoids the drama of a courtroom battle over his beliefs and whether they amount to heresy. Shortly before Christmas he was suspended by the Bishop of Meath and Kildare, who hoped he was providing the dean with time to ponder and to reflect. Instead, Dean Furlong used that time as an opportunity to extend the controversy, setting up a new website, emailing a wide audience of friends, colleagues and journalists, offering interviews and seeking publication in journals and magazines.

These were hardly the responses of a priest accepting his bishop's invitation to think again. And so, it was unlikely the Court of the General Synod could impose a lesser sentence of admonition or suspension. Dean Furlong was facing removal from office, and even the loss of his right to practise as a priest. His resignation saves him greater embarrassment, and saves the Church of Ireland from the possibility of an unseemly debate at next week's General Synod.

No one can doubt the dean's pastoral and professional skills. Everyone who speaks about him praises his care of his parishioners, and undoubtedly he will have no difficulty in finding fruitful opportunities in the caring professions. His views are exciting and challenging; when views like his are held by lay members of any denomination, they challenge clergy and theologians alike to find fresh and stimulating ways of ensuring the teachings and traditions of the Church are conveyed with relevance and challenge to a new generation. But his beliefs are not acceptable among the clergy, who are both the agents and the guarantors of those same traditions and teachings.

Dean Furlong's resignation allows his parish and parishioners to have a fresh start after weeks of public controversy. He has saved himself and the Church of Ireland from an unedifying spectacle. And he has cleared the ground so the Bishop of Meath and Kildare can be considered as a serious candidate to become the next Archbishop of Dublin.

The Irish Times **(11 May 2002)**

This Week they Said
A selection of quotes from around the globe

I have always grieved when I left a parish but I am also grieving for the Church of Ireland because I feel it is missing out. – Dean of Clonmacnoise, Very Revd Andrew Furlong, resigns over his controversial belief that Christ was not the Son of God.

Appendix H

An interview with *The Church Times* (2002)

FAITHFUL ARE 'OUT OF TOUCH': INTERVIEW BY BILL BOWDER,

CHURCH TIMES (12 APRIL 2002)

AFTER the Court adjourned, I asked the Dean whether there was a way forward – whether he could modify his position.
There is a great deal in what I believe that is central to the heart of Christianity, and is orthodox Anglicanism. I believe we are created in love, for love, by a God of love. I believe that Jesus is an unforgettable part of our tradition, an outstanding member of the ancient community of Israel. Without Jesus there would never have been a Christian tradition, which is an evolving tradition.

Has Christ still a central role to play in the Christian faith of which you are part?
Theologians distinguish between the Jesus of history, who is open to the investigations of a historian, and the Christ of faith, whose stories may be connected, in one way or another, with some of the historical stories, but have a large faith component.

Are you saying you still believe in the Christ of faith?
I believe in the Christ of faith, in the sense that the stories of the Christ of faith are stories about this mysterious God that we reach out to adore and to serve; the God who finds us forgivable, infinitely loveable and reconcilable.

The Christ stories speak to us about God, because they connect to the Jesus of history. He teaches us about a God of unconditional love and endless forgiveness.

Is there anything that you believe as a Christian minister which should preclude you from ministering in the Church of Ireland?
No, I don't think there is. I am very concerned about the people of the parish of Trim and Athboy, whom I love dearly, and whom I remember in my prayers nearly every day.

Some people in the parish have been hurt by all this. Do you understand that hurt?
Yes, I do.

Is there anything you could have done, or the Church could have done to have prevented this hurt?

I think the leadership of the Church as a whole is guilty of a sort of paternalistic love, a desire not to rock the faith of the faithful. But what it has meant is that the faithful have got out of touch with the results of honourable theological investigation.

Is there room for the whole spectrum of views?

Anglicanism has tried to be as accommodating of people and their views as possible. The majority has had to have the tolerance to live with the minority, and the minority has had to respect the fact that they are a minority and respect the view of the majority. The history of the Church is partly a history of doing that successfully. But it is also one of failing to live successfully with the conflicts and the tensions.

Are we going to be in the same position when we come back to court on 10 May?

Individuals, be they theologians, bishops, clergy, lay people or whoever, have a human right to do their own theological thinking and research. The clergy, particularly, need to do their own exploring, doubting, thinking and searching, without fearing that the hand of authority is going to take them by the scruff of the neck and throw them out

Appendix I

Christianity's self-scrutiny: a conversation between friends
(*The Church of Ireland Gazette,* 1978)

This article has been slightly modified for inclusion here.

INTRODUCTION

Over the last few years the clergy and laity as well as the general public have become aware that a serious debate is being pursued among certain theologians of the Church. It is a debate about Jesus. There have been some television and radio programs which have attempted to explain the issues involved in this debate, and a number of books have been written which indicate what conflicting views are now held by these theologians about who Jesus really was. For many people the debate seems near to blasphemy, indeed they see no reason for a debate, they are convinced that their experience of the risen and living Christ is no delusion and they believe him to be their Savior, their Lord and their God, in a literal sense. Some people find it very difficult to be tolerant, indeed they feel that the Church is much too tolerant for its own good, and they think that theologians who no longer accept the traditional claims about Jesus should be asked to leave the Church; on the other hand, it is recognized that the theologians have a job to do, and that no generation of Christians should regard their beliefs as somehow exempt from probing questioning and deep searching. If their beliefs are true, then there is nothing to fear if someone wants to see how those beliefs arose in the first place, and to see what the reasons are for thinking these beliefs to be true. The debate about Jesus going on within the Church today is a complex one, in what follows I have tried to bring out some of the issues involved, though it has not been possible to include every viewpoint.

I probably have made many mistakes in my presentation and some people will say I have not balanced the different viewpoints very well. I have used the form of a dialogue between two people whom I have called Alistair and Susan, both of these people reflect the spirit of the age we live in for they have deeply questioning minds. The dialogue will be in six parts.

PART ONE

Alistair: We are going to be thinking about what is contained in the writings which go to make up our Bible, I think it would be wise first of all if we shared what we think it means to say that the writings in the Bible are inspired by God.

Susan: Some people believe that every word of the Bible is inspired by God, indeed they think of God as virtually dictating word by word what he wanted to be contained in the Bible, so the people who actually wrote its contents were really just like a modern secretary taking down dictation from her boss.

Alistair: There are plenty of problems with this view of what inspiration means, not least because the Bible contains a considerable number of inconsistencies, but also because this view leaves out of account the fact that in so many areas of life our knowledge has increased, old ideas are no longer seen to be correct or to be credible, new ones have taken their place; I suppose a good example of our changing and growing knowledge would be the discoveries by scientists of the early history of mankind, their theories of evolution and of how the whole universe has been changing and expanding.

Susan: I feel you have put your finger on an important point: does it not all depend on what estimate you put on the God-given faculties of mind and brain, of religious imagination, insight, and reflection with which we have been endowed? The view of inspiration that I have described makes us very passive, the writers just took down what God dictated, and they did not really use the powers with which God had endowed them.

Alistair: Here is another view which I believe to be the correct one: I consider that, first of all, to say that the Bible is inspired by God is to acknowledge that our powers of religious insight, imagination, and reflection, whether we use them correctly or not, are powers with which God has endowed us when he made us as human beings. Secondly, I think it is impossible to distinguish between what you might call the divine and the human factors in the writings of the Bible. Let me take two illustrations from ordinary life: in the case of a great musician it is not possible to distinguish in his make-up and his work between musical genius and divine creativity, nor in the case of a great poet is it possible to distinguish between poetic ability and divine inspiration. Likewise in the case of the Bible we want to say that the writings are both inspired by God and also the product of human thought and labor.

Susan: I agree with you, and it seems to me that it leaves room as you indicated for the misuse of our God-given powers; a musician, however great, can at times write poor music with many mistakes, a poet can achieve sublime heights in his poems, but also write very inadequately at times, and our religious ideas and our insights can also turn out to be mistaken in part and need correction.

Alistair: We have mentioned that modern science makes certain parts of the Bible no longer credible; I expect you agree that the seven-day story of creation would be a good example, though there are certain insights in that story about man's relationship with God and the place God has given him in the created order that would appear to be of perennial significance.

Susan: Another example would be the story of the crossing of the Red Sea by Moses and the people of Israel: some scholars today seem to think that the story contains considerable exaggeration, they say that the people of Israel passed through a swampy region which was negotiable by foot, but too muddy for the Egyptian chariots to get through. Some theologians also consider that the book of Jonah is really not a true story, but a kind of novel with an important message; the famous whale is a symbolic figure whose significance would have been clear to the people to whom the writing was addressed, in other words Jonah was not literally swallowed by a whale.

Alistair: Let us not over-emphasize new understandings of the Bible or corrections that we think need to be made at the cost of overlooking the enormous achievement of these writings of the Jewish people. Their insights into the character and purpose of God, their peaks of loyalty and faithfulness to God, their grasp of the highest and best values to which a human being can aspire and by which he should try to live – I believe these are what makes the Bible such a source of strength and a continuing vision for life and for faith.

Susan: I agree that we must never lose sight of the greatness of the Bible. Perhaps I might summarize the position that we have reached so far: our discussion of what we understand the inspiration of the Bible to mean has led us to making the point that the Bible is both divinely inspired and the achievement of human insight and reflection and as such is, like the products of every other area of human life, prone to be fallible and mistaken in various ways.

Alistair: I think you can detect within the Bible itself considerable development and growth as the Jewish people from one generation to another searched for the reality of God. At first they seemed content to believe that every nation had its own god whom they worshiped; gods were like patron saints with, as I have said, each tribe or nation having their own gods. Later in their history, the Jewish people became conscious that it was really only credible to believe that there was one divine reality who was the Creator of all life. They believed they worshiped the one true God and criticized the other nations for worshiping idols that were not gods at all.

Susan: I disagree with this attitude, it seems to me to be fairer to say that these other nations also were searching for the one divine reality, these nations believed too, for instance, that he was a caring God and that he was the sustainer of all life. Their concepts of God may not have been so advanced as those of the Jewish people, but I do not consider it right to believe that they alone had found the one true God.

Alistair: I mentioned when we were talking about the different views of what it means to say the Bible is divinely inspired that there were inconsistencies within the Bible; I would also say that certain beliefs that the majority of Christians hold today conflict with the ideas that are in the Bible. This would seem to justify the outlook we both share that the Bible is not exempt from a questioning and searching mind.

Susan: Perhaps you would give some illustrations of what you mean.

Alistair: Let me illustrate the conflict between beliefs held today and the beliefs in the Bible: most people believe that when a Christian dies he or she goes to heaven. We speak about people going to the nearer presence of God when they die, and we mean that God has given them new life beyond death and has brought them into an eternal future in heaven. If you look at some of the ideas in St Paul's first letter to the Thessalonians you will see that in chapter 4 he thinks of Christians who have died as being what he calls "asleep". They are in their graves waiting for the end of this age. Paul believed it was about to come, and he speaks of Jesus as about to return to this world; the dead, he believes, will be raised to eternal life first and those who are still alive will join them, then everyone will go with Jesus, to live with him forever. Now there is a clear conflict here, who is mistaken? I imagine most Christians would say that Paul's views are wrong, it is more likely that the moment we die God takes us into heaven and gives us everlasting life. The second area of conflict concerns inconsistencies within the Bible itself: for example, in St John's Gospel the cleansing of the temple is placed as an event towards the beginning of Jesus' ministry, in the other three Gospels it happens during his last visit to Jerusalem shortly before his betrayal, trial and death. Is St John's Gospel correct or incorrect in this particular instance?

Susan: I am glad you took an example from the Gospels, because more people today seem to be aware of what a gospel really is. It is such a pity that the work of scholars and theologians seems to take so long to permeate into the general consciousness of the whole Church, but at least people's understanding of what a gospel is seems to be known more widely today.

Alistair: You mean that a gospel is more than what in journalism might be called "straight reporting". St John's Gospel is certainly much more than such "straight reporting": most of the long speeches in this Gospel should not be regarded as the real words of Jesus, if only for the reason that the style of the speeches and the concepts expressed in them are so different from the distinctive means of speaking and teaching that the three other Gospels show that Jesus used: for example, he loved to use parables and short pithy sayings to get his message across, in St John's Gospel nothing like this is contained; and concepts such as "the bread of life" and "the light of the world" which are in St John's Gospel are not found in the other three.

Susan: I like to compare St John's Gospel with what Shakespeare was doing. For instance, in his play, *Julius Caesar*, he wrote the famous speech that Mark Antony delivers to the citizens of Rome after Caesar's murder and makes Mark Antony say what he felt would have been appropriate for the occasion. In a similar way the author of St John's Gospel wrote speeches and put them on the lips of Jesus in order to bring out what he believed was the full truth about who Jesus really was.

Alistair: In St John's Gospel, though not in the other three, Jesus "says": "Before Abraham was, I am"; now that is a clear illustration of what scholars would take to be a saying never actually uttered by Jesus, but which the author of the Gospel felt it appropriate for Jesus to "say" in his Gospel, because it expresses his convictions and his fellow-Christians' convictions about who Jesus really was.

Susan: Some people have said that there are just two alternatives: they assume Jesus really said, "Before Abraham was, I am" and they conclude that either this is true or else Jesus was some kind of madman. We are suggesting that there is a third possibility, namely, that Jesus did not actually say this, but St John's Gospel says it about him. The questions for us must be: what does this saying imply about what they thought about Jesus, how did they come to believe this about him and were they correct to do so?

Alistair: We are both impressed by the teaching of Jesus, does it mean though that no questions are permitted to be asked about the truth or adequacy of what he said?

Susan: I don't think so. We have just seen that we have to ask questions about what in the Gospels really was said by Jesus and what on the other hand the Gospel writers claim he said. I want to ask questions about his teaching too; for example, when Jesus was asked what was the essence of right living, he answered that it consisted in obeying the commandment to love God and the commandment to love your neighbor as yourself. As a Jew, Jesus regarded these commandments as given by God. In human relationships a husband cannot command his wife to love him, her love is freely given to him by her own choice. Is it really adequate to conceive of a God of love commanding us to love him? I believe that God has given us free will, partly because he knows that if we are to love him, it can only be because we choose to do so; true love cannot be commanded or demanded from a person – so there is one question I find myself asking about the adequacy of Jesus' teaching.

PART TWO

Susan: You and I, Alistair, are not professional theologians, even still perhaps we can share some of our ideas and understanding about this debate which is being conducted within the Church today about who Jesus really was; though needless to say we will hardly express every viewpoint.

Alistair: Where does your thinking on this issue begin?

Susan: It is difficult to know where to start, but let me begin by saying that I always have been puzzled by one of the claims made about Jesus, namely, that he died for the sins of the world. Sometimes people say that Jesus' death was God's punishment for sin that he bore in our place. St Paul said that Jesus bore the curse of the law; do you believe this?

Alistair: Yes, I certainly do. The Old Testament contains two verses which sum up for me what Jesus did: we have all sinned, "cursed be he who does not confirm the words of this law by doing them" (Deut. 27:26), Jesus bore that curse for us on the cross, "a hanged man is accursed by God" (Deut. 21:23).

Susan: Would a judge be right to punish a person for someone else's misdeeds?

Alistair: No that would not be right.

Susan: I am sure that you would agree that since God is good and just, he never would punish the wrong person.

Alistair: I can see where your argument is leading to; you are going to say that this means we cannot interpret Jesus' death as the punishment he bore for our sins. I am not sure if I can see a way around your argument, but remember Jesus' death was also a sacrifice to God for our sins. Another author, the writer of the letter to the Hebrews, called Jesus a high priest, there is a verse which says "he entered in once for all into the Holy Place, taking not the blood of goats and calves, but his own blood, thus securing an eternal redemption".

Susan: I disagree with two things in this concept of sacrifices. First, it seems to be suggested that God will not forgive people their sins until his anger has been placated by a sacrifice; I object especially to any suggestion that a God of infinite love and boundless goodness would ever require the sacrifice and death of a human life before he would forgive his people. Secondly, I think that if Jesus' death was a sacrifice and was made as a sign of repentance to express our sorrow for our sin, it was pointless; I can understand people wanting to make up for the wrong they have done and wanting to express their intention to mend their ways, but that is something each person has to do for himself. For example, if I offend a friend, I will ask for his forgiveness and try to make it up to him by being more kind and thoughtful to him; nobody else can do that for me.

Alistair: So you think it is mistaken to say Jesus' death was the punishment for our sins, which he bore for us, and that it is mistaken to say that his death was a sacrifice to God for our sins.

Susan: Yes that is what I have come to think.

Alistair: I do not know what to say to you, except that in my mind sin and death have always been connected. I have believed that Jesus' resurrection from the dead was his triumph over sin and death, he defeated death and opened the gate to everlasting life.

Susan: You will find these ideas in St Paul's letters. As you know he considered that disobeying God's laws, which everyone has done, meant that we were all under the sentence of death – this was the punishment. He believed that Jesus accepted and endured that sentence in our place, laying down his life for us. I find it a little difficult to understand St Paul's thinking at this point, but I think that he felt that once the punishment had been borne, then as a criminal is let go after he has served his sentence, so Jesus was free, and set the rest of mankind free from death as well. So God could give Jesus new life. It is a curious argument; I think that St Paul believed that Jesus had lived a life without sin, and therefore had not deserved to die; Jesus' life provided God with good grounds for raising him to new life. Paul certainly speaks of Jesus as the first fruits of the resurrection from the dead. He thought that death was soon going to be a thing of the past, for shortly God was going to begin the resurrection of the rest of those who had died and the changing to immortality of those still alive.

Alistair: You are not the only one who finds St Paul hard to understand, but did you not notice that he was saying just what I have told you that I believe? Jesus is our savior, for without his death and his acceptance of the punishment of the law none of us would be raised to everlasting life, death would still rule over us and keep us in its grip.

Susan: You may wonder that I should disagree with St Paul, but I am sure you remember, Alistair, that I have told you already why I do not think Jesus' death should be seen as a punishment for sin, for it goes against all the principles of justice. Anyway, I do not agree that death has come about because people sin; it seems to me that death is part of all life: flowers fade and die, animals grow old and die, birds and fish die, and human beings grow old, wear out and die too. Death is part of the world as God has made it.

Alistair: What do you think about the resurrection and eternal life?

Susan: I like studying human history and learning about the different ideas that people have held about death and an afterlife, though I must say that some of them have been horrifying. You know that many of the Jewish people, at the time Jesus lived and before him too, did not think of people going to heaven, they expected a new kingdom back here in this world; so they thought of dead people as going to a place below the earth, and waiting there for the day when God would hold his judgment, and give righteous people new and everlasting life in the Kingdom which he would establish. On the other hand, I do not envisage a new kingdom in this world, as I expect you don't either. I believe the future God has for us is in heaven; but you see where I differ from you is that I see no reason why God should not have been raising people to eternal life from the beginning of man's history. I believe that the moment we die, God will give us new life in eternity, and he will want us to go on growing to be the people he wishes us to become, so fulfilling the loving purposes of his creation.

Alistair: In what we have discussed so far, Susan, it seems to me that I place greater importance on the life of Jesus than you do. I see him as the one who destroyed death, as the first person to be raised to everlasting life, as the one who bore the punishment for our sins and as the one who opened the gate for us to everlasting life; you disagree with me in all these beliefs. I wonder, in fact, whether you see any connection between Jesus' death and God's forgiveness.

Susan: I do; when I think of Jesus' death I think of a human being showing love and offering forgiveness in very difficult circumstances. I say to myself that if human love and forgiveness can be offered when a man is dying painfully on a cross, then there can be no limit to divine love and divine forgiveness. I also see that if human love and forgiveness are costly and involve a measure of suffering, so too it is reasonable to believe that divine love and divine forgiveness are costly and also involve a measure of suffering.

PART THREE

Susan: Who was Jesus? That is the question that theologians are debating in the Church today. I have told you, Alistair, why I do not believe it is correct to describe Jesus as the savior of the world who died for the sins of the world. Who was Jesus then?

Alistair: Let us start with some basic facts: he was a Jew, his Bible was the Old Testament. We call him "Jesus"; in fact, it would be a more direct translation from his Hebrew name to call him "Joshua", it sounds more Jewish, the word "Jesus" comes from the Greek translation of his name. So, if you like, he was "Joshua of Nazareth", a man who was an untrained though gifted teacher, a man of great spiritual insight and deep faith, a man shaped by the religious traditions of his people, but who thought for himself as well, a man with healing gifts, a loving, compassionate person of strong character and courage who died while still comparatively young.

Susan: I think that we should say that he was a prophet as well. People sometimes say that he was a man of his own times, we ought to look at what that means.

Alistair: It is often taken to mean that he could not have possessed the sort of scientific knowledge that we have today, his knowledge was limited by the age he lived in.

Susan: I agree, and it also means that he shared broadly speaking in the religious outlook and ideas of his day. For instance, he believed in the Jewish ideas about death and an afterlife: the dead were waiting below the earth for the day of judgment and resurrection. He preached that this day was not now far off. Like John the Baptist, Jesus seems to have thought that God's new kingdom would soon be established on earth. He highlighted the need for repentance before this impending judgment and he emphasized God's mercy and forgiveness towards the sinner.

Alistair: So far as we can tell the time in which Jesus lived was a time of religious excitement and expectancy, there were groups of Jewish people

waiting for God to bring in a new age. Although I imagine that many other
people assumed that life would go on much as before.

Susan: Such people were right, weren't they? No new kingdom was
established, no new world order was begun. The person that Jesus said he
expected to come and execute God's judgment never arrived; I am referring
to the Son of Man, who it was believed would sort out the "sheep" from the
"goats".

Alistair: Do not forget that some theologians say that Jesus himself thought
he was the Son of Man; there are divided views on this question, though all
agree that the first Christians believed that Jesus was the Son of Man and
that he would return some day to judge the world. I have a feeling that you
may be rather critical of this religious outlook and beliefs.

Susan: I am, Alistair. I do believe that God is king, and that he has a future
for his people beyond death. However, I think the Jewish ideas that Jesus
shared about a new kingdom being established on earth and people enjoying
everlasting life in it are mistaken. So I also consider that the Jewish idea of
dead people waiting in some shadowy place below the earth for the day of
judgment and the hope of being given everlasting life in the new kingdom is
incorrect. As I said to you before, I believe that God gives people new life in
heaven when they die. Furthermore, I do not think there is any such figure as
the Son of Man; the origin of this belief in a human figure coming on the
clouds of heaven to judge the earth can be found in the visions of the book
of Daniel, chapter 7. Those visions belong to a time when the Jewish nation
was hard-pressed by foreign powers; the visions are full of hope because they
proclaim that God will stand by his people, they will triumph in the end and
be able to pass sentence on their enemies. The vision of a Son of Man
coming in judgment is a symbolic, not a literal, way of expressing this belief.
As the centuries went by, Jewish people like Jesus seem to have come to
believe there really was a human figure waiting to come to judge the world.

Alistair: We seem to be spending quite some time on what people mean
when they say Jesus was a man of his own times; is there anything else
which you think we should say?

Susan: There is; you know, I am sure, how the Old Testament reflects the fact
that the Jewish people looked back on the reign of King David as a golden
age when their nation lived in peace, with their enemies defeated and kept
at bay. The Old Testament also records that in the midst of their tragedies
and persecutions of their long history, they came to long for a new leader
who would have powers like King David of old and be able, under God, to

secure for them a kingdom in which they could live in harmony and peace. The leader they looked for was called very simply the "Anointed One" or to use the Hebrew word the "Messiah".

Alistair: We want to be careful that we do not present too simple a picture of this hope for a "Messiah"; some people in Jesus' day gave it a political interpretation, meaning that they wanted a leader who would get rid of the Roman Empire of which they were now a part, while others gave it a spiritual meaning and talked in terms of a leader who would prepare a purified and pardoned people ready to receive the new kingdom of God; I suppose you would say that Jesus inclined towards the spiritual or religious interpretation.

Susan: Yes, I think that is right, but let us not forget that his ministry and teaching included much that relates to social and political life. However, what I want to ask you is whether you think that such a concept of a "Messiah" who would act either in a political or a spiritual manner is a plausible concept. We have traced the background to the Jewish hope for a kingdom of peace in which to live, even if that kingdom is seen as a spiritual one, is it really possible to imagine that one person is going to be chiefly responsible for bringing it about?

Alistair: I believe Jesus deserves the title "Messiah" because he played a unique part in the working-out of God's purposes for humankind. He died for the sins of the world, to make us a purified and pardoned people, through his death we have forgiveness of our sins. He is and was the long-awaited one, sent to be the savior of the world.

Susan: I do not agree with you, for as I have explained to you already, I do not think it is correct to believe that Jesus' death should be interpreted as a bearing of the sins of the world. As you observed before, I place less importance on Jesus' life than you do. For me the concept of a "Messiah" is a dream that will never be fulfilled, no individual either in a political or a spiritual way will bring about peace between man and God and between man and man – that is a work not solely for an individual, but one in which the whole human family with God's help has its part to play.

Alistair: I know from other discussions which I have had with you how much you value the teaching about how to live that is contained in the Old Testament and in Jesus' sayings in the New Testament; I know as well how profound you think are many of the ideas about God and the insights into his character which may be found in the Bible; I know how the sheer record of human hopes and fears, and the diversity of human living contained in the Bible have a strong appeal for you, and are a source of strength and inspiration; but do you not feel that the Bible is saying much more than this, much more about Jesus than that he was a Jew, a gifted though untrained teacher, a man of real spiritual insight and strong faith, a man with healing gifts, a loving and compassionate person, and a man of courage? Do you not see that we are being told that the first Christians felt compelled to acknowledge Jesus as divine, the record of their experience in the New Testament shows that for them to be led, guided, and filled by the spirit of Christ was the same as being led, guided, and filled by the spirit of God himself? Do you not see that the first Christians came to the astounding realization, as one recent writer has put it, that "the same infinite Creator God who brought into being the evolving galaxies disclosed himself to us in human personality"? God has lived a human life; he has experienced its joys and sorrows, its happiness and its suffering and death. From the emphasis you have been placing on the kind of human being Jesus was and from your failure to see him as the savior who died for our sins, I am beginning to wonder whether you believe he was both human and divine.

PART FOUR

Susan: The last time we were talking together, you raised some very important questions about Jesus and about God, which people regard as the central questions in this debate, and which theologians are pursuing at present within the Church. Here is one way to put the main question: was Jesus just a man or was he God come among us to live a human life and to disclose himself to us?

Alistair: I want you to tell me who you think Jesus was.

Susan: Let us look at the evidence in the New Testament and let me explain how I understand that evidence. First, let us consider the belief in the resurrection of Jesus. I do not know whether it is a distinctive twentieth-century outlook that has been produced by the influence of science, but I am wary of supernatural events. God has endowed us with brains to think with and the history of man's knowledge shows that some events, that were once thought to be supernatural, are now known to have natural causes. When I come to look at the evidence concerning Jesus' resurrection, I do not rule out the possibility that God might have raised him from the dead, in such a manner that he could go and meet and speak with his disciples again, and eat with them; but my wariness of supernatural events makes me look first for natural causes to explain the belief in his resurrection. I want to make two more brief points: first, I do believe that Jesus is alive again, because I believe that God gives everyone new life the moment they die; and second, the fact of someone being raised from the dead does not prove that they are divine.

Alistair: I realize that this is a difficult issue to discuss and understand, but please try to do it as clearly and simply as you can.

Susan: I will certainly try to do so. Perhaps it would be easier if we reminded ourselves once again of some of the ideas and expectations that Jesus shared with many of his contemporaries concerning the Jewish faith. We know that in Jesus' day hopes were high among certain groups of people that what some Old Testament prophets called "the day of the Lord" was about to come. There was a group of Jews who withdrew to a place near the Dead Sea; there they waited expectantly for God's new kingdom to arrive. John the Baptist and Jesus also shared this expectant outlook. Jesus rightly emphasized the mercy of God and showed a particular concern for those people of his day who were regarded as especially sinful and evil. It really was a matter of some urgency that they should put their lives in order and accept God's gracious forgiveness.

Alistair: I think it is very hard for us to recapture their sense of crisis, their sense of foreboding and yet also of excitement and glad looking forward. Do you remember when Jesus sent his disciples on a tour to heal and to preach about the coming of the kingdom, how he said to them that the Son of Man would come before they had been through all the towns of Israel?

Susan: In fact the Son of Man did not come, though this does not seem to have deterred Jesus from his preaching and his beliefs. It is very difficult to detect changes and development in his thinking, but he seems to have come to realize that the opposition he was arousing would lead to his being put to death; and he seems to have come to believe that this was part of God's plan to be fulfilled, before the Son of Man would arrive, and before the new kingdom would be established. His death would be for the forgiveness of sins.

Alistair: During his trial before the chief priests and elders he expressed his certainty that the Son of Man was about to come, did he not say that they would see the Son of Man sitting on the right hand of Power, and coming on the clouds of heaven? The new kingdom was about to be established.

Susan: Yes, that is right, that is what he believed; we should remember also that at the Last Supper and on other occasions he was concerned to impress on his disciples that his death would not be the end of him. At the Last Supper he looked to the day when he would drink wine again, it would be in the new kingdom of God.

Alistair: This brings us to the resurrection, at last.

Susan: May I remind you that I said I was wary of supernatural causes and preferred to look first for an explanation due to natural causes. I know you will regard what I have to say as very speculative, but please bear with me. There is no doubt in my mind that Jesus' disciples were very frightened when he was arrested; but you have to remember he had done his best to prepare them for it, especially he had shared with them his firm conviction that his death would not be the final reality for him; they would soon drink wine together again in the new kingdom of God, indeed his disciples would have thrones from which to judge and rule over the tribes of Israel in this new kingdom. When people die those close to them are in a state of shock. They cannot take it in that their loved one has died; they still feel they are alive. For weeks and maybe longer they feel the dead person's presence with them, perhaps they think they hear the dead person's voice or footsteps or they have some vivid picture of them in their minds. Maybe a widowed housewife will imagine she has heard the key turn in the front door, it is teatime and she thinks her husband is arriving home. These bereavement experiences can be very upsetting, people sometimes feel as if they must be going mad.

Now I want to suggest to you that Jesus' disciples interpreted their bereavement experiences to mean that Jesus had been raised from the dead, and was alive again. It is very likely that like other bereaved people they could not take it in that he was dead, but still felt he was alive. This experience, together with the conviction that Jesus had impressed on them that he would be raised to life again, enabled them to believe that this had really happened. Certain passages of the Old Testament were felt to be very reassuring because they reinforced Jesus' belief that his death was part of God's plan and not just a great mistake; now just before the judgment day came, a new covenant had been established between God and man, Jesus' death was the sacrifice for sin that brought about God's forgiveness of people. So Jesus could be proclaimed as God's special "Messiah", the person who in one way or another the Old Testament prophets had expected would be the one to prepare for the day of the Lord and to enable God's new kingdom to be established. Surely too the courage of Jesus that had enabled him to face death now had its influence on the disciples as they preached their message boldly, despite much opposition.

Alistair: I once read an article by a radical theologian who did not take the resurrection stories literally, but you have surpassed even his views. I expect you think that the resurrection stories were constructed and told as a means to get across the disciples' belief that Jesus was alive again.

Susan: Yes, that is what I think; for example, I consider the story in St Luke's Gospel concerning the two people going to Emmaus to be a story constructed by St Luke to make the point that if the Old Testament is interpreted in the right way then the beliefs of the first Christians about Jesus will be seen to be justified. You may call my views on the resurrection radical, but remember one point which I regard to be of fundamental importance: we can have no certain knowledge that God exists, his existence cannot be proved, it will always be a matter of faith and belief. It follows that if the disciples had absolutely certain knowledge that Jesus was raised from the dead, then this would prove that God exists, for only God can give new life beyond death. However, I have just said that God's existence can never be proved; so the disciples, I would suggest, cannot have had certain knowledge that Jesus had been raised from the dead, for them it can only have been a matter of faith and belief. My account of how their belief in the resurrection arose makes it clear that they did make a leap of faith, because they interpreted their bereavement experiences and the related sense of the presence of Jesus to mean that he was alive again. As it happens, and as you can no doubt guess, I do not think that they were really justified in interpreting their experiences in this way, because I think the only real ground for believing that people have been raised to new life is that this is the kind of God we believe in and find credible, namely, one who gives new life after we die. We do not know for certain if we will have life beyond death, but it is our belief and faith that we will. I repeat that the human condition is one of faith and not of sight: we have no certain knowledge where God is concerned.

Alistair: I agree that we have to live by faith and that in human history this always has been the case, but with one exception, and that exception is the resurrection of Jesus. I believe that the disciples really did meet and talk with Jesus, and ate with him too; they did have certain knowledge that he had been raised from the dead, faith was not needed, their eyes told them the truth. I allow that this proves that God exists, for only he can give life beyond the grave. However astonishing it may seem, yet this is what I believe that the resurrection stories are saying; and I think that the disciples would not have claimed that they talked and ate with Jesus unless they really had done so. You mentioned that the first Christians turned to what, as Jews, were their scriptures, namely, the Old Testament. I would like you to explain how you think that they used the Old Testament in their preaching and in their understanding of what Jesus' life and death were about and for what the future might now be expected to be.

Susan: When the disciples became convinced that Jesus was alive again, they felt sure that everything was working out according to what they understood God's plan to be. They proclaimed that Jesus' death had been a sacrifice for sin and was available to all who would repent and ask to be forgiven. They said Jesus was the Messiah, he was the long-awaited leader who would prepare the way for God to bring in his new kingdom and establish it here on earth. While nobody knew exactly when this would be, it could be expected confidently in the very near future. The final offer of forgiveness, the final call to people to put their lives in order before the judgment day, was being made. The disciples now proclaimed Jesus as the Son of Man, though whether Jesus had thought of himself as the Son of Man, as we noted before, is open to question; they said he would be returning soon with power to judge the living and dead. They considered that many parts of the scriptures were really about Jesus: so for example, in Acts chapter 2, they quoted Psalm 110 verse 1, and deduced from it that Jesus was now exalted to the right hand of God, and in Hebrews chapter 2, they quoted Psalm 8 verses 4-6, and deduced from them that Jesus was second-in-command to God, ruling over all creation.

Alistair: Do you not think that this is the wonderful fact about the Old Testament; do you not see that God enabled his prophets to speak about Jesus long before his life on earth?

Susan: If I am going to be honest with you, Alistair, then I must say that I believe the first Christians were mistaken to interpret and understand the Old Testament in this way. Look at the two examples that I have just given you: Psalm 110 is from an ancient Jewish coronation service or perhaps from the yearly enthronement service; it says that the king will have God beside him to help him, especially in any battles he may have to fight against other nations; Psalm 8 is a meditation on the wonder of God and his power as Creator, it expresses man's sense of being small and humble before such a God and yet also of being highly privileged by the position given to him above the animal kingdom and the world of nature. These Psalms have nothing to do with Jesus, except in so far as they apply to him as an ordinary human being.

Alistair: Perhaps the Old Testament has to be seen then as having two meanings: certain passages have both their original meaning as intended by their writer and the new meaning found in them by the first Christians which applies in a special way to Jesus.

PART FIVE
Susan: You know, Alistair, that there is a sense in which God exists outside space and time; technically we call this the transcendence of God, he is eternal and exists outside and independently of his creation. However, human faith and experience speak of God as in his creation too, he is active in human history and can be encountered in our everyday lives; technically

we call this the immanence of God. I want to look with you at some of the ways the immanence of God is understood in the Bible.

Alistair: The Bible is full of people who encountered God in their lives, people who heard the word of the Lord like the prophets, and people who were filled with the Holy Spirit like Barnabas and Paul.

Susan: You have just mentioned two ways people described their experience of God: hearing the word of the Lord and being filled with the Holy Spirit. I am sure that you agree that we do not hear God speak to us in the same way as I hear you, when you speak to me. Rather a prophet, for example, may detect another meaning or message in the thoughts going through his mind, he may say to himself, these ideas are not just my thoughts, they are a message from God, and they are the word of the Lord. He will announce that he has heard the word of the Lord and he will tell people what he believes God wants him to say. The Jewish people were sure that God was powerful and in particular they associated his "word" with power. The word of the Lord which came to a prophet was often a powerful judgment on the society in which he lived; they also thought of the story of creation; had not God just issued a command, spoken a word, and everything came to be, such was the power of God's word. God said: "Let there be light" and there was light. The Jewish people placed considerable emphasis on another way of expressing their encounter with God: they spoke of the spirit of God filling them, what does this mean? You can imagine a prophet being stirred to anger and righteous indignation against the injustices of his society or a prophet being filled with a great desire to fulfill God's will, to do justice, to love kindness, and to walk humbly with God. In these cases the human emotions and desires that fill the prophet and his moral conscience are interpreted as being the spirit of God: God has stirred his conscience and filled him with righteous indignation or a desire to be holy.

Alistair: This is one of the features of religious experience that I find difficult to understand. The divine and the human seem impossible to distinguish: is the prophet's indignation a human emotion or is it the divine spirit of God? We seem to need to say it is both; in a similar way, as we once noted before, you cannot distinguish in a poet's make-up what is poetic ability and what is divine inspiration, or in a musician what is human genius and what is divine creativity.

Susan: You are right, and do not forget that it applies also to "the word of the Lord"; the prophet has his own thoughts, but in them he detects the thoughts of God as well. We have thought about God's word and his spirit, there is another way of expressing our encounter with God that I want to mention.

This is called God's wisdom. When people sensed that they needed God's help for their thinking and planning, they said that they desired God's wisdom. Sometimes, too, as they looked at the beauty and order of the world around them, they came to realize that God had done everything very wisely; he had acted with wisdom.

Alistair: Is there some reason why you have chosen to speak about these three things: God's word, God's spirit, and God's wisdom?

Susan: It is rather interesting that you should speak of them as "things", for are they not all ways of speaking of God himself encountering us in our lives? God's word, spirit, and wisdom are not something different from God, they are God himself, acting and communicating with us. However, I say it is interesting that you should call them "things", because that is what the Jewish people did as well. At times you would think that they thought that they were separate from God; they speak of God's word, spirit, and wisdom existing with him from eternity before the world was created. However, they never thought of them as indeed separate from God; when they spoke of God creating the world with his word, it was God himself who created the world, not some separate entity, agent, or mediator called his "word". They just meant that God created the world out of nothing, he did not have to make it out of anything as a potter makes vessels out of clay; rather God just said: "Let there light" and there was light.

Alistair: I follow all you say, but I am still not sure where you are leading our discussion. Does this have any bearing on Christian experience of God, and on what the New Testament records of the experience of God, and on what the New Testament records of the experience of Christ?

Susan: Yes it does. I now want to see if I can explain to you how I think some of the astonishing claims about Jesus in the New Testament came to be made. When he died on the cross, we know some people regarded him as guilty of death, but in their preaching the disciples and other Christians proclaimed a different viewpoint. He had died for the forgiveness of sins; and now, so it was believed, he was seated at the right hand of God. I have shared with you my suggestion as to how the belief in his resurrection should be understood. I also suggested to you that the first Christians used their scriptures, our Old Testament, in a way that I consider to be mistaken; it seems, for example, that they deduced from the imagery of Psalms 110 and 68, and perhaps from Daniel chapter 7, that Jesus was seated at God's right hand and had been given power and authority by God. Jesus could now be believed to be the Son of Man, who according to Jewish thinking would come to carry out God's judgment in the world. We have noted before that some theologians think that when Jesus preached about the Son of Man, he was in fact referring to himself; whether this view is right or not, it is clear that his disciples expected the Son of Man to come very shortly and they believed that Jesus was this Son of Man. In the Jewish religious thought-world this supposedly real figure called the Son of Man was a human figure, waiting on the clouds of heaven to come and judge the world. Here is one starting-point for seeing Jesus as having a life which began before he came to earth, so maybe the Son of Man should be regarded as a divine being, and therefore Jesus also should be believed to be human and divine.

Alistair: I am following you, Susan, though I do not like your line of argument. Might it not be that even by imperfect means the disciples were discovering the real truth about Jesus: that he has existed from eternity, and is divine as well as human?

Susan: Let me come now to St Paul's thinking and experience. You remember that I find his argument, that Jesus' death should be interpreted as his bearing of the punishment of the law for us, a mistaken argument. However, Paul believed it; and as he thought about the cross, he saw not just a loving, forgiving man dying on it, but he felt that here he was encountering the loving, forgiving grace of God. He believed that Jesus loved him and had given himself for him; Jesus' love and God's love seemed to be fused together as he reflected on the meaning and the purpose of the cross. This was to affect how he spoke about his religious experience, as we will see in a moment. The death on the cross for sin, so Paul believed, had been God's idea; God's forgiveness and love were now newly and completely offered to mankind, at this crucial stage of world history before the judgment day began. Paul thought of Jesus as a man who had been full of love and self-giving, and as one who had shown the true nature of trustful, obedient sonship in relation to a heavenly Father; Jesus had been filled by the spirit of God. Paul writes in his letters about his own experience of God and says that he too is filled by the spirit of God; however, he also says he is filled by the spirit of Christ, or just refers to the love and life which fill him as Christ himself, but in both these latter cases he is still referring to the spirit of God, that spirit of God which he believed also filled Jesus.

Alistair: You mean that these different terms are interchangeable, don't you? Paul can write of the spirit of God filling a person, or the spirit of Christ being in a person, or Christ himself dwelling in a person and mean the same as his Jewish forefathers when their prophets spoke of being filled by the spirit of God.

Susan: Yes, that is correct, though to Paul's mind Jesus' life, love and self-giving created an enlarged vision of what it means to be filled by the spirit, love, and grace of God. I have pointed out that Jesus' death on the cross for the forgiveness of sins was of crucial importance to Paul. He therefore considered that Jesus could rightly be thought of as a mediator between God and mankind. So Jesus was no mere insignificant individual, he was the one through whom God had acted toward the whole world. Once again, I repeat that I consider it mistaken to interpret the death of Jesus as achieving the forgiveness of sins and as bearing the punishment of the law; however, I am going to suggest to you that these staggering claims about Jesus, especially his role as a mediator between God and man making peace by the blood of the cross, led on to even more astounding beliefs. You recall that Jesus was identified with the Son of Man by his disciples and that the Son of Man was believed to be someone who was waiting on the clouds of heaven to come and judge the world. This identification suggested that Jesus "existed" before his life on earth. If that was the case, and if he was the mediator between God and man, then who could he be said to be?

Alistair: I believe the answer in the New Testament is clear: "In the beginning was the Word, and the Word was with God, and the Word was God ... all things were made through him ... the Word became flesh and dwelt among us."

Susan: I am glad you chose to quote from that particular passage from St John's Gospel. You recall what we said about God's word, it was one way that the Jewish people had of expressing their encounter with God. The prophet heard the word of the Lord; you remember we said as well that the Jewish people also thought of God creating the world with his word, for through his simple word of command everything came to be.

Alistair: How does this relate to St John's Gospel and his description of the "Word"?

Susan: Can you imagine the "Word" being thought of as a kind of mediator between an eternal God who exists outside space and time and his creation? The "Word" is like a bridge between God and his creation; through his word he contacts and encounters his people, indeed through his word he created everything. So the "Word" is the great mediator between God and us. Now the first Christians thought of Jesus as the great mediator, to my mind mistakenly, and the staggering deduction that they made was that he must be this "Word". So St John can write that "in the beginning was the Word, and the Word was with God and the Word was God ... all things were made through him ... the Word became flesh and dwelt among us." Remember though that I suggested to you that while Jewish thinking sometimes regarded the word of God, or the spirit or wisdom of God, as separate entities from God, yet basically it was recognized that there was no separation, God's word was God himself so, for example, when it was said that God created through his word, it simply meant that he himself created, the reference "through his word" expressed the manner of his creating: it was solely by a word of command.

Alistair: It is rather different for Christian thinking, because Jesus is in a sense separate from God: after all, there is God the Father, and God the Son. Wasn't the thinking of later generations of Christians addressed to this problem, of how to speak of the unity of God and also of different persons within the Godhead; how to allow on the one hand that "in the beginning was the Word, and the Word was with God and the Word was God", and on the other hand to allow that God the Father and God the Son were distinct parts of the one Godhead?

Susan: This problem is not a problem for me, because I consider that Jesus neither died for the sins of the world, nor is he the mediator between God and man, nor therefore is he the word of God, nor is he "the only-begotten Son of God, begotten of his Father before all worlds, God of God, Light of Light ... being of one substance with the Father", as the Nicene Creed expresses it.

PART SIX

Alistair: You and I hold rather different beliefs about Jesus; that much has at least become clear. I believe that the person who recently wrote the following words is expressing the truth: "The same infinite Creator God who brought into being the evolving galaxies disclosed himself to us in human personality." I believe that what St John's Gospel expresses is correct: "In the beginning was the Word, and the Word was with God, and the Word was God ... and the Word became flesh and dwelt among us." You, on the other hand, Susan, see Jesus as just a good man; you have explained to me how you think that the first Christians came to believe that Jesus was divine and why you think that they were mistaken. I have listened patiently to you; you would say that the story of God humbling himself, becoming a man, sharing our human experience, being the victim of our human sin, suffering and dying is a beautiful story, but simply not true; I almost feel like saying to you that it is not only a beautiful story, but a compelling and appealing one that simply must be true. Do you not see that this is just what a God of love would do for humankind; do you not realize that love involves identifying with others and that is what God did in becoming a man? Do you not see what a difference it makes when you realize that you are speaking to someone who has lived a human life and really understands it?

Susan: I know what you mean, but let us not forget that we have been concerned where we can to get at the facts. What may we legitimately believe about Jesus? The traditional claim about Jesus, which you accept, is an astounding one to make about a human being. It was not as if he went about with a badge saying, "I am God" or gave infallible proof of divinity. I have tried to scrutinize the beliefs which arose about Jesus, to see whether they are likely to be correct; but as we both know, people more professionally qualified than us are, at present, engaged in examining the claims about Jesus, and no doubt these theologians will make the issues a good deal clearer than we have made them, so that the Church at large may be surer about what faith it wants to teach to future generations.

Alistair: There are a few questions that I want to ask you: first of all with the beliefs you hold, what does such a central service as the Holy Communion mean to you now?

Susan: I have said to you that I recognize in Jesus the spirit of self-giving love: he embodied this eternal virtue. This for me is the true spirit and manner in which human beings should live. In the Holy Communion service I am reminded of Jesus' generous and self-giving life and love, and this helps me to become conscious of what it is that I seek for myself from the God who is the source of all love: I want and need more of this same self-giving love in my life. In the Holy Communion, I show God my desire to grow deeper and stronger in love by accepting and receiving the bread and wine, for they are the symbols for me of this generous and self-sacrificing love; bread is a symbol of the life God gives me and wine is a symbol of the self-giving spirit in which I try to live. Since love is so central in this service, I find myself strengthened and upheld by God's love for me and his forgiveness of my weaknesses and failings.

Alistair: I too find Jesus' life a deep influence on me: it constantly inspires and challenges me, but my understanding of the Holy Communion is of Christ coming into my life to inspire and strengthen it. I want to ask you as well whether you agree with the belief expressed in the New Testament that Jesus lived a perfect life without sin.

Susan: We have noted many times that Jesus' death was interpreted as a sacrifice for sin, one way in which the belief in his resurrection was understood was as God's approval that the sacrifice had been made satisfactorily; so the deduction was made that, if it was a perfect sacrifice, then Jesus must have been perfect and without sin himself. As you know, I do not think it is correct to interpret his death as a sacrifice for sin, so I do not make the deduction about his sinlessness. Anyway, I do not think that human beings are in a position to make this sort of judgment on another human being; only God knows the full truth of our lives. I would have strong doubts as to whether any human being has ever lived a perfect life; it seems most unlikely from what we know of the struggles and weaknesses of our own lives and the lives of others.

Alistair: Traditional Christian belief claims that Jesus led a perfect human life and that in that life we may see the fullest revelation of God that is possible for us in this temporal and mortal life. Don't your beliefs make it harder to see who God really is?

Susan: I think I know what you mean. For instance I can imagine many Christians looking at an artist's painting of a man hanging on the cross. The man who was painted, of course, was not Jesus, but a model for the artist; nobody except those who saw Jesus in his lifetime knows what he looked like. Somehow, though, this does not seem to matter, and the Christian can say about that picture: "There is my Savior, my Lord, and my God." Well I would not say that nor believe it; in that sense it is harder for me to see or visualize God. In fact, of course, God is an unseen God, we cannot see him; and if the person looking at a picture of a man hanging on a cross was asked to say whether he was really looking at God, he would answer, "No, I am not"; rather what the outer eye sees is a help to what the inner eye of faith is turned toward, namely, a loving, suffering, and forgiving God. But who is God, what a big question? God has created us with a mind and an imagination to think about him, yet none of our ideas or pictures of God are anything but analogies from our experiences of the world around us.

Alistair: You mean, for instance, that when we say that "the Lord is my shepherd", we do not mean that God really is a shepherd, because shepherds look after sheep, and clearly we are not sheep, but human beings. We call God a shepherd, or strictly speaking say he is like a shepherd, because he cares for us. The shepherd caring lovingly for his sheep gives us a clue about God; it gives us an analogy or picture, so that we can say that since God cares for us he is like a shepherd.

Susan: That's it. Please listen carefully to what I learned recently: there are some societies in the world in which the men stay at home and bring up the family, while the women go out to work. It would not be surprising if people of religious insight and spiritual depth in such societies reflected on the fact that the women were the bread-winners and sustainers of family life and concluded that the divine reality and sustainer of all life is a goddess, a heavenly mother who watches over her creation and sustains it continuously.

Alistair: What implication do you draw from this?

Susan: I think the implication to draw is that the divine reality is neither male nor female. You notice I use the words "divine reality", because even the word "god" has masculine overtones. As we have just remarked all words about God are used by analogy, concepts such as "heavenly father" or "heavenly mother" are like signposts, they point us to a divine reality who creates us, cares for us, and loves us. We may also infer that the divine reality, being neither male nor female, is not literally "composed of" an eternal father and an eternal son, any more than it might be thought of as being "composed of" an eternal mother and an eternal daughter.

Alistair: Your illustration of the society in which women go out to work and in which divine reality might be conceived of as a goddess and heavenly mother certainly shows the influence which the society we live in has on the analogies and pictures we use for thinking about God. The society in which the Jewish people lived was patriarchal or male-dominated and God was conceived of primarily as a father, a king, and a shepherd, which are all masculine images.

Susan: Perhaps I may explain that I believe it is possible for people to speak about their experience of God in terms of an experience of Christ. As you know I do not believe that Jesus was the eternal, only-begotten Son of God; indeed I have suggested to you that I do not think of God as having an eternal Son, so you might wonder how I could allow that what I regard as just a man, namely, Jesus, could be such a vital part of many people's experience of God.

Alistair: How do you understand this?

Susan: I consider that most people's account of what they describe as an experience of the risen and living Christ is an account of an experience in which God is pictured as a close friend and as something like an older brother. These pictures or analogies are useful because God's love for us and our love for him are like a friendship; furthermore, to picture God as like an older brother gives us a sense of someone we can look up to for support and understanding, sometimes an older brother is closer than a father; for one reason or another then, some people cultivate their experience of God, maybe not consciously, in terms of Christ rather than in terms of a heavenly Father though both pictures, "father" and "brother", express certain truths about our relationship with God and help us to think about him and to communicate with him. We always need to remember that God is beyond our words and thoughts; he is not literally a father or an older brother.

Alistair: I would like to widen our discussion about God and ask what you think the other world religions have to contribute to our understanding of God; and what you think their relationship to Christianity is.

Susan: I am no expert on such religions as Hinduism, Buddhism, Islam, or the Tao faith, though we both can say we know something about the Jewish faith. However, the views I have shared with you about who Jesus was preclude my assenting to the traditional Christian doctrine that only inside Christianity will true salvation be found, because Jesus is believed to be the savior of mankind. I regard all the religions, Christianity included, as evidence of the long search through human history for the truth and reality of God. It is a search that is still continuing. God has created us as human beings with minds and imaginations to think about him and each religious tradition shows how one generation has sifted, examined, and developed the ideas held by former generations. From the little I know about other religions I would say that they do contain much true insight into the character of God and his purposes of love as well as a vision of the eternal virtues such as self-giving love, truthfulness, justice, reverence for life, humility, gentleness, and compassion which are embodied in a true, good, and holy human life. I think that all the religious traditions, Christianity included, contain in their long development and history many misconceptions and mistaken outlooks. I am sure you would agree with me that each generation, each person, must decide for themselves what they believe the truth about God to be; and they ought to search fearlessly for the truth and be prepared to go wherever that search may take them. I feel it is essential to uphold certain approaches to religion: I mean there must be a place for freedom of thought, a place for reason, a tolerant outlook, and space to change and grow.

Alistair: Isn't it sometimes said that if you read the writings of the saints and mystics of the different world religions you will find that there is a common pattern to their religious experience of God?

Susan: Yes, I think that is correct. There seem to be two distinct kinds of experience of God: in the first kind, God is thought of as another person whom we may picture as a heavenly Father or a divine friend; this kind of encounter with God is called the "I-Thou" relationship, it is like a person-to-person relationship. However, the second kind of experience of God is rather different and is in a way more profoundly mysterious; you know that there is a sense in which God is in each one of us, indeed he is present everywhere in the whole universe.

Alistair: Yes, and sometimes people say not just that God is in us, but that we and his whole creation are in him: "In him we live and move and have our being"; have you heard the phrase someone used, "the everywhere-ness of God"? I should say that these are two ways of speaking of the experience that you call the second kind.

Susan: I agree. This kind of experience of God as present in us has been pictured in a number of ways; it is like the relationship between an ocean and a wave, or the sun and the rays of sunlight, or a spring of water and the stream that flows from it, or a tree and the branches; do you see what is meant? The experience of God as being present and active in each of us is as if God was an ocean and we were the waves, or as if God was the sun and we were the rays of sunlight and so on.

Alistair: You were right to call this experience of God profoundly mysterious. I do not remember being conscious of anything but the faintest glimmerings of a sense of God dwelling in me and in other people and being present in all life, though I do believe it is true. The model of an ocean and a wave does strike me as a helpful way to illustrate what we once talked about, namely, the fact that it is impossible to distinguish between the human and the divine in a musician or a poet: we asked, what is musical genius and what is divine creativity, and what is poetic ability and what is divine inspiration? The model suggests that as the wave would not exist and be what it is unless the ocean existed, so a musician or a poet would not be who they were unless God was present and active within them in this deeply mysterious sense.

Susan: The same goes for us as well: you and I would not be the people we are unless the infinite Creator of all life was present and active in us. Let me read to you from this book which I have here a little of what a famous twentieth-century contemplative monk wrote: "The message of hope the contemplative offers you is that whether you understand or not, God loves you, is present to you, lives in you, calls you, saves you ... The contemplative has nothing to tell you except to reassure you and say that if you dare to penetrate your own heart you will understand what is beyond words and beyond explanations because it is too close to be explained: it is the intimate union in the depths of your own heart of God's spirit and your own secret inmost self, so that you and he are in all truth one spirit." Those words are worth pondering over. The two experiences of God that I have been trying to talk about are expressed in two lines of the well-known hymn, 'Be thou my vision'; here they are: "Thou my great Father, and I thy true son", that is the first kind, the person-to-person relationship; "Thou in me dwelling and I with thee one", that is the second kind, in which God is sensed as within us and we feel at one with him. The truth of faith that these experiences of God point to is what I would like to call the true meaning of the Incarnation: a truth not just about Jesus, but about every human being.

Alistair: We must end our conversation now. I feel it is very hard to put into words just what I believe. I think that God knew beforehand what a difference it would make to us if he became one of us and shared a human life. I believe this happened. Jesus was God incarnate, God come among us to live a human life. This belief helps me to believe that God really loves us and cares for us, he has shared our suffering, he has become more personal. My prayers would not be the same if I could not pray to Jesus; I believe he really understands me, for though he is God yet he has also lived a human life. I know you claim the evidence or the facts do not justify these astounding beliefs about Jesus, you say he was just a man; I have not been convinced by you, in particular the first Christians would not have said Jesus was divine unless they were absolutely sure he was, I still think that the New Testament shows that their experience of him compelled them to make their astounding claims.

Susan: I once loved, as you do, to use prayers, hymns, and anthems addressed to Jesus for my worship of God; it was hard to give them up. You say that the Incarnation makes God more personal; I feel that the God of the Jewish faith, the God of the Psalms, for example, could not be more personal. I think of Jesus as one of a number of human beings whose lives have expressed and embodied the highest values. I believe in the unseen God whose face is the face of eternal love; the God I believe in is too big and too great to understand completely. Like a close friend, God shares in our lives, in joy and in suffering; in a profoundly mysterious sense I believe that the God I worship fills his whole creation and is close to each of us, closer than our breath, but he also reaches out beyond his creation into eternity.

God's existence cannot be proved; the human condition is always one of faith. In the Old Testament the nations whom the Jews encountered were criticized for believing that God could be located and be especially present in idols of wood or stone; the Jews themselves showed the same desire to locate God by saying that he dwelt in the ark of the Lord or in the Temple. I ask myself whether Christians have given in to the same human desire to locate God and to know where he is by proclaiming that his special dwelling place was and is in Jesus. The debate about who Jesus really was seems set to go on for a long time within the Church and it will need much tolerance while it lasts; "Whom do men say that I am?" Jesus himself asked this question; as people of other faiths and of none look on, the Church asks itself in our day, "Is the traditional belief about Jesus the truth?"

Epilogue

I began to write this book in July 2002. The world is a different place now from how it was then, nine months ago. For, as I write this epilogue, it is March 2003, and the war in Iraq has begun. It is a frightened and angry country. In the rest of the world as it follows this war, millions of us also feel fear and anger. Among staff and students on my Peace Studies course in Dublin are people with differing perspectives on war and in particular on the current situation in Iraq. Some of us are pacifists, but others are not. In political theory some are realists, some are liberals. Many of us are social constructivists. Not all of us, but many of us, come from a Christian background. Since September 2002, when we came together to start the course, we have discussed, analyzed, and debated the state of the world, with a growing awareness of its complexity, and a deepening appreciation that there are no easy answers to many of our human problems. Virtually all of us we against the war.

I had wanted to see our UN arms inspectors continue their work in Iraq. I have felt deeply suspicious about the hawkish position in the USA. It has not rung true to me. I dislike and disapprove of the precedents being created by this war in a new century. I am appalled and saddened at the loss of human life, the maiming of human beings physically and psychologically, and the trauma and grief experienced by so many. The anti-war marching of millions of people worldwide gave us a new sense of power, and many of us were reminded of the street marches that helped end communist rule. There is both a sense of power and a sense of powerlessness in the face of the military might of the USA and its allies. We can have an influence, but in other ways we are simply ignored. This war is complex, but undoubtedly, to my mind, is partly about oil. I feel that the more powerful countries must accept the moral demands of sharing the earth's resources more fairly amongst the whole human family. I do not know how long this war will last and I feel for the Iraqi people as their cities and towns and people are bombed. At the same time I am deeply mindful of the political oppression that they have suffered from, as so many millions of people do in other countries such as Zimbabwe where I used to work.

I can imagine that next year when the Olympic Games take place in Athens, this global event will be politicized, as world leaders try to heal some of the divisions this war has created. They will try to use the coming together of sportsmen and women from the nations of the world to compete in peace against each other in a spirit of sporting friendship as a symbol of a united world. As a sportsman myself, the Olympic Games appeals to me. I like the sense of the love of sport bringing people together, and of that love transcending borders and boundaries, ethnicity and gender, religion and class, languages and nationalities, and age and wealth. The sense of a shared humanity and of a common aspiration to achieve the highest standards comes through strongly in the Olympic Games, as it will do in the Special Olympics in Dublin in June 2003.

All these Games remind me that my own identity is as a human being, first and foremost. Being European or Irish or white or male or anything else comes much lower down on my scale of priorities. Within my identity as a human being is a spiritual component – my quest for and trust in God and my commitment to ethical values. The different religions have each seen their God as carrying a passport that provides an identity as a Christian God, a Muslim God, a Hindu God, or a Buddhist God, etc. I think of God today as traveling without a passport of any kind. God simply travels under his or her own hidden and mysterious identity. In a globalized world a search for an authentic spirituality for such a world has begun. I believe it will be based on a sense of the sacred precious worth of human life and on a moral appreciation of our inter-dependence on a precarious eco-system. It will be a spirituality closely connected with a life of action, a spirituality of engagement in the muck and mess, as well as the beauty and wonder of our world. For this vision people will wager their lives, for this they will live and die. For some it will be a spirituality that points beyond the known limits of life and of our universe to some great and good mysterious power. I submit that my understanding of religion and belief, based on the assumption that God is not knowable to us, can contribute to peace among people of a religious outlook in our world. For it inevitably means that all belief is speculative and conjectural, no matter how profound the reflection and reasoning underlying it or the human experiences that have helped create new insights of a spiritual or moral nature. My position requires that I be tentative, provisional, and accepting of alternative viewpoints.

Globalization brings our world together and increases the commonalities – whether through the commodities we buy or through a sense of a shared humanity in suffering and care. However, it is also being recognized how the human spirit reacts against homogenization. There is a new emphasis on cultural diversity as an enrichment of our world. This, to my mind, will mean that while a common language for a global spirituality may be constructed, such a spirituality will be expressed in diverse ways through the world's varied cultures. Those involved in the religions would do well to try to create a more pluralistic and democratic atmosphere. In the past there have been huge tensions among the differing sects and strands within each faith tradition. They have been compared to unhappy, dysfunctional families where much hate and mistrust has flourished. It is likely that the conservatives and traditionalists in the future will continue to have their place in the world of spirituality, but so too will the liberals and the radicals. Perhaps we can learn from the past, and learn to be more tolerant of each other and less threatened by each other.

I imagine many an author comes to the end of writing a book, and as they do so, comes to hear about another book that they wish they had discovered earlier. In my case it is the book *Worlds within a congregation: Dealing with Theological Diversity* by W. Paul Jones. This book is both a plea and a challenge to the Churches that they recognize diversity and welcome it. In particular Jones writes about five diverse theological worlds in one of which a believer may find themselves most at home. Part of the task of the Church today is to help both clergy and laity become more aware of which world they most naturally fit into, though it should be remembered that a 'theological world' cannot be separated from political, social, and cultural realities. He writes:

> *There has never been either a unified Christian Church, or a common Christian theological position, in the light of which diversity can be faulted.* What is new in our era, then, is not the fact of diversity, but the call of the Church *to celebrate this diversity in a gesture of rare and expectant honesty.* (p.36)

> Research indicates ... that these overlapping theological Worlds tend to cluster in five composite, alternative Worlds. All five are viable, with none more faithful, more preferable, or more mature – except to each person. (p.38)

Jones emphasizes the way a religion functions in people's lives – especially what it means for them and how it meets some of their deepest needs. People prioritize these needs differently.

My book comes out of an Anglican ethos. Anglicanism has never been easy to define. L. William Countryman wrote "It is relatively clear who is Anglican: anyone who claims the history and is claimed by the family. That said it is less clear what is Anglican" (*The Poetic Imagination*, p. 31). My bishop brought me to the highest court of our Church on a charge described in the media as a charge of heresy. In doing so he seemed to be saying that the family could no longer claim me as one of its own. I think Richard will prove to have been mistaken, for I suspect he has not become sufficiently aware of those five theological worlds described by W. Paul Jones and the approach to religion adopted by Jones, which emphasizes how a religion, rather than doctrinal beliefs, functions in a person's life and actions. It would be good to have a greater self-awareness of the way our religion functions in our lives, and an appreciation of which theological world we inhabit and its similarities with and differences from other such worlds. However, no matter how well we understand all this, there will still be the challenge of welcoming diversity. There will be the difficulty both of accepting that we do not well understand some of these other worlds, and of accepting other people's right to live within them. Such an approach to religion might well be followed in the world of politics – for there is not just one way of organizing the life of a nation. History, culture, and the rich diversity of humanity support a pluralist vision for the social and political realities that we construct.

Bibliography

Some suggested reading for further exploration and reflection

Marcus Borg and Tom Wright, *The Meaning of Jesus: Two Visions*, 1999

David Boulton, *The Trouble with God: Religious Humanism and the Republic of God*, 2002

Joan D. Chittister, *Heart of Flesh: A Feminist Spirituality for Women and Men*, 1998

Richard Clarke, *And is it True?*, 2000

L. William Countryman, *The Poetic Imagination: an Anglican Spiritual Tradition*, 1999

Lloyd Geering, *Christianity without God*, 2002

Daphne Hampson, *After Christianity*, 1996

Richard Holloway, *Doubts and Loves: What is left of Christianity*, 2001

John Hunt, *Daddy do you believe in God?* 2001

W. Paul Jones, *Theological Worlds: Understanding the Alternative Rhythms of Christian Belief*, 1989

W. Paul Jones, *Worlds within a congregation: dealing with theological diversity*, 2000

Hans Kung, *Christianity: Its Essence and History*, 1994

Mark Oakley, *The Collage of God*, 2001

Jonathan Sacks, *Celebrating Life*, 2000

Bernard Brandon Scott, *Re-Imagine the World: an introduction to the parables of Jesus*, 2001

Elaine Shepherd, *R . S. Thomas: Conceding an Absence, Images of God Explored*, 1996

John S. Spong, *A New Christianity for a New World*, 2002

R. S. Thomas, *Collected Poems 1945-1990*, 1993

Teresa Wallace et al. (eds.), *Time and Tide: Sea of Faith Beyond the Millennium*, 2001

Maurice Wiles, *Reason to Believe*, 1999

WEBSITES

The Center for Progressive Christianity: www.tcpc.org
The Sea of Faith Network: www.sofn.org.uk
My site: http://myhome.iolfree.ie/ ~ andrewfurlong

Endorsements

It is doubtful that Jesus thought he was divine. Thus Andrew Furlong is in good company with his questioning of this Christian dogma. It is unfortunate that Christian churches are not broad enough to allow such questions.

Rosemary Radford Ruether. Carpenter Professor of Feminist Theology, GraduateTheological Union, Berkeley, California

Running alongside the central argument of this book is a profound challenge to patriarchal accounts of Christianity. The author is confident that Christianity has the capacity to transcend its male-oriented past. Out of this he envisions a Christian tradition that is prophetic and inclusive, one that affirms and celebrates the goodness of human life in all its diversity.

Dr. Linda Hogan, Lecturer in Peace Studies, Irish School of Ecumenics, Trinity College, Dublin

This heresy story needs to be read alongside the Sea of Faith Network's groundbreaking study on doctrine and diversity.

David A. Hart. Lecturer in Religious Studies at Derby University, UK

The original conflict between Jesus and institutional religion repeats itself frequently today, as church authorities refuse to let Christian doctrine evolve naturally to fit a rapidly changing intellectual climate. This is the well documented and passionately told story of one such encounter.

Lloyd Geering, Emeritus Professor of Religious Studies, Victoria University, Wellington, New Zealand.

Living with differences has been said to be the genius of the Anglican Church. But this book gives a sad picture of one corner of that church, the Church of Ireland, and its current unwillingness to allow different ways of expressing Christianity. All who are concerned that witch hunts and heresy trials should not become the norm in Ireland would do well to read AndrewFurlong's story.

(Canon) Hilary Wakeman, Church of Ireland

Andrew Furlong provides a fascinating account of his struggle with the religious establishment and his theological journey to a radical interpretation of the Christian message. It is a gripping story of bravery and pain.

Rabbi Professor Dan Cohn-Sherbok. University of Wales

Andrew Furlong will not soon forget Monday 8 April 2002 when he was to be tried for heresy. And those who read his book will not soon forget his story. One can forgive the parishioners who had not been made aware of the findings of modern biblical and theological scholarship, but cannot forgive Mr. Furlong's ecclesiastical superiors who had. Bishops who traffic in feigned ignorance and deception are in this volume held to account by simple testimony to honesty and integrity by the author. It makes one weep to witness the truth crucified all over again by the church and then in the name of Jesus of Nazareth. Congratulations to Andrew Furlong for his courageous stand.

Robert W. Funk. Founder of the Westar Institute and of the Jesus Seminar